Reengineering and
Total Quality in Schools

■ ■ ■

SCHOOL LEADERSHIP AND MANAGEMENT SERIES

Series Editors: Brent Davies and John West-Burnham

Other titles in the series:

Effective Learning in Schools
by Christopher Bowring-Carr and John West-Burnham

Middle Management in Schools
by Sonia Blandford

Strategic Marketing for Schools
by Brent Davies and Linda Ellison

Forthcoming titles:

Human Resource Management for Effective Schools
by John O'Neill and John West-Burnham

Management Development
by John West-Burnham

Managing Quality in Schools
by John West-Burnham

Resource Management in Schools
by Sonia Blandford

Strategic Development Planning for Schools
by Brent Davies and Linda Ellison

Reengineering and Total Quality in Schools

■ ■ ■

How to Reform and Restructure your School to Meet the Challenge of the Future

Edited by
BRENT DAVIES AND
JOHN WEST-BURNHAM

FINANCIAL TIMES
PITMAN PUBLISHING

This book is dedicated to Linda Ellison

FINANCIAL TIMES

MANAGEMENT

LONDON · SAN FRANCISCO
KUALA LUMPUR · JOHANNESBURG

*Financial Times Management delivers the knowledge,
skills and understanding that enable students,
managers and organisations to achieve their ambitions,
whatever their needs, wherever they are.*

London Office:
128 Long Acre, London WC2E 9AN
Tel: +44 (0)171 447 2000
Fax: +44 (0)171 240 5771
Website: www.ftmanagement.com

A Division of Financial Times Professional Limited

First published in Great Britain in 1997

© Pearson Professional Limited 1997
© Chapter 12 John Marsh 1997

The right of Pat Collarbone, Brent Davies, Pam Dettman, John Lewis,
Ian McKenzie, John Marsh, Alan Murphy, Geoffrey Samuel,
Charles Sisum, Nayland Southorn, Suzanne Taylor, Claire Trott,
Richard Wallis, Dave Weller and John West-Burnham
to be identified as authors of this work has been asserted by them
in accordance with the Copyright, Designs and Patents Act 1988.

ISBN 0 273 62410 5

British Library Cataloguing in Publication Data
A CIP catalogue record for this book can be obtained from the British Library

10 9 8 7 6 5 4 3 2

Typeset by Phoenix Photosetting, Chatham, Kent
Printed and bound in Great Britain by Redwood Books, Trowbridge, Wiltshire

The Publishers' policy is to use paper manufactured from sustainable forests.

Contents

■ ■ ■

Contributors

■ ■ ■

Co-editors

Brent Davies. Brent is Professor and Director of the International Educational Leadership and Management Centre at the Lincoln University campus. Brent taught in the secondary school sector in London for ten years before moving into higher education. He is a member of the National Council of the British Educational Management and Administration Society and chair of their International Committee. His specialist interests are devolved school management, school finance and reengineering in education. He is a Visiting Professor at the University of Southern California (USC) where, as co-director with Professor Brian Caldwell (University of Melbourne) and Professor David Marsh (USC), he runs an annual International Principals' Institute. Brent has lectured and published widely, with seven books, including ones on school development planning, marketing schools, financial and resource management in schools, and over fifty articles and conference papers on many aspects of self-managing schools in Australia, the UK and the United States.

John West-Burnham. John is Professor of Educational Leadership and Management at the Lincoln University campus. He taught in secondary, further and adult education for fifteen years before moving into higher education. He has worked as an education officer responsible for management development and was director of the first distance learning MBA in Educational Management. He has published widely on topics relating to quality management in education and human resource management. John has provided training and consultancy to a wide range of schools and organisations in the UK, Australia and Africa. His research interests include managing quality in education, the relationship between management and learning and models of leadership.

Contributors

Pat Collarbone has worked in education in Inner London for twenty-seven years. She was appointed to the headship of Haggerston School in 1990 where she has established a national reputation for innovation and achievement. Pat has delivered INSET on school improvement and effective leadership to a wide range of audiences. She was a member of SCAA's Key Stage 3 advisory group. Currently she is a member of the DFEE Advisory Committee on Improving

Schools. Pat completed her MBA in September 1995. She holds a fellowship at the Lincoln University campus and she is a fellow of the Royal Society of Arts. Currently she is the London President of the NAHT. In January 1997 she took up the post of Director of the London Leadership Centre.

Pam Dettman is the headteacher of Woodlands Girls' School in South Australia. She has taught at primary, secondary and tertiary levels and is well known for her work in technology, especially, in relation to laptop computing programs and their effects on teaching and learning. Pam has a Masters Degree in Evaluation and is completing a doctorate at the University of Melbourne in the area of 'Strategic Leadership in Schools'. She is a visiting fellow at the Lincoln University campus.

John Lewis is Principal of Dixons City Technology College in Bradford. John studied history at Queens' College Cambridge before entering teaching. He has started two new schools from scratch, Birchwood Community School in Cheshire and the innovative Bradford CTC. John received the OBE for his services to education in 1996.

Ian McKenzie has been a teacher for twenty-five years and is currently assistant principal at Endeavour Hills Campus of Eumemmerring Secondary College. He is a strong supporter of the team/small group model of teaching and learning because he believes it develops the whole child, and it builds relations with students and teachers which foster learning. Ian has facilitated a number of workshops in change management, accountability, school charter and team development. Currently he is looking at the changes in work organisation and practice which lead to improved learning outcomes for students.

John Marsh's aim is to help release people's creativity by applying Total Quality principles and methods within industry, education, government, the voluntary sector and ultimately throughout whole communities. He spent five years with ICL, one of the UK's leading practitioners of Total Quality. In 1991 he became TQ manager for WESTEC, formally Avon Training and Enterprise Council. He currently directs Total Quality Partnerships, providing a wide range of services to all types of organisations and communities both in the UK and abroad. John has had two books published, along with many papers. He has co-authored several British and International standards.

Alan Murphy is the headteacher of St Edward's School, a joint Roman Catholic–Church of England comprehensive school in Poole, Dorset. He has significant experience in management and leadership training and has contributed to a wide range of management development courses. He is an associate tutor for the Leicester University MBA in Education Management and has tutored summer schools for the Open University Business School. He leads a training organisation – TEAMS (Towards Excellence: Applied Management Seminars) – which offers weekend courses and school-based in-service training.

Geoffrey Samuel has just retired as headmaster of the Heathland School which he opened in 1973. He has contributed to a number of books on school management and has written and lectured widely on appraisal and TQM. He is a regular contributor to the education press. As a consultant he is also specialising in staff appointments and development, institutional planning and target setting, the training of heads and governors. He was for many years a councillor and chairman of governors and is currently deputy chairman of the local Bench.

Charles Sisum is currently the headteacher of Wisewood Secondary School in Sheffield. During 1994–95 Charles was seconded to the Quality Directorate of the Royal Mail as part of the Warwick University-based headteachers into industry scheme. Charles has been a regular contributor to journals and in-service events on the topic of school improvement. He is an executive member of the Sheffield Centre for School Improvement and a headteacher representative on Sheffield LEA's Raising Achievement and Participation Project.

Nayland Southorn is deputy headteacher at Sir John Talbot's School in north Shropshire. Previously Teacher Advisor for geography in Cheshire, he introduced the cross-curricular European Airbus education business programme to schools in the North West. Demands placed on his current rural, 11–18 comprehensive school, with limited staffing flexibility, prompted an innovative design and delivery of the curriculum. He has significantly reengineered the timetable structure with distance learning/video conferencing opening up many exciting possibilities in teaching and learning. He is currently studying for an MBA in International Education Management and is working closely with the US Department of Education 'blue riband' cross-phase project in Texas.

Suzanne Taylor is currently Professional Development Co-ordinator at Endeavour Hills Campus of Eumemmerring Secondary College. She is interested in innovative and progressive educational alternatives. In particular she is working on the extension of staff collegiality to extend the students' co-operative work and their ability to direct their own learning. As part of her work she is developing co-operative classroom cultures that function on trust, not only on what the teacher wants but also on what the students recognise they need.

Claire Trott has worked across the educational phases. Having trained as a drama specialist she began her career at Stantonbury Campus in Milton

Keynes. After working as a Buckinghamshire advisory teacher, in 1990 she was appointed deputy head of Mereway Middle School, a new 9–13 Northampton School. During a year's leave of absence studying for an MA, she worked as an Honorary Research Associate at Leicester University. As a deputy head she has led a number of initiatives: recent areas of interest and responsibility include leading the school's development as a learning organisation of teacher researchers, involving two projects funded by the Teacher Training Agency.

Richard Wallis is currently deputy headteacher at Hugh Christie Technology College, Tonbridge, Kent. Over the past ten years as a deputy headteacher, he has worked on numerous curriculum and organisational initiatives. These include flexible learning and electives programmes. He has played a significant role in the school becoming a technology college and in it becoming involved with the American-based Coalition of Essential Schools, a school improvement organisation. He believes that there is no 'silver bullet' for effective schools. It requires organisational structures to be constantly challenged while simultaneously focusing on improving the teaching and learning in the classroom.

Dave Weller is in the Department of Educational Leadership at the University of Georgia. He teaches and researches in the area of Total Quality Management and allied administrative theories. He has experience as a secondary school teacher, a middle school principal, and a marketing representative for Xerox Corporation. He co-ordinated the school desegregation of Dallas (Texas) Independent School System and served as a consultant for the Educational Testing Service. Dr Weller was a visiting lecturer on Total Quality Management at the University of Lincolnshire and Humberside and has written several book chapters, has over fifty research articles published, and is chairing a national commission on Total Quality Management.

Preface

■ ■ ■

Education, and especially leadership and management in education, has gained increasing importance in the 1980s and 1990s and has generated a rapid explosion in publications in the field. This has happened during a period when the university sector has been subjected to the research assessment exercises which have increased the pressure for research. In this system, original research gains a points ratings for a university department. Gaining points is often considered more important than the value of the research to improve practice which, in education, surely should be the improvement of children's learning. Knowing how to dissect things and to be critical gains academic respectability as does quoting other people's work. It would seem that it is possible to have an original academic idea as long as forty sources can be quoted who have had similar but slightly different ideas before. This way the idea can be grounded in the literature of the field. No more significant example of this is leadership. Once we were able to talk about 'leadership' but the academic researchers have divided it up and we can read about transactional leadership, transformational leadership, invitational leadership or even educative leadership (isn't all leadership in education supposed to be educative?). As we constantly divide, we often lose the main purpose of our study.

We believe that ideas are not only found in the painstaking process of research of other people's work but that ideas also come very powerfully from individuals in schools who use their intuition and judgement to dare to do things differently, knowing only that what they are doing at the moment is not sufficient or adequate. By using their judgement or intuition they can move their organisations forward. Waiting for the outcome of a five-year research process may be too late to affect the lives of their pupils, thus they develop and implement brave new ideas.

This book is an account, management by storytelling if you like, about pioneers who have tried to do things differently to improve their schools and about the opportunities open to their pupils. Our approach has been to let them share their experiences on their personal journeys with you and we have provided the framework and the commentary to accompany those journeys. John Stuart Mill said that one man with a commitment is worth ninety-nine with an interest. Columbus would not have sailed to the New World in 1492 if he had had to provide forty academic referenced accounts of previous journeys. Thinking differently, he used the ideas of the time and undertook a new journey. We believe that these accounts provide, in their small way, ideas by individuals who have undertaken their own journeys of discovery from which the reader can gain insights to improve his/her own school. Reengineering and total quality have provided a useful way of stepping out of traditional thinking to use ideas from a different context and to look afresh at the challenges facing schools. Being reflective and proactive depends on developing key ideas for action. We believe that the chapters provide examples of individuals who have used the power of ideas to change their schools and the lives of the pupils within them.

We are involved in a long-term study and partnership with key practitioners in the field of reengineering and total quality approaches. In this volume, by taking a random sample of the individuals with whom we have been working and researching, we have provided a framework for them to share their very significant insights and experiences with other practitioners. As this is part of a long-term study of work in this field we would wish to hear from other schools who have been working in the same field. We can be contacted at the International Educational Leadership and Management Centre at the Lincoln University campus.

The structure of the book

The book is structured into seven major sections. Part One considers some of the basic tenets of reengineering and total quality to provide a framework for analysing the chapters that follow. These chapters are grouped into five major sections (Parts Two to Six):

- Reengineering: whole school approaches
- Reengineering: learning and teaching
- Total quality perspectives in schools
- Quality strategies
- International perspectives on quality.

These chapters are then followed by a conclusion (Part Seven) which draws the ideas in the book together to map possible future scenarios for leadership and management in schools.

Brent Davies and John West-Burnham

■ ■ ■

PART ONE

The nature of reengineering and quality management

The nature of reengineering and quality management

BRENT DAVIES AND JOHN WEST-BURNHAM

Introduction

We have in the UK undergone a decade of educational reforms which are familiar to all in the education service and can be summarised as:

- a national curriculum for all children
- standardised assessment and testing of pupils at key age stages
- vastly increased powers for schools with consequent reduction in the power of Local Education Authorities (LEAs)
- delegated school decision-making and the operation of school site management through the delegated budget scheme, Local Management of Schools (LMS), with funding linked directly to pupil numbers
- the facility for schools to 'opt out' of LEA control and be funded by a direct grant from central government (as grant-maintained schools)
- the establishment of City Technology Colleges (CTCs) funded by central government and industry in inner city areas
- restructuring of the governing bodies of schools to give much greater power to parents and local industry and commerce
- a policy of open enrolment to enhance parental power of choice.

The change can be seen to be one of polarisation with increased power at the centre and at the schools with the intermediate layer (LEAs) marginalised. Caldwell and Spinks (1988, p. 7) note this trend:

An echo of this perspective from organisation theory may be found in the work of such people as Peters and Waterman, whose studies of excellent companies led them to the identification of 'simultaneous loose-tight properties'. They found that excellent companies are both centralised and decentralised, pushing autonomy down to the shop floor or production team for some functions but being 'fanatical centralists about the core values they hold dear'. The parallel in education is the centralised determination of broad goals and purposes of education accompanied by decentralised decision-making about the means by which these goals and purposes will be achieved, with those people who are decentralised being accountable to those centralised for the achievement of outcomes.

As such these changes should be seen not necessarily as a peculiarly UK phenomenon. Davies (1997) argues that they are part of a much wider reform and restructuring of education systems and outlines a number of cross-national trends that can be identified.

- The development of state and national curriculum and testing frameworks is providing measures of output and value-added, thus increasing information for parental choice.
- Relating value-added educational gains to resource levels allows schools to be compared in terms of 'value for money'.
- Increased differentiation between schools encourages more specialised provision.
- Significantly enhanced levels of parental choice.
- Considerable changes in staffing patterns and arrangements, more para-professionals, core and periphery staff, fixed-term performance-led contracts, school-site pay bargaining.
- Radical changes in the nature of teaching and learning as the impact of the new teaching and learning technologies gathers pace; the role of computers, the place of work – school or home, the development of teachers as co-ordinators and facilitators managing technology and, with the use of technology, the ability to provide high quality all the time.
- Greater varieties of finance with blurring between state-only and private-only funding of schools.
- Contracting out of educational as well as service elements of schooling.
- A reexamination of the boundaries between different stages of education and between education and the community.
- Redefinition of the leadership and management functions in schools.

What is happening in education is only a reflection of changes in the wider global economy. Hammer and Champy in their seminal book, *Reengineering the Corporation* (1993), suggest that three forces are driving companies into a new and unfamiliar operational context. Those forces are *Customers, Competition,* and *Change.*

Customers

The mass market developed in the 1950s, 1960s and 1970s. During this time customers were glad to receive any product, but this situation has now broken down into a 'quality product' approach aimed at individual customers. The following factors can be seen to be emerging:

- customers have experienced quality and good service and expect more and better quality in the future;
- customers are better informed, having more data on which to make their decisions;
- customers know their legal rights in cases of dispute;
- customers are less deferential;
- customers dictate what they want, when they want it and how they want to pay for it;
- customers want to be seen as individuals and to receive a customised product;
- customers are aware that there is plentiful supply and that they can pick and choose.

The parallel trends in the education sector in general, and the school sector in particular, are almost identical. State curriculum and testing frameworks are providing benchmarks to help parents to measure the quality of education received and the achievement made by their children. The culture in which the school knew best and parents were kept at arm's length has been replaced by a move to a more equal home/school relationship. Selection of school through open enrolment legislation has, in several countries, increased choice and given more power to the parent as customer.

Competition

Good performers drive out the inferior, because the lowest price, the highest quality, the best service available from any one of them soon becomes the standard for all competitors. Adequate is no longer good enough. If a company can't stand shoulder to shoulder with the world's best in a competitive category, it soon has no place to stand at all. (Hammer and Champy, 1993, p. 21)

What are the features of the intensified competition that is sweeping through companies and forcing them to reassess their position? The following highlight some of these:

- The nature of the competition is increasingly global: low wage economies of the Far East and China are allying themselves to high technology to threaten traditional firms and there are more recent forms of competition from Eastern Europe and the old Soviet Empire.
- Technological leaders are emerging with new firms starting up without the 'baggage' that traditional firms have in terms of structures and costs and they are driving the traditional firms out of business.
- Niche targeting of specific markets means that entrepreneurial firms are establishing bridgeheads in markets previously dominated by large corporations.

5

Does any of this apply to education? Isn't education somehow different from the business world? While it may be different, education is not isolated from the pressures and trends that are making themselves increasingly evident. Global competition has a profound impact on the future of our children. Unless they develop high quality thinking, problem-solving and technological skills to compete with the best in the world, they will be competing for the low wage/low skill jobs. Also, competition between existing suppliers of education (schools), while in itself increasing, is being joined by competition from non-traditional sources including technology.

Change

Change has become normal and persistent. We have come out of an age in which change took place and then we were on a plateau and nothing changed again for a while. Now constant change, and increasingly rapid change, can be seen to be the norm. Indeed we may be undergoing a very fundamental change which Peter Drucker describes as

Every few hundred years in Western history there occurs a sharp transformation ... Within a few short decades, society rearranges itself ... its world view; its basic values; its social and political structures ... We are currently living through such a transformation (Drucker, 1993, p. 1).

Drucker goes on to state that 'knowledge is fast becoming the sole factor of production, sidelining both capital and labor' (Ibid, p. 33). For those of us employed in the knowledge industry the implications are profound. The key points to consider are:

- change has become pervasive, persistent and normal
- there is an accelerating rate of technological advance
- the business cycle and the economic cycle are no longer predictable and thus
- the nature of work, the economy and employment in the future are also uncertain
- all products have shorter life-cycles, reducing from years to months.

One of the big myths in education is that the changes initiated in the 1980s have worked their way through the system and that we are now in a stable pattern for the next few years. It would seem that the expectations of customers, the nature of competition and the ongoing rate of change itself is unlikely to leave education in a backwater. Education is at the forefront of society's attempts to come to terms with this new reality. It is difficult to imagine that education, and the nature of schooling, will not itself have to change radically.

The impact on leadership and management

Given all the pressures that are impinging on schools they have, by and large, failed to change *how* they manage in proportion to the changes in *what* has to be managed. In very general terms schools are isolated as institutions, with teachers isolated within them. Large schools are often hierarchical and bureaucratic with ill-defined roles for managing and with an emphasis on reaction. If this were a result of an uncompromising focus on students as learners then it might be acceptable. However, the inconsistencies between schools and, more importantly, within schools in terms of student performance, might be seen as indicating a lack of integration of leadership and management with the core purpose of the school.

It is very difficult to find a rationale for the way in which most schools are currently structured. In many ways they resemble nineteenth-century organisations. It is difficult to see how a focus on learning, as opposed to the efficient delivery of the curriculum, justifies existing roles, structures and systems. Many schools have elaborate management structures but then provide no time to manage. Virtually every school has a set of aims but it is often difficult to see how core values inform every aspect of school decision-making. Most significantly schools rely on hard work and on the gifted amateur. The failure of individual schools, and the education service in general to develop an approach to management and leadership that is value-driven, appropriate and effective has only been possible because of panglossian culture – we are doing as well as we possibly can.

This failure to begin the process of moving towards an integrated under-standing of the nature of, and relationships between leadership, management, administration and learning accounts for the dysfunctionalism aspects of many schools. Not least of these is the reliance on hard-work and goodwill.

Schools are almost unique in failing to engage in a process of fundamental reconceptualisation of how they should be designed and how they should function. This book provides exceptions to this situation. Of course there are many others but the issue is the extent to which the need to change has been recognised.

We will only achieve effective education if changes in educational frameworks and structures are matched by changes in attitudes and processes within schools. This change in attitudes and processes is considered by Davies (1997) to be the second wave of reform. In this chapter we draw on concepts and ideas from the reengineering and total quality management movements to construct a framework that highlights the key elements that are necessary to implement reform at the school level.

The vehicles we use to examine fundamental change are those of reengineering and total quality. A more detailed analysis of these two concepts now follows.

What is reengineering?

Two significant books were to influence much of the thinking in the 1990s. In *Reinventing Government*, Osborne and Gaebler (1992) fundamentally rethought the role of government in society in the USA. A parallel book in the business sector is *Reengineering the Corporation* by Hammer and Champy (1993). Michael Hammer, with Steven Stanton, published a sequel, *The Reengineering Revolution – A Handbook*, in 1995 by which time the concept of reengineering had spawned a series of books and brought a new concept and language into common usage. So what is reengineering?

Hammer (1995, p. 3) describes reengineering as 'the fundamental rethinking and radical redesign of business processes to bring about dramatic improvement in performance'. In unpacking the definition Hammer makes a number of key points. It is important to understand each one of these.

First, and of utmost significance, is that reengineering is about the *'redesign of business processes'*. The aim is not to focus on reengineering organisational units or structures but on reengineering how work is done. In a school context, the process might be the child's learning but to improve that, instead of seeing the holistic nature of the process and seeing how improvements can be made from the learner's point of view, school strategies are often more concerned with organising curriculum groupings in terms of departments or faculties.

The second point concerns *'fundamental rethinking'*. Reengineering is not about incremental improvement or incremental thinking but about 'radical' changes and radical rethinking. It is tearing up the old ways and seeking totally new ways of doing things. This is difficult because it is necessary to reengineer 'mind sets' in terms of how people think before being able to undertake the rethinking of the process. In schools, focusing on how children learn and on the role of technology allows schools to reassess fundamentally the place of learning and the role of the teacher; it is no longer adequate to consider another computer in the classroom but, rather, whether traditional classrooms will still be required.

Finally, reengineering is about *'dramatic improvements'*. Marginal improvements in performance are not seen as adequate in a rapidly changing world but rather, as Hammer (p. 4) states, we seek 'dramatic breakthrough performance' with significantly enhanced levels of performance. Davies (1997, p. 21) provides a useful case study of applying reengineering thinking.

A school in the UK, 'Moortown', is oversubscribed by sixty pupils each year. It is an 11–18 school with no other school nearby. The Local Education Authority refuses entry to these extra pupils each year, stating that the school is full to capacity. How does this relate to schooling in the future? A closer examination of the case study school reveals some interesting factors. The school opens for pupils for 190 days a year (i.e. 52 per cent of the time), and during those days pupils operate an 8.30am to 2.30pm day (25 per cent of the time). As a result the building, as a fixed asset, is used for 13 per cent of the total possible time. This raises some interesting questions. Do children only learn in that 13 per cent or does learning also take place in the other 87 per cent of the time? The answer is obviously the latter. Once the perspective of schools being facilitators of learning and not the sole providers of education is accepted, then a little more creative thinking can be encouraged. Can Moortown school only be expanded by extra capital expenditure which produces buildings that are used only for 13 per cent of the time? Or can different patterns of attendance for different age groups be used? Can staff have different working hours and conditions. Can greater use be made of technology so that 'learning' takes place when teachers are not there? Can other adults be used as coaches as well as fully trained staff? The ideas that can be generated are many but our traditional way of thinking usually does not encompass them. We need far more radical interpretations of possible future scenarios. Will all the children be attending five days in ten years time? Will part of the lessons be conducted at home using the computer? Will traditional libraries become information centres bringing all pupils the best of the best all the time by using available technologies? Will the teachers work in support teams and facilitate the access to differing learning resources? Will the internal organisation in terms of buildings look like traditional classrooms as four hundred years ago or be radically different? Redesigning learning processes needs a radical shift in the 'mind set' of our educational leaders.

This case study illustrates how traditional thinking can be redefined by a reengineering approach.

What is TQM?

Total Quality Management, or as is more common now, Total Quality, lacks the clear and uncomplicated pedigree of reengineering. Total Quality's antecedents can be found in a range of sources; the introduction of statistical process control in the Second World War, the focus on the customer and the emphasis on a philosophy of continuous improvement that emerged from Japan and the emphasis on corporate culture found in many American multinational corporations. Out of these sources grew a number of quality 'philosopher-kings' notably Deming, Juran and Crosby. Although broadly consistent there are significant differences between them which at times appear to the outsider as somewhat theological in the distinctions made. This is one of the strengths and weaknesses of the total quality movement.

It is a strength in that the movement is catholic in the range of interpretations it permits. This means that few organisations have adopted a stereotypical model, rather they have modified it to suit specific circumstances. This flexibility can be interpreted as a weakness in that the multiple definitions have allowed critics to argue that there is a lack of integrity and coherence in the concept of Total Quality. Equally, Total Quality has become a term of approbation which is used as a PR slogan rather than an accurate description of organisational processes. There can be no one authoritative definition of Total

Quality but it is possible to argue for a minimalist model which exhibits the most frequently cited characteristics.

Four key components can be identified: the status of customers, the emphasis on values and vision, the management of processes and the significance attached to the management of people. However, there is a fifth component, often ignored, which transcends the other four. This is the integrative and holistic view of Total Quality which means that the four are all present and perceived as of equal significance. Many organisations achieve some of the elements but few achieve the high level of interdependence that characterises Total Quality in its most sophisticated manifestation. Thus, if it is possible to achieve high levels of customer care but without a perception of employees as internal customers, then it could be argued that Total Quality does not exist. Most theoretical models are only partially adopted; Total Quality is unusual in the rigour it places upon the integration of all elements.

Although the model is made up of symbiotic elements it is possible to extract the distinctive features of each. The status of customers is best exemplified in the fact that it is the customer who defines quality. Juran is uncompromising: 'Quality is what the customer says it is'. This is closely relevant to the most widely used definitions of quality; the notion of quality as 'fitness for purpose', where purpose is the customer's and fitness is defined by the customer. This challenges an authoritarian supplier-led definition and the notion that quality exists as an abstract entity. If customers are defined as 'anyone to whom a product or service is provided' (West-Burnham, 1992) then customers are both external and internal to the organisation and the relationship is defined through the process rather than the relative status of those in the relationship, i.e. a quality lesson is defined through the child's understanding rather than the teacher's effectiveness.

However, the focus on the customer has to be placed in an explicit moral context. This is where the emphasis on vision and values is central to total quality. Vision is significant in the extent to which the core purpose of the organisation is defined and made axiomatic to every component of organisational life. If visions is *what* the organisation exists for then values are the *how*. A distinctive feature of total quality is the pervasive and consistent nature of the moral basis for action. This recognises that no action is value-free and that a consistent code is necessary if core principles are to be translated into the experience of those coming into contact with the organisation. Two specific features emerge from this approach. These are first, an emphasis on planning in order to translate principle into practice and, second, the notion of transformational leadership. Total Quality requires leadership rather than management.

Although a customer focus expressed through visions and values is central to Total Quality these are not enough to ensure quality. Hence the shared emphasis on process management which is manifested in three ways. The first is through the significance that is attached to prevention, i.e. an approach which seems to minimise the possibility of error through definition of standards. This is reinforced by the second component which is measurement in order to understand the extent to which a process conforms to an agreed specification. Such measurement also facilitates the third notion, that of continuous improvement by which every process is subject to review in order to enhance it.

These first three broad categories are bound together by the fourth, the importance attached to the management of staff. This is exemplified through an emphasis on development, the use of appropriate working structures, e.g. teams and the creation of high levels of trust, involvement and the acceptance of personal responsibility.

As has already been mentioned, this abstract model is capable of a wide range of interpretations, in some cases purely semantic, in others quite fundamental shifts of emphasis. There is evidence of some standardisation of definitions emerging such as the Baldrige Award in the USA and the European Quality Award in the UK and the rest of Europe. The use of the ISO 9000 services and the Investors in People Award in the UK have again helped to produce an apparent consensus as to the nature of certain elements of Total Quality.

However, two factors raise doubts as to the applicability of Total Quality as an organisational panacea (and the high failure rate of organisations seeking to introduce it would appear to confirm these). First, Total Quality is derived from the premise of the possibility of homogeneity in beliefs and actions. This contrasts strongly with phenomenological perspectives of organisations and assumes that in school management high degrees of consensus are possible and desirable. Because of its insistence on specification and conformity it could be argued that Total Quality potentially denies the heuristic process that is the hallmark of a learning organisation. This is balanced by the second concern which is the centrality of the notion of continuous improvement. On the one hand this offers the possibility of modification and development but this is counterbalanced by concerns about incrementalism. The slower a change process the more likely it is to be distorted and corrupted.

Although the components of Total Quality have been demonstrated to function well in schools, colleges and universities there are few examples of *Total Quality*. Significantly, it is possible to demonstrate that there are high levels of congruity between Total Quality and the school improvement and effectiveness movements.

Are reengineering and TQM contradictory or complementary?

Fundamental differences between TQM and business process reengineering are outlined by Carr and Johansson (1995, p. 16).

Table 1: Fundamental differences between TQM and business process reengineering

Factors	TQM	Reengineering
Type of Change	Evolutionary – a better way to compete	Revolutionary – a new way of doing business
Method	Adds value to existing processes	Challenges process fundamentals and their very existence
Scope	Encompasses whole organisation	Focuses on core business processes
Role of Technology	Tradition support, e.g. Management Information System	Use as enabler

However, we do not necessarily see these as contradictory as Carr and Johansson would suggest. Instead we would propose a number of factors which would suggest they are rather more complementary than would at first seem.

1. The decision to introduce total quality may well constitute a decision to reengineer the organisation, thus challenging the status quo.

2. The issue of disjointed incrementalism is a key area. Any innovation will be distorted over time if historical legacies are not addressed. This varies the need for a fundamental realignment of organisational culture – the paradigm shift. Because of its potentially diffuse nature total quality could well be compromised so that it only results in cosmetic changes. In this instance it may well be that reengineering is necessary to achieve the break with historic patterns of operating, i.e. the reconceptualisation of the organisation's purpose and nature. Thus quality implementation may better follow reengineering.

3. If Total Quality is seen as a way of achieving organisational effectiveness by the use of integrated approaches, then reengineering is the strategy to create the propitious circumstances to allow the components of Total Quality to function to optimum effect, and then to provide a means of regular reappraisal in order to prevent incremental drift.

4. Total Quality was at its most successful in organisations that were functioning in a context of relative social and political stability and economic growth. The Japanese experience in recent years would appear to suggest that Total Quality is not helpful if the context is less than propitious. If an environment is turbulent or undergoing radical and profound change then Total Quality may not be an adequate means of developing a response. An addiction is not cured by incremental withdrawal, there has to be a profound and sustained change in behaviour. This requires reengineering personal constructs of priorities, understanding, use of time and so on. If the environment in which schools have to function is undergoing profound

change then it may be necessary to reengineer in order to break historical modes of functioning and then to introduce an integrated system that consolidates the changes.

5. The danger with Total Quality is that it will produce efficient management that does not impinge on children's learning. For example, a school could earn the Investors in People Award and not apply the principles to children – who are not people in terms of the award's criteria! Reengineering may balance this tendency by focusing on core processes.

Findings from research

We report in this book twelve accounts of reengineering or quality initiatives. While we initially thought that quality and reengineering were opposing perspectives we now consider this not necessarily to be so. In the case studies two factors become clear.

1. It is very difficult to introduce total quality to one section of the organisation. By its very nature it has to be adopted by all of the organisation to be effective. Thus our case study schools that have adopted Total Quality approaches successfully have had all the staff and pupils involved in the process. This exemplifies one of the problems of Total Quality – that it is very difficult to change the attitudes of all the individuals and, as a result, Total Quality often fails.

2. Reengineering, on the other hand, can focus on one section of an organisation and reengineer it. One case study school we have investigated that reengineered the teaching of one subject area for 16-year-olds by the use of interactive technology, improved pupil performance by 25 per cent while reducing teacher input time by 60 per cent. However, the limitation of this approach is that it can be partial and not driven through the whole organisation. The advantage, on the other hand, is that schools can make significant shifts in patterns of operation and create a climate for change.

*   *   *

Each of Parts Two to Six will conclude with an analysis and commentary drawing out key points. Part Seven will put forward perspectives on Total Quality and reengineering to aid leaders and managers in schools to operate effectively in the next millennium.

References

Caldwell, B. J. and Spinks, J. M. (1988), *The Self-Managing School*, London, The Falmer Press.

Carr, D. K. and Johansson, H. J. (1995), *Best Practices in Reengineering*, New York, McGraw-Hill.

Davies, B. (1997), 'Rethinking the educational context – a reengineering approach', in B. Davies and L. Ellison, *Educational Leadership for the 21st Century – A Competency and Knowledge Approach*, London, Routledge.

Drucker P. F. (1993), *The Post-Capitalist Society*, New York, Harper Business.

Hammer, M. and Champy, J. (1993), *Reengineering the Corporation*, New York, HarperCollins.

Hammer, M. and Stanton, S. A. (1995), *The Reengineering Revolution – A Handbook*, New York, Harper Business.

Osborne, D. and Gaebler, T. (1992), *Reinventing Government: How the Entrepreneurial Spirit is Transforming the Public Sector*, Reading, MA, Addison-Wesley Publishing Company, Inc.

West-Burnham, J. (1992), *Managing Quality in Schools*, Harlow, Longman.

PART TWO

■ ■ ■

Reengineering: whole school approaches

1

■ ■ ■

A journey of a thousand miles … the Haggerston journey

PAT COLLARBONE

Introduction

To begin with a single step but always keep the end in mind is invaluable advice when embarking on a journey. In order to plan the route you need to know the destination. The challenge for those who wish to engage in school reform is that the destination does not always remain static. Consequently, constant rerouting takes place and valuable energy can be consumed in wrong turnings. To enjoy and appreciate a journey one also needs to be able to look out of the window and take in the 'big picture'. As educators the need to keep in touch with the wider picture of education and learning is essential. I increasingly feel that we have spent too long on the educational tube and not enough time on the cross-country train of lifelong learning.

Starting out – a new headteacher

The first step in my journey came in spring 1990 when I was promoted from deputy and took over the headship of Haggerston School, a single sex girls 11–16 comprehensive school, maintained by Hackney Local Education Authority. The school is a tremendously exciting, challenging place to work, being located in a borough high on all the indices of social deprivation. It is both culturally and ethnically mixed with Bangladeshi pupils representing the largest minority. It is almost inconceivable, looking back, that I took over a school with no development plan, no mission statement and no public consultation process regarding change and development.

For me, the journey through headship has been a series of 'awakenings', of lessons learned along the way, people met and articles stumbled upon that have made all the difference. It is these 'awakenings', these milestones and signposts along the journey, that I want to share with you.

The concept of homography

Immediately prior to my appointment as head, the school had just taken part in a series of seminars at the Grubb Institute where we were introduced to the concept of mission statements and school aims. I seem to remember that a great deal of time appeared to be spent in the minutiae of discussing the significance of words and phrases in an aim statement. At that time it felt slightly unreal, divorced from reality and didn't seem to have an awful lot to do with running a school. The aim we eventually decided upon was:

> At Haggerston School we aim to give girls a variety of opportunities to achieve – intellectually, personally, socially and creatively – so that they are able to develop the knowledge and skills necessary to make confident and responsible choices when they leave school.

It served us well at that stage. There was one concept introduced at the Grubb Institute that stuck in my mind and has remained with me ever since and that was the concept of homography. Behaviours, we were told, run through the institution from the top to the bottom and the senior managers can have a profound impact on the workings of the institution by the way they behave towards each other and to others. The old adage 'smile and the world smiles with you' suddenly had value as a management tool. It is this message, that as a manager 'you are what you say and do', which has remained with me and has become one of my core management principles.

But I divert from my journey. When I became head in April 1990 how many of us really knew what happened on that road we travel every day – our classrooms? As a new headteacher with a number of years of experience in the school I wasn't sure how confident I felt about what went on in the classroom. Another idea I borrowed from the Grubb experience was the notion of the professional pupil. To understand that pupil experience, one of the first exercises I put in place at the start of my new headship was a series of pupil trails. The opportunity to trail pupils was open to all staff and cover would be provided for one day to allow them to do this. They were encouraged to take on the rôle of pupil for the day and to share their experience through a piece of descriptive writing and reflection.

> 'It is now lesson 6 and we are greeted by the teacher – this is the first time today that this has happened. It feels good, I feel as if the teacher wants to be there and wants to be with us and this is the last lesson of the day.'

'The pupils stand behind their chairs at the start of this lesson and wait to be asked to sit down. Entirely different to the last lesson. I'm amazed at how these different expectations on the part of the teacher are automatically transferred into different behaviours on the part of the pupil. I feel totally at sea about what is expected of me from one lesson to the next.'

Looking back on the pupil trails a number of issues stood out for me. One was the importance of never losing contact with the daily classroom experience – since then I have come across the metaphor of the 'ballroom' in the art of watching pupils and staff at work. As school leaders we sometimes dance on the floor, weaving and interacting with all the other 'dancers'. Sometimes, however, we must stand on the balcony and watch quietly, better able to decipher and understand the patterns we see from the seemingly complex movements below us.

Another issue was the importance of giving teachers time and space to watch other teachers at work and to truly experience the learning process. The 'sameness' of the classroom diet, the joy of a teacher with creative insight, and the importance of talk and discussion in enhancing learning were all insights gained through the pupil trail process.

Developing confidence

Linked to this was the notion of confidence – a confident headteacher breeds confident staff and confident children. My appointment as head coincided with the demise of the Inner London Education Authority (ILEA) and the birth of Hackney LEA. Like many heads at that time I felt the self-confidence and morale of my staff plunge. It was a time of uncertainty and staff turnover was high. Indeed in September 1990 there were 34 staff new in post at Haggerston.

Media attention was being focused on inner city schools with a vengeance and, with cries of falling standards, such negative publicity was very damaging. Being told that we 'could do better' simply angered teachers. We needed strategies to succeed. Out of this sense of frustration and isolation the idea of the Haggerston Conference was born, with its theme of raising achievement in the inner city.

The Haggerston Conference

Setting up and facilitating these conferences gave us the opportunity to work with and learn from a richly stimulating group of people. Professor Eric Bolton, speaking at the first Haggerston Conference, reinforced our belief that schools *can* make a difference and that the goals and purposes of education are the same for all pupils. This message coincided with our first year as a Phase 1 pilot LMS school. Brian Caldwell and Jim Spinks (1988), in their work on the 'Self-managing School', added to the voices raised at the first conference when they stressed the necessary focus on teaching and learning, a framework for accountability, the involvement of staff, pupils and parents and the importance of professional development. This phase in the school's development was strengthened the following year when Roland Barth travelled to Haggerston from the Harvard Graduate School of Education and encouraged us to develop the art of conversation in our schools.

The art of conversation

Since working with Roland Barth, I have reflected many times on the art of conversation and its place in school improvement and quality management. To truly engage in rich dialogue with staff and pupils has been an enormous learning experience for me as headteacher. It has led me to experiment with the notion of conversation as a means to school improvement.

Most of us listen with the intent to reply, not to understand. We listen from a paradigm limited by habit, tradition, and personal experience and knowledge. Seeking to understand this goes beyond this narrow form of conversation. (MacManus, 1993)

The writer of this is Joanne MacManus, a school principal from Massachusetts and perhaps she speaks for us all when she says:

With regard to school leadership, what does this mean? For me it has meant my rôle as principal has changed dramatically. I find that I am now more a seeker of information than a giver. I try hard to be an empathetic listener, I make time for personal and small group conversations.

Roland Barth also enjoined us to grow into a 'learning community'. He talked about schools being places where the learn*ed* taught the learn*ers* and until we could all see ourselves as learners, then an achievement culture within a school would never flourish.

School is not a place for important people who do not need to learn and unimportant people who do. (1990)

He also encouraged us to see student achievement, staff development and the professional growth of principals as complementary; he challenged us to make learning endemic and mutually visible throughout the school.

He reminded us that principals, preoccupied with expected outcomes, desperately want teachers to breath in new ideas yet are not themselves visible and voracious learners. He used the powerful image of flight attendants giving information regarding oxygen masks to passengers:

in the event of oxygen failure, those of you travelling with small children should first place the oxygen mask on your own face and then – and only then – place the mask on your child's face. (1990)

He reminded us that we as teachers must be alive in order to keep the young people alive. How many of us are suffocating for lack of oxygen while desperately wanting others to live and breathe?

Since the second Conference with its emphasis on improvement as a continual quest, I have endeavoured to see myself, not as headteacher, but as lead learner in my school. This can have its painful moments, but I believe that if we as teachers are not willing to put ourselves in risky situations where we stand up to be tested and sometimes struggle, how can we expect our pupils to do similar, day after day? I truly believe that the best learning happens in an environment which is free from anxiety and where all are encouraged to make mistakes and to learn from them. That for me is the bedrock of quality management.

The Socratic dialogue

The third Haggerston Conference was planned as a symposium, in the style of Ancient Greece and influenced by the ideas of Socrates. We attempted to emulate the Socratic dialogue with no 'experts', where beliefs and assumptions are open to perpetual questioning, firm conclusions have no special status and you end up with, not a firm answer, but with a much better grasp of the problem than you had before. We invited Professors Peter Mortimore and Michael Barber to engage in a conversation in front of 200 delegates who were encouraged to interrupt, challenge and question each other and the two 'experts'.

We also spent many hours videoing pupils and parents talking about effective teaching and learning. These video clips were used at strategic points in the conversation allowing us to open up the dialogue to many more people than we had previously. All shared with us the risk in doing this and reinforced for me the power of conversation as a tool for clarifying and gaining a greater understanding of issues.

The Haggerston Conferences found us travelling in unmapped regions. Not only did we stand to lose a great deal of money if they were financially unsuccessful but we also ran the risk of failure in the eyes of the wider educational public. As a school leader I learned the value, and the worry, of taking calculated risks. There is a poem by Robert Frost that was quoted to us during the planning phase of the first Conference and has remained with us ever since:

I shall be telling this with a sigh
Somewhere ages and ages hence:
Two roads diverged in a wood, and I –
I took the one less travelled by,
And that has made all the difference (1969)

The poem has become a great friend to Haggerston School, staff and pupils alike, inspiring us to take risks along our journey, for who knows what opportunities lie round the next bend.

When pupils and staff shared the platform with professors, policy makers and politicians, an achievement culture gained momentum. The pupils in particular, began to feel proud that they were members of a Hackney Comprehensive and began to gain confidence in their potential. Roland Barth had urged them to believe that 'they are the best'. He believed that they were and he thus inspired self-belief. When asked for their vision of a good school, a group of pupils presented a paper to delegates:

> *Many people on hearing the name Haggerston will ask 'where's that?'. When told that it's in Hackney they will immediately start making judgements based on common stereotypes of inner city schools. The way the inner city schools are given bad reputations can only make matters worse. By giving students the impression that they are getting second best they are made to feel that they are less able to achieve and therefore become less motivated than students in schools that are better financed.* (1993)

The challenge for me was very clear. We too had to show the pupils that we believed in them and that they had unlimited potential. Specious stereotypes had to be dismantled. As well as raising achievement in the inner city we had to raise the profile of inner city schools in general and celebrate our joint successes.

The development and articulation of vision

We articulated the vision whenever possible: at meetings, in newsletters, in conversations. We sought to use the vocabulary of success to drive us forward. The message became powerful when we encapsulated it in one word: ACHIEVE. Used as an acronym, displayed in school and used regularly in assembly it has enabled us to communicate and share our vision with the school community. The ACHIEVE word is used as a yardstick against which to measure practice.

A   ttendance

C   ommitment

H   omework

I   mprove

E   ffort

V   alue

E   veryone

Professional pupil

The Haggerston Conferences also led us to pay much more attention to the pupil voice in the management of the institution. Regular 'conversations' between pupils and beginner teachers are organised where the pupils talk about what makes an effective learning environment – what motivates them and helps them to learn.

> *'I think that the teacher should be organised and have homework marked. I find that really important because they say to us – they say, write this essay over the weekend. So you try really hard all weekend and bring it in and you think, I put all my hard work into this, it's really gonna be recognised now cos look what I've done. Well in the lesson you say, aren't you going to collect the essay and – well not everyone has done it so next week ...*
>
> *Then later on – have you marked my essay yet – "not yet, not yet, next week"*
> *Then next week comes, "not yet, not yet" – you know, you start to feel a bit let down. You forget about it – the essay – you don't feel proud of that work because she isn't proud of it – if she isn't proud of it then why should you be?'*

> *'Another important thing is – you wanna be a teacher – then show us you wanna be. Don't give the impression that you're there because you have to be, it's the only job you could get and you don't like your job – you wanna get out of it, you wanna quit. Show them – yeah I chose this, I chose this profession because I enjoy it and I enjoy being with you and that's everything. That comes before everything I reckon.'*

> *'You see, teachers have to take into account we're not all as able as each other. I think when it comes to writing – yeah, I can get on with it and I am pretty able, but maybe I'm not as good as the others at sport and I really need encouragement. This one teacher in particular, he showed me that and it was really good – he told me, you've got enthusiasm and that's what counts and from here you can do anything Natalie, and so I thought yeah. Every week I look forward to that lesson and that's just the most brilliant teacher for me.'*

In their conference seminar paper they conclude:

> *As pupils of the school we are always the first to notice when classmates start losing their enthusiasm for certain lessons. This is usually a result of lessons having the same structure from one week to the next, and as pupils lose interest, their attendance begins to suffer. This is a problem which needs to be addressed by both teachers and pupils. The teachers must make a conscious effort to make their lessons interesting and imaginative, while pupils must be self-motivated and willing to learn. It is also the task of the pupils to tell the teachers what they want, either through the school council or through their tutors.* (Haggerston Conference, 1993)

This work with pupils has now led to a reconstituted pupil council with an active rôle in school development. The next conference is being planned by the pupils in partnership with a school in Leicester and one in Birmingham. Not only is this a tremendous opportunity for the young people to exercise their voice but it also allows them to develop the skills of problem-solving, decision-making, team work development, reflection and evaluation – the essential skills of a good manager in fact!

The pupils have also shared their thoughts, feelings, hopes and fears through poetry and art work published in 'Haggerston Voices' (1995):

> *We look before and after and pine for what is not,*
> *We've come beyond the laughter,*
> *Now in store lies what?*
> *We blame our state on the folly of youth and try to turn back time.*
> *We wish we'd known the simple truth,*
> *That ignorance is a crime.*
> *We regret our hasty actions and see how cruel life can be.*
> *We look back in dejection and think again,*
> *If only.*

Forida's poem launched the 1993 Haggerston Conference. This extension of audience for pupil work is essential in building up pupil and staff confidence. Seeing their work in print has had a measurable impact upon the self-esteem of the pupils. It is clear to me that if pupils feel they are poor learners, they believe they are; if they believe they are then they will behave as if they are. As leaders of learning our most important task is to encourage pupils to find their own signposts, chart their own course through learning, and believe in their highest goals.

Multiple intelligences

Our approach to teaching and learning has been informed by the work of Howard Gardner and his extended view of achievement through the development of multiple intelligences. He urges us to transform a uniform school to one where individual strengths are brought to the fore. His advice that 'students are smarter when the teachers are smarter. Teachers are smarter when they don't treat all students the same' (1995), is salutary. His message was brought in charismatic style to the fourth Haggerston Conference through Professor Tim Brighouse. His message from Birmingham was to encourage all to 'achieve on previous best' and to delight, nurture and publicise those small nuggets of good practice that make such a difference to the daily life of a young person. This notion of 'butterflies' in the everyday life of a school is attractive. As lead learners I believe it is our job to find them, delight in them and learn from them.

As we explore different approaches to teaching and learning to encourage success for all, pupil confidence has grown. One measure of this growth in personal confidence and the development of intra- and inter-personal intelligence is manifested for us in the growth of pupil working groups. This has included the setting up of a pupil antiracist/antibullying council. Activities undertaken include designing an antiracist mural, designing and producing antiracist posters and consulting on and piloting a pupil incident referral form. The antiracist policy on every wall in every classroom, they told us, was written by teachers for teachers. The language, they said was far too difficult for the younger pupils to understand.

> 'The school antiracist policy and statement was written by teachers for teachers – the pupils didn't understand it. Especially the younger ones, they didn't understand the words in it.'

We were chastised by our arrogance as policy makers – another lesson on the road to a true learning community.

Early in my headship I travelled along a steep learning curve when pupils staged a sit-in in response to the construction of additional security fencing. On reflection I learned how much the pupils cared about their school and wanted to share in the decisions which affected their school life.

Of course, empowerment can be risky. In the early days of the school council a boycott of school lunches was planned. Every day I see the value of encouraging the pupil voice but see also the need to promote responsibilities as well as rights. Learning about the nature of delegation, representation and negotiation took us into a new phase where the voice is appropriately raised and discussion can take place.

The learning community

The development of a learning community was further enhanced through the work done in the Initial Teacher Training partnerships which we set up with Institutes of Higher Education. Through setting up mentoring programmes with beginner teachers and involving many more staff in facilitating beginner teacher seminars, the notion of all teachers as learners was strengthened. It also added a dimension to our desire to become a learning community which facilitated the development of reflective practitioners, something for which teachers in the past have had precious little time. One could say that on the journey they have been so busy trying to read the map that they have had no time to look out of the window and really take stock of the scenery.

A recent development in enabling teachers to join the wider educational debate has been the growth of action research projects led by teachers. An able pupil project and home/school partnership research project were planned and developed by two teachers in consultation with other staff members. Presentations at staff meetings and to senior management followed as a result of the project and the recommendations have now been taken up by working groups in the school. Conversations on the value of this work have clarified our belief in teachers as leaders, the need teachers have to exercise leadership, and the rôle of the headteacher in allowing that leadership to develop. I am constantly reminded of the fact that an effective principal is more a hero maker and less a hero.

Priorities

The other milestone on this journey to a learning community was finally getting to grips with the issue of priorities. A fellow traveller who helped with this was Steven Covey (1992). His description of a rock experiment is vivid and salutary. Consider this: a jar filled with rocks, not yet full but no more rocks can fit it. Now fill it with gravel – still not full but no more gravel will fit in. Carry on – fill it with sand and finally, when you think it's full, pour in the water. What a wonderful visual metaphor! When I asked the delegates at the 1995 Haggerston Conference including the pupils what they made of this metaphor their suggestions were fascinating.

- that one person is filled up with diverse elements
- however you feel, there is always room for improvement
- that what is going on inside is just as important as outside
- that education is not one thing; that full education required many different things
- the order in which the elements were put in affected the outcome
- first things first, prioritise!

For me the jar of rocks signifies one thing: decide what your big rocks or priorities are and fit them in first. They are the most difficult to lift, they have sharp edges and can hurt, but if you don't get them in first you won't have a chance of squeezing them in later. Like all managers I sometimes avoid my big rocks – the things that are truly standing in the way of quality. Isn't it easier sometimes to play around with sand and water! I now have a large rock on my desk as a visual reminder – prioritise and deal with the big rocks first.

A practical embodiment of shifting the big rocks for me has been putting in place the systems we have for reviewing curriculum delivery. A system of curriculum review, department by department with target-setting and follow-up for both pupils and staff has been put in place. Regular review of the teaching and learning experience in the school is a rock which requires effort and commitment to keep it high on the agenda but one which focuses the Senior Management Team (SMT) firmly on the quality of teaching and learning, the one factor above any that has a direct impact on the achievement of the young people in our school.

Clarity of systems is all important so that everyone can focus on the big rocks efficiently. To that end the nature of meetings was changed. Staff meetings, that were once largely one-way information exchanges, have become workshop-oriented discussion sessions where school policy and procedures are discussed and reviewed. The nature of the information we give to staff has changed. It must be accessible, readable and succinct – information overload is a subtle way of disempowering staff who then feel bewildered into accepting a system they didn't fully understand. That is no way for a learning community to behave.

My other big rock is teacher development, working particularly to motivate teachers to continue learning. Roland Barth encouraged us to be aware of 'at risk educators' – those who leave school at the end of the day or year with little possibility of continuing learning about the important work they do.

As headteacher I do not believe that we can lose teachers in the profession; they are our greatest resource. If a teacher has lost his/her way it is our job to bring them back onto the path. But nevertheless, it is a big rock. The philosophy of 'improving on previous best' holds true for teachers and pupils alike. The continued development of long-established patterns of partnership teaching has done much to move the school away from professional isolation to shared problem-solving, risk-taking and consequent celebration in the classroom. Roland Barth (1990) once again reminds us that 'There can be no community of learners where there is no community and no learners' and again that 'our primary responsibility is to promote learning in others and in ourselves. That is what it means to be an educator.'

Leader and lead learner

What have I learned about myself as lead learner and leader on this journey? I have learned that every single member of this institution is a person of value. For me this is embodied in my schoolkeeper, who has displayed tremendous vision and skill in the area of multimedia presentation used to full effect at the Haggerston Conferences. Seeking out and nurturing professional growth and development for every member of the community is an essential aspect of leadership. Improving schools without extending learning for all within them is a hollow concept. The words of Eric Hoffer quoted on the door of a school in Connecticut ring in my ears:

> *In times of change, learners inherit the earth, while the learned find themselves beautifully equipped to deal with a world that no longer exists.*

My own learning has led me to complete an MBA in Education Management. The opportunity to reflect on my own management style, keep a management diary and explore the relationship of management and leadership theory to practice has been immensely valuable. The dissertation topic I elected to pursue on 'High Performance Teams' led to an examination of the SMT – were they a high performance team, indeed were they a team at all? A number of staff agreed to complete a questionnaire and to take part in lengthy taped interviews exploring these questions. For the SMT this was also a time of individual and team self-review, a difficult but necessary exercise for key members of a learning community. My own conclusion from the research was that:

> *The single most important issue emerging, if the school is to grow as a learning organisation, is the need to learn to listen. Almost all of the recommendations emerging from the research would fall into place, enabling the completion of the jigsaw, if listening became a priority.* (Collarbone, 1995)

A significant stopping-off point for me was this summer, when I took up residency at the Harvard Principals' Centre for two weeks. In the tradition of all travellers I kept a diary and discover new insights into my rôle as school leader whenever I return to it. I was led to the work of Max De Pree (1993) who cautioned us that 'we cannot become what we need to be by remaining as we are'.

I was encouraged to spend time on developing the art of reflection and reflective writing. The message 'we write to live', was a powerful one, as was the realisation that our schools are full of stories waiting to be told by pupils, teachers and parents. I left Harvard convinced that listening to and telling each other stories is not an indulgence but, when melded with research and current educational thinking, a rich and intellectually powerful medium.

Efficacy

So where has this journey led us? I recently came upon the work of Jeff Howard of the Efficacy Institute and was struck by his work on the efficacy paradigm. The unshakeable belief that all young people are capable of success, the challenge in setting exit standards exceptionally high and allying everything we do in our school to meet them and the joy of creating a school 'without failure' are powerful ideas. Nevertheless, having met such ideas on a professional journey, one cannot ignore them. As we journey forward we are now aware of all the signposts that we ignore at our peril:

- Develop a common vocabulary that encapsulates the vision – a common language that all can understand.

- Set the exit points high.

- Believe fundamentally that you can meet the exit points and make sure that all your initiatives are focused on that end point.

- Look for examples of good practice and make sure everyone knows about them.

- Talk up the school, the pupils, the parents and the staff at every opportunity and make sure that they hear it.

- Review, review, review at every stage and act on the information you receive.

- Above all, be confident, be bold, be determined.

The next step

As we now embark on the next stage in our journey I believe that we have two choices. We can either pursue with all our energies the development of life-liberating classrooms in our schools or we can live with classrooms that are life-limiting. We can live with classrooms where children are left unenergised, where their talent is unexplored, where learning is something to endure rather than something to rejoice in. Or we can seek out, promote, develop and build life-liberating classrooms, classrooms without failure where young people learn to learn through taking risks and through developing a relationship with an adult who really believes they can learn and cares passionately that they do.

What is the rôle of the head in ensuring that this destination is within the reach of every member of the institution? This journey now continues with Peter Block (1993) and his notion of 'stewardship' as a companion. He believes that strong leadership does not have within itself the capacity to create fundamental changes in our organisations. Strong leadership, he says, localises power, purpose and privilege in the one we call leader. Stewardship, on the other hand, asks us to be deeply accountable for the outcomes of an institution without acting to define purpose for others, control others or take care of others.

In order to truly change our schools into institutions 'without failure' we need to create passion and commitment in employees. It is Andy Hargreaves (1994) who reminds us that 'Good teaching is infused with desire, pleasure, creativity, challenge and joy' and again that 'Educational change must engage our hearts as well as our minds'.

The learning community which is Haggerston School needs to find ways of enabling all its members to believe that they have a hand in its evolving creation. As a leader I have to move beyond the security and safety of my 'leadership' rôle and accept the challenge of 'stewardship'.

We now have the Haggerston statement of belief to guide us on the next stage in our journey:

> *'Haggerston School is a creative community of learners where everyone can succeed and improve on personal best.*
> *A love of learning is our priority.*
> *We believe in developing confident, responsible citizens who will contribute to and lead society in the 21st century.'*

References

Barth, R. (1990), *Improving Schools from Within*, San Francisco, Jossey-Bass.

Block, P. (1993), *Stewardship: Choosing Service over Self-Interest*, San Francisco, Berret Koehler.

Caldwell, B. J. and Spinks, J. (1988), *The Self-Managing School*, London, The Falmer Press.

Collarbone, P. (1995), *High Performance Teams in a Learning Organisation*, unpublished dissertation, MBA Education Management, Leeds Metropolitan University.

Covey, S. R. (1992), *The Seven Habits of Highly Effective People*, London, Simon & Schuster.

De Pree, M. (1993), *Leadership Jazz*, New York, Dell Publishing.

Frost, R. (1969), 'The Road Not Taken', *The Poetry of Robert Frost*, Jonathan Cape.

Haggerston pupils (1993), *What Makes a Good School*, Haggerston Conference seminar paper.

Haggerston School (1995), *Haggerston Voices, an anthology of poetry*, London, Haggerston School.

Hargreaves, A. (1994), *Changing Teachers, Changing Times*, London, Cassell.

MacManus, J. (1993), 'The Art of Conversation' in *Reflections*, Boston, Harvard University Press.

2
■ ■ ■

Reengineering at Hugh Christie Technology College

RICHARD WALLIS

Introduction

Hugh Christie is now an 11–18 Technology College, for boys and girls with a roll of about 1,100 students. In addition it is the first International Affiliate of the Coalition of Essential Schools (CES). This American-based organisation is committed to exploring methods by which learning can be made more effective and meaningful. Two years ago the school was a successful high school, with GCSE and A level results among the best in the country for a school of this type. So why change? There are seventeen secondary schools within the catchment area competing for the same students and the 11+ system is still in operation. The mind set of the community is one of a strict pecking order of schools, driven very much by social class. At the top are the private schools which reflect one's social status, closely followed by the six single sex grammar schools which, even here, are ranked. Denominational schools are next and bottom of the pile are the high schools.

Parents continually press for a curriculum and *modus operandi* aping the grammar schools, who, to some extent, model themselves on the prestigious private Tonbridge School. Despite being a successful high school, there is always a feeling by students, staff and parents of being inferior. This does little for morale and motivation for all concerned. Also, Hugh Christie has a very successful special education programme which attracts many children who have learning difficulties, thus, further distorting the ability profile.

There became a growing tension between following the agenda set by the other schools, and setting our own agenda essentially challenging the local education system. Also, the advent of national league tables of performance and the intake ability profile heavily skewed to the lower ability, would always endorse the school as being unsuccessful despite there being considerable value added. Therefore, the school had to look towards achieving a more balanced intake if it was ever to be regarded as a successful school.

A new headteacher was appointed in January 1994. After analysing the situation we knew that we must challenge the system. We were aware that research suggests that collaboration and collegiality are pivotal to the orthodoxies of change and knew that we wanted to move from a traditional to a modern learning paradigm. We had to face the huge question of how to get from where we are to where we want to be. Even more fundamental was 'where do we want to be and what would it look like when we got there?' We embarked on a voyage of reengineering the organisation into a learning organisation. Instead of following the current rules we would be writing new rules on how to run a school.

The local politics is just that, local. However, the world is changing and, so too, are the assumptions of how we think about and perceive the world. Newtonian and Cartesian paradigms are being challenged and there is a growth of Chaos and Complexity theories in a post-modernist, post-capitalist society. Everything hangs together, the ecology of everything is where all is interrelated, a connectedness: the globalisation of the economy; the phenomenal growth of nanotechnology; the predicted doubling of the human life span; completion of the human genome project and the blurring of the boundaries of humans and machines. All this suggests that we need to look to the future. The 'tools' of the past or even the present are inappropriate for the future.

> *What is more, to educate young people as though the present patterns of thinking and living, or past ones for that matter, provide a sound basis for confronting the future is quite plainly dangerous. No curriculum can afford to overlook this prospect.* (Beare and Slaughter, 1993, p. 7)

Current thinking concerning the structures of organisations and leadership styles, proclaimed by Senge (1990), Fullan (1993), Drucker (1993) and Hargreaves (1994) suggest that successful schools should focus on the qualities needed to become a learning organisation, such as collegiality, empowering staff, encouraging them to take on new ideas. A central requirement is, that leadership must be transformational rather than transactional and all must strive for personal mastery.

What are needed are some theoretical concepts and models to help an organisation look to the future and cope with these turbulent times. The need for strategic thinking and planning. What is meant by a strategy? Johnson and Scholes (1993, p. 7) define this as:

> *the direction and scope of an organisation over the long term: ideally, which matches its resources to its changing environment, and in particular its markets, customers or clients so as to meet stakeholder expectations.*

It seems then that strategic management is the process of matching the school's activities to the current and emerging environments, within the resource capability of the organisation. This process has three domains: strategic analysis; strategic choice and strategic implementation.

Strategic analysis aims to 'form a view of the key influences on the present and future well-being of the organisation and therefore on the choice of strategy' (Johnson and Scholes, 1993, p. 17). It has four influences: the *environment*, which can be very complex as the introduction to this chapter suggests, as included here are the commercial, economic, political, technological, cultural and the social world; *strategic capability* is effectively the resources of an organisation in its broadest terms; *organisational culture* and *stakeholder expectations* are important because they will affect what will be seen as acceptable in terms of the strategies suggested therefore, to understand the influence of culture is a vital part of a strategic analysis.

> *Organisational culture needs to be analysed in detail in order to understand the paradigm of the organisation. This enshrines its culture and is a powerful force in preventing or facilitating change in the organisation.* (Johnson and Scholes, 1993, p. 198)

A SWOT analysis (strengths, weaknesses, opportunities and threats) is of value in this process. Here in two quadrants the internal 'Strengths' and 'Weaknesses' of the organisation are listed whilst in the other two quadrants the external Opportunities and Threats are recorded. These are not just listed in terms of a manager's perceptions, but a more structured analysis is undertaken to yield findings which contribute to strategy formulation. This model itself has sometimes been modified to carry a fifth dimension, 'Unknown' where the impact of external influences on the organisation are yet unknown. This process is a simple way to gain an understanding of the position of the school and the environment in which it has to function.

Strategic choice, the basis of which is provided by the strategic analysis, has in (Johnson and Scholes', 1993, p. 20) model, three parts: the generation of options; the evaluation of strategic options and the selection of the strategy. This decision-making process usually has to satisfy three criteria: suitability, acceptability and feasibility. A suitable strategy may be one that is commensurate with the principles and aims of the school, whilst utilising its strengths via a window of opportunity and yet at the same time reducing its weaknesses. An acceptable choice involves the value system of the school such as ensuring equity of teaching and learning for the students. The feasibility is often related to the project being financially viable or the targets being realistic.

Strategic implementation and the associated school development plans would be seen as the critical stage. Also up to this stage the process is purely academic. Traditionally in schools, governors and senior managers are extensively involved in the more strategic aspects of planning. Now the staff and pupils will need to be more involved in creating the development plans. It is common for a senior member of staff to set up a planning group which translates the strategic decisions into actions at a rate that allows for ongoing activities to continue. This free communication flow ensures that the plans are realistic as well as contributing to the achievement of the strategic aims and the strategic options chosen. Communications between the various teams such as curricular areas, key stages, school council and support staff while essential, in reality, are nevertheless very difficult to achieve.

This model of strategic planning provides a useful conceptual framework. It has much support as school-based planning is still in its infancy. The model itself is fundamentally hierarchical, forming a self-fulfilling prophecy which supports the hierarchical structures that exist in many schools. Thus, most schools are content with such planning models as they are linear and rational and seem to foster a false sense of a planned and secure future – just what is needed in a school where the organisation is to provide a secure planned future for its students. This form of strategic planning is also supported by the National Audit Office (1995, p. 23) who 'looked for a timetabled, analytical and consultative approach to planning with a review of the past performance, leading to strategic plans'. They then provide a model (1995, p. 24) which would lead to a plan meeting their criteria. What is occurring is the predominant application of the familiar and the attempt to avoid or reduce uncertainty or ambiguity.

However, in these times of rapidly increasing rates of change, strategic planning is being placed under closer scrutiny. In these turbulent times, while not totally discredited, strategic planning is no longer regarded as the queen of managerial disciplines. Indeed, Henry Mintzberg (1985) suggests that there is confusion between strategic planning and strategic thinking. Strategic planning is not strategic thinking. Indeed, strategic planning often spoils strategic thinking, causing managers to confuse real vision with the manipulation of numbers. This confusion lies at the heart of the issue: the most successful strategies are visions not plans.

Another problem arises from an assumption that the current environmental conditions relating to the school will continue to affect it in the same way as the past. Max Boisot (1995) also argues that the failure to treat strategy and organisation processes interactively, rather than sequentially, has led to a growing divergence between theory and practice. This in turn is influencing current thinking concerning the structures of organisations and leadership styles.

> *They [Massachusetts Institute of Technology] were engaged in building new types of organisations – decentralised, non-hierarchical organisations dedicated to the well-being and growth of employees as well as to success. Some had crafted radical corporate philosophies based on core values of freedom and responsibility. Others had developed innovative organisation designs.* (Senge, 1990, p. 15)

The fundamental task of managers is, according to O'Brien 'providing the enabling conditions for people to lead the most enriching lives they can'.

(Senge, 1990, p. 140) Senge believes that there should be personal mastery, where there exists a culture of personal growth and learning. People with a high level of personal mastery live in a continual learning mode. They never 'arrive' . . . It is a process. It is a lifelong discipline . . . 'the journey is the reward'. (Senge, 1990, p. 142)

How is a school to plan when everything is changing? If the way forward is to become a learning organisation what sort of planning is going to be relevant? Max Boisot (1995, p. 32) argues that, in addition to *strategic planning* as outlined above, there are three other strategic options:

- *emergent strategy*, a term coined from Henry Mintzberg (1985) to describe the organisation-wide process of incremental change to environmental states that had not been anticipated via previous analysis. The 'unknown' influences of the modified SWOT analysis. Fundamental to emergent strategy success is that the organisation learns at least at the same rate as the discontinuities and that all the employees are involved in learning.

- *intrapreneurship* after Pinchot (1985) relies on the managers at a local level to deal with any discontinuities as they think is appropriate, irrespective of the positive or negative effects on other parts of the organisation. Success in this Heraclitan world of intrapreneurship is for the organisation to be loosely coupled and the managers empowered and trusted.

- the fourth option, *strategic intent*, copes with turbulence through direct, intuitive understanding emanating from the top leadership. Strategic intent is holistic and deals with turbulence through intuition rather than analytical understanding. It would rely on a common vision or perhaps a set of principles that orientates the staff. Covey (1989) would claim that one's life should be lived by following timeless principles.

Although Boisot's (1995, p. 41) hypothesis points to strategic intent being the distinguishing mark of the learning organisation, he also suggests that, as the turbulence is so varied, all the strategic options together should be regarded as a form of 'strategic repertoire' to be drawn on according to the needs of the moment. Therefore, it seems that a successful, future-focused school will enhance its survival by expanding its strategic repertoire to cope with the divergent environmental turbulence. This will only succeed if all managers include strategy in their personal mastery.

Inextricably linked with strategy planning is the management of change, which is one of the main reasons for having strategic plans in the first place. What is challenging and fascinating about change is that the culture of the organisation will reflect how change is managed. More significant is that if the culture itself is changed, then this is a more holistic approach to change as opposed to making changes in a piecemeal fashion. Hugh Christie has embarked on the former and, as it is reengineering itself into a learning organisation, it seems eminently sensible to focus upon this process of change. One of the reasons for such change is, again, the tension between the post-industrial, post-modern world, with its accelerating change, compression of both time and space, cultural diversity, technological complexity, national insecurity and scientific uncertainty on the one hand and, on the other hand, a modernistic, monolithic school system that continues to pursue anachronistic purposes within inflexible structures.

At the heart of reengineering lies the notion of *discontinuous thinking* identifying and abandoning the outdated rules and fundamental assumptions that underlie current business operations. (Hammer and Champy, 1993, p. 3)

To change the behaviour of the system one must identify and change the limiting factor. This may require actions that have not been considered, choices that have never been noticed, or difficult changes in rewards and norms. Although, reengineering is a concept borrowed from industry it is the process which is the focus for change that is so valuable rather than the person.

> *Reengineering, properly, is 'the fundamental rethinking and radical redesign of business processes to achieve dramatic improvements in critical, contemporary measures of performance, such as cost, quality, service and speed.' ... The focus in any force field analysis is on the process. Why do we do what we do? And why do we do it that way?* (Hammer and Champy, 1993, p. 32)

In schools, to ask these simple, yet powerful questions leads to people working smarter not harder, as when a process is reengineered, jobs evolve from being narrow and task-orientated to being multi-dimensional. People who once did as they were instructed now make choices and decisions instead. 'The learning organisations of the future will make key decisions based on shared understandings of interrelationships and patterns of change.' (Senge, 1990, p. 204)

This is all fine but crucial to the success of reengineering and the learning organisation is the vision. This must be simple and communicated to all in the organisation. Shared vision is vital for the learning organisation because it provides the focus and energy for learning.

> *A shared vision, especially one that is intrinsic, uplifts people's aspirations. Work becomes part of pursuing a larger purpose.* (Senge, 1990, p. 207)

Instead of separating decision-making from real work, decision-making becomes part of the work. Classroom teachers now are trusted and empowered to do what middle managers once did. Reengineering demands that teachers deeply believe that they work for their students, not for their bosses. Work is organised around the learning processes by the teams that perform them. People communicate with whoever they need and control is vested in the people performing the task.

After reengineering the issue of structure is considerably diminished in importance. So, the organisation becomes more open, the climate is dominated by merit rather than politics, where doing what is right predominates over who wants what done.

Freedom to create the results we truly desire. It is the freedom that people who pursue personal mastery seek. It is the heart of the learning organisation, because the impulse to generative learning is the desire to create something new, something that has value and meaning to people. (Senge, 1990, p. 286)

Fullan (1993, p. 31) suggests that there are four personal qualities for greater change capacity: personal vision, enquiry, mastery and collaboration. These are matched by the organisation's shared vision building, organisational structures, norms and practices of enquiry; a focus on organisational development and know-how and collaborative work cultures. He intimates that successful continuous change needs a dual approach working on individual and institutional development. By this he is emphasising the importance of everyone in the organisation being an effective change agent. In addition, reengineering identifies information technology as another essential enabler of change. Applying information technology to school reengineering demands inductive thinking, the ability to first recognise a powerful solution and then to seek the problems it might solve, problems which the school probably doesn't even know it has.

How can we use technology to allow us to do things that we are not *already doing?' Reengineering unlike automation is about innovation.* (Hammer and Champy, 1993, p. 85)

Thus, to succeed in a period of ongoing technological change, schools need to make technology exploitation one of their core competencies. Change is something that people usually readily strive for. People like change but do not like being changed. Too often, change management simplifies the process, relying on cause and effect, seeing things as a snapshot rather than the reality of the complex systems in which we operate. Strategies for managing change have been described as having three stages: unfreezing, changing and creating the new culture. For continual success to occur, the new culture must not become refrozen. There is a paradox here: where there exists a culture of change, change is normal, an everyday activity. This is, of course, one of the many components of a learning organisation.

So how useful has Hugh Christie Technology College found the strategic planning, reengineering and management of change theories in becoming the first international member of the Coalition of Essential Schools, and a technology college. The arrival of the new head was the focus for reviewing the future direction of the school. Although everything looked good, an analysis of the environmental situation from a different mind set concluded that something radical had to happen, otherwise the school would always be regarded as second rate. The challenge was on: how to simultaneously challenge the local education system and make the school significantly different. All the senior management team were encouraged to read Handy's *The Age of Unreason* (1989) and the books by Ted Sizer *Horace's Compromise* (1984) and *Horace's School* (1992). Our quest is neatly put by Hargreaves (1994, p. 261):

the possibilities for establishing more vibrant and vigorous teacher cultures are seriously limited by the existing structures in which many teachers work. If teachers are to interact more flexibly, learn from each other more extensively, and improve their own expertise continuously, then new structures need to be created pre-emptively which make these learnings and interactions more possible.

At this point the vision of the future was unclear, other than the need to find some unique course of action encompassing a moral-rich principle of improving teaching and learning. This made the Coalition of Essential Schools as an organisation an attractive proposition. At this stage it was important to involve as many stakeholders as possible in assessing the effectiveness of this reform group. Their nine principles were circulated to all staff. A cross section of staff, including governors, visited CES schools in America. Following this extensive evaluation exercise we proceeded with an application to become the first international affiliate member of the CES. At this stage of cultural reform, we received considerable support from Brown University, Rhode Island, USA, and from Ted Sizer the founder of the organisation, who views restructuring as about nothing more or less than helping the student to 'learn to use one's mind well'. (Sizer, 1992) Indeed, the network of Coalition schools has been a catalyst for much restructuring and for many curriculum initiatives. It is not to say that it would not have occurred without such support but at a time of inevitable risk-taking it is some comfort to share one's ideas with other professionals who are following the same principles.

Distinguishing characteristics of Hugh Christie Technology College directly related to CES influence include:

- increased student participation in the curriculum via an electives programme – short courses on any subject which students may wish to learn about, taught in non-age-related groups; assessment is via exhibition, where the students exhibit their work for assessment by their peers and adults including representatives from the local community;
- collapsing the conventional timetable approximately every ten days, for similar electives type courses;
- advisory groups where most adults working in the college have a small group of students, and engage them in a focused dialogue about themselves and their academic progress;
- an increased focus on learning;
- new heterogeneous groupings and the development of collaborative group-work;
- staff and students attending the 'Fall Forum' conference and hosting the first international CES conference outside the USA in July 1995.

At this stage 'Internationalism' became a part of the new vision with staff and students networking, resulting in many collaborative curriculum initiatives as well as several exchanges. Thus, although the original vision was somewhat vague, the principles helped to remove the mist clouding the navigating star.

Simultaneously, the government had launched the Technology College Initiative. This, provided an ideal opportunity to create a fundamentally different school. All stakeholders were consulted on the technology college issue, although, the short time span for the application was really insufficient for detailed analysis. There is something of an irony here. If the consultation period had been longer, an in-depth strategic analysis on the strategic capability would have cast doubts on the school pursuing technology college status.

It is hard to think now of these two significant developments as separate. The CES provided a clear set of teaching and learning principles while the Technology College Initiative is more of an enabling agent, a catalyst for radical pedagogies using modern technologies and telecommunications.

This metamorphosis of the school into a technology college would not fall neatly into the models of change as described above. Quite simply, it seemed an excellent opportunity, so 'let's do it'. The school was awarded technology college status, just seven months after the new head arrived. This supersonic rate of change has been criticised by many staff. The consultation period was too short and regarded as superficial, so causing some resentment. The critical implementation stage of the changes has not been smooth, yet from this there has been a paradigm shift for most staff. Previously, all change would have expected to follow a set pattern and not be implemented until all the problems were resolved but now, fine tuning as the changes evolve is more accepted as part of the culture. Nevertheless, the new status clarified a second vision: the use of the latest computer and communication technologies throughout the whole organisation.

The increased focus on improving teaching and learning has led to the acquisition of modern technologies for flexible learning, the creation of a flexible learning centre, and the development of supported self study. The use of closed circuit television (CCTV) for the conventional reasons such as security has had an interesting spin-off. It is modifying the students' behaviour along corridors and in the flexible learning centre. This in itself has helped to transform the role of the teacher from 'supervising' students in the flexible learning centre to coaching or supporting the students in their learning. Technology is doing the supervising.

Technologies now touch all the stakeholders in the college. These include: a college-wide computer network; a school radio station run by the students; a TV bulletin board system capable of showing students' work, using video clips; a new telecommunication system making the switchboard post almost redundant (while on the other hand communications into the school have been enhanced). Student services have also been enhanced by creating a homework help-line. Video conferencing facilities further develop our international connections and multi-cultural and language initiatives, while quite a revolutionary change is that some 'A' level courses will be taught as a distance learning package using this video conferencing facility. A swipe card registration system has redirected significant time from mindless administration to more active academic learning. All these initiatives show that technology college status has a significant enabling function in terms of resource capability. Cultural change is also occurring at the college, some as a latent function of the two major initiatives. The focus on learning begs the question, do the college buildings reflect this cultural change? Are there subliminal messages around the college which emphasise the main function of the organisation? There is evidence of this in the considerable amount of artwork around the college. This falls into two distinct domains: the first supports the function of the college with slogans such as 'learning is the most important thing you do today and every day', or depicts the value or relevance of particular subjects; the second is where students have been encouraged to create their own pictures signifying that it is their college and that they are reinforcing their sense of belonging by contributing to their working environment. Both continue to have a significant influence on the changing culture.

As a technology college we develop such personal qualities as proactivity, responsibility, collaboration, flexibility, interpersonal and groupworking skills, a willingness to use modern technologies and generative learning. However, to operate within a framework of reductionism, a subject-based curriculum, a schedule of subject time slots and small classrooms does not facilitate collaborative teaching teams or flexible teaching and learning styles. To facilitate the latter, in terms of the building, walls have been removed and replaced, if at all, with small screens to create the requirements as outlined above. Traditional organisational structures could not respond to the pace of change and sheer volume of initiatives. Staff are trusted and empowered and encouraged to take on new ideas. The leadership is far more transformational than transactional. All are encouraged to become leaders, to become involved with projects of all types with appropriate financial incentives. There is an emphasis on horizontal structures where the stress is on flexible collaborative curriculum teams, responsible for all the child's education. These teams go under the banner of PITs (Planning and Implementation Teams). The Year 7 PIT is challenging the intellectual chaos provided by compartmentalised subject based curriculum and time slots with the aim of creating a more coherent learning paradigm. Decisions about these changes were made by the appropriate staff.

In the sixth form the teaching and learning is undergoing similar transformations. There are modular courses at 'A' level, incorporating less teacher directed and more flexible learning, with small groups, or one-to-one tutorials. The teacher is coach and the student is the worker. Some 'A' level courses are outsourced via video conferencing and other computer-based technologies. The swipe card registration system facilitates more effective use of the college's resources while students capitalise on the flexible day with community work and industrial placements.

The international dimension of the organisation's vision is realised by a cohort of foreign students who spend as little as a term, or stay for a full two-year sixth form course. They come mainly from EU countries such as Germany, Holland and Sweden although some students come from Japan. These students provide many linguistic and cultural exchange opportunities for all. The Romanian student and teacher exchange is most revealing for all those involved. The Romanians have barely become an industrial nation, let alone wrestled with the implications of the post-industrial society.

So how, over the past two years, do the theoretical models of strategic management and the management of change correspond to the practical processes in operation at Hugh Christie Technology College? Many of the events can be identified as the stages of strategic management. The strategic thought process formulated an agenda for action. The interesting concept of vision has been crucial in setting the college on the road to success yet, in itself, the original vision was more holistic and intuitive than based on hard rational analysis. It was strangely both precise and yet fairly vague: 'we must do something different focusing on teaching and learning'. This then encapsulates the theory of 'Strategic Intent' as espoused by Max Boisot (1995). Strategic analysis was used in the SWOT process which formed the platform for the strategic choice. That is, become a member of the CES which was both different and focused on learning. Similarly, this initiative would partially satisfy Henry Mintzberg's 'Emergent Strategy' theory although he would suggest that, during the implementation period, unanticipated opportunities and threats will emerge which have to be dealt with incrementally (Mintzberg, 1985). Nevertheless, the changes as a result of becoming a technology college would fall more in the reengineering camp of transformational change. The turbulence of the external environment fuelled by an impending OFSTED inspection would satisfy emergent theory. Despite plans associated with the curriculum reform being transformational in nature, the impending OFSTED saw a return to a short-term incremental approach to developments, sticking with the tried and tested, deferring some of the radical change, rather than encompassing the strategic vision. It could be argued that OFSTED was a powerful agent against change at that time. Yet, post-OFSTED, their agenda for action becomes a powerful agent of change. This schizophrenic influence on change could form the basis of further research.

What about the claims that the organisation is undergoing reengineering? Certainly there is much evidence to suggest it is, such as the 'A' level courses being delivered by video conferencing and the work of the PIT group. However, as yet the outputs of these new modes of practice have not shown the great savings or significant increases in performance that would be claimed by true reengineering.

The results from student and parent surveys are generally positive: for example students are happier, feel valued and know that learning is important, and at 16+ the stay-on rates have improved yet hard indicators such as attendance and examination results have only made slight improvement. It could be that these changes have only enhanced those already committed students and have not, as yet, reached the disaffected. Or perhaps it is that the learning process is a long-term activity and real improvements are occurring in personal management skills, such as positive attitudes and behaviours, responsibility and adaptability, and team work skills, rather than in the traditional performance indicators. Could it simply be that teachers are so involved in meeting highly diverse INSET needs that staff are frequently out of school and classes have supply teachers, which is undermining the students' learning? Much of this is sheer supposition and more research is needed to evaluate the effectiveness of these changes. Another divergence between the top-down model of reengineering and practice at Hugh Christie is that many new initiatives were teacher inspired. So, change at Hugh Christie is instigated both top-down and bottom-up. Other examples derived from successful change management include: a simple vision regularly communicated to all; the unfreezing of the old culture by dialogue and debate; and encouraging all to look beyond the organisation for successful practice. Staff have been empowered to take on responsibilities and make changes in harmony with the vision and principles. An example is the work of the PIT group. No longer is it the role of the organisation to set out the learning requirements for the staff, but they are encouraged to set their own lifelong learning agendas. More staff than ever before are encompassing the concept of personal mastery, for example being involved with higher degree courses.

There is no doubt that a new culture is being created with many ongoing changes, but where are the weaknesses? Ironically, they appear at the most crucial level. The implementation of these changes in the classroom is variable. For example, changes in pedagogies such as increased individualised learning via flexible learning and the creation and use of the flexible learning centre have been an outstanding success. This can be attributed to: a significant lead-in time; the Prince's Trust who provided detailed implementation plans, and a network of other organisations for ongoing support; and the professional guidelines on flexible learning provided by Waterhouse (1990) and Hughes (1993).

This has not been the case for the use of IT across the curriculum. No detailed implementation plans were evident, too much was left to chance, it really had been delegation with disassociation. It seems that schools who have extreme development profiles are, on the whole, good at plan construction but much weaker on audit and evaluation. A lot of energy goes into the first phase of constructing the development plan while this is not necessarily taken further into action plans which sustain implementation and lead to evaluation. A way ahead is to use more detailed action planning which slows down innovation, follows it through and evaluates it. However, there is a 'catch 22' situation here. Without the equipment one cannot raise the level of IT. But once the equipment is there, everyone wants to use it. The enormous INSET requirements and implications are beyond the resource capability of the college. It is unable to provide adequate INSET and time for staff to collaborate or network with other schools. This has resulted in dramatic improvements occurring in a few areas, while in others no authentic use of IT is happening.

Reflecting on the 'Empowered School' (Hargreaves and Hopkins, 1991) the analysis of the poor level of IT development could be innovation overload. Maybe it is because the head and senior management team enthusiastically embrace individual innovations as they arrive, and some staff may conse-quently engage in so many innovations that they become overwhelmed by them. It is the responsibility of the leaders within the college to rethink this most crucial area and for example, to formulate a new IT implementation plan, which of course is all part of the iterative planning process. The introduction of ILS (Integrated Learning Systems) provides an ideal window of opportunity for this. Normally once implementation takes place the plan goes on automatic pilot and little on-going support is given. Working groups using action plans should be able to overcome this difficulty.

Thus, it can be seen that at Hugh Christie Technology College there are links with theory and practice and that such theories do provide a useful theoretical framework for strategic management and managing change in a school. However

Restructuring is not an end to our problems but a beginning chance to set new rules for new purposes and new learnings in a newly constructed world. (Hargreaves, 1994, p. 261)

References

Beare, H. and Slaughter R. (1993), *Education for the Twenty-First Century*, London, Routledge.

Boisot, M. (1995), 'Preparing for turbulence: the changing relationship between strategy and management development in the learning organisation', in B. Garratt, *Developing Strategic Thought: Rediscovering the Art of Direction-Giving*, London, McGraw-Hill.

Covey, S. R. (1989), *The Seven Habits of Highly Successful People*, London, Simon & Schuster.

Drucker, P. F. (1993), *Post-Capitalist Society*, New York, Harper Business.

Fullan, M. (1993), *Change Forces: Probing the Depths of Educational Reform*, London, Falmer Press.

Hammer, M. and Champy, J. (1993), *Reengineering the Corporation: a Manifesto for Business Revolution*, New York, Harper Business.

Handy, C. (1989), *The Age of Unreason*, London, Arrow Books.

Hargreaves, A. (1994), *Changing Teachers, Changing Times*, London, Cassell.

Hargreaves, D. and Hopkins, D. (1991), *The Empowered School*, London, Cassell.

Hughes, M. (1993), *Flexible Learning Examined*, Glasgow, Network Educational Press.

Johnson, G. and Scholes, K. (1993), *Exploring Corporate Strategy*, Hemel Hempstead, Prentice-Hall.

Mintzberg, H. (1985), 'Of strategies deliberate and emergent', *Strategic Management Journal*, pp. 257–72.

National Audit Office (1995), *Examinations of Value for Money at Grant-Maintained Schools 1994–1995*, London, HMSO.

Pinchot, G. (1985), *Intrapreneuring*, New York, Harper & Row.

Senge, P. M. (1990), *The Fifth Discipline*, New York, Doubleday.

Sizer, T. (1984), *Horace's Compromise: the dilemma of the American High School*, Boston, MA, Houghton Mifflin.

Sizer, T. (1992), *Horace's School: Redesigning the American High School*, Boston, MA, Houghton Mifflin.

Waterhouse, P. (1990), *Flexible Learning: an Outline*, Glasgow, Network Educational Press.

3

■ ■ ■

From a blank sheet of paper

JOHN LEWIS

In the spring of 1989 I was happily ensconced as the headteacher of Birchwood Community High School in Cheshire. Nearly five years previously I had been delighted to be appointed there for my first headship. This was particularly so because it was to be something that I had always wanted – a brand new secondary school.

This opportunity was rare in the 1980s, which had been a decade characterised by falling birth rates and educational contraction: mergers and staff redundancies were much more the order of the day than the building of new schools. Birchwood went against this national trend because it was part of a new town development: in this case, Warrington. The rapid growth associated with this had already led to the building of new secondary schools at Great Sankey and Padgate and to the establishment of four new primary schools in Birchwood itself. A secondary school was now deemed necessary to provide educational continuity for these children after the age of eleven.

I was under no illusions about headship. I recognised that every school is different and that each requires a particular type of headteacher to guide it to its full potential. The type of personality required to turn around a failing school, or even one with major problems, is not necessarily the same as that needed to guide an institution through its vital early years. I felt that my own character was better suited to providing a vision and being supportive of a committed and optimistic staff than having to deal ruthlessly with a difficult and suspicious group of colleagues in a situation of low morale.

Five years later, almost to the day, I was appointed the Principal of Bradford City Technology College. Again this was to be a completely new institution and once again I was to be given a full year to plan its launch before a single pupil would set foot in it. I considered myself to be exceptionally fortunate: to be given such an opportunity once in one's life was marvellous – for it to happen TWICE was almost beyond the bounds of credibility!

In each case I was given what was virtually a blank sheet of paper and encouraged to design a school on it. There are, of course, different ways of looking at such an uncluttered document. On one side can be seen all the vast problems which are undeniably associated with such a situation – unruly pupils, dissatisfied parents, fractious governors, meddlesome local authorities and an increasingly demanding DfEE. This is a prime recipe for continuous tension, extreme stress, potential nervous breakdown and possibly even an early grave! Who in their right mind would want that?

Most fundamentally I have introduced and integrated a particular ethos into both schools. The latter has been neither a task nor a duty – rather it is a process which any headteacher will be associated with whether s/he likes it or not. It is well documented that every school takes on, to a considerable degree, the personality and characteristics of its head. I believe that mine have been no exception to this general rule.

With the advantages which hindsight brings, the Birchwood headship was far easier than what was to follow at Bradford. There were many reasons for this difference. The most important was that Birchwood was a school which was actively desired by the entire local community; indeed many prospective parents had previously demonstrated with placards outside County Hall at Chester when the existence of the new school had been in doubt.

I know that when I announced that I had been offered a new post it took everyone by surprise. In fact I had not been seriously contemplating an alternative; I felt happy and fulfilled at Birchwood. However, as so often happens in life, fate played a part. My wife came from Yorkshire; her parents were not in good health and so there were strong family reasons for moving to that county. It was she who saw the TES advertisement for the post of Principal of Bradford City Technology College and who encouraged me to apply for it.

As CTCs were expected to establish a uniquely pro-active working partnership with commerce and industry I half expected to be in competition at interview with senior executives from outside the education sector. When it became clear that this was not the case, I knew that I stood an excellent chance of being appointed. My experience in starting a new school would inevitably stand me in good stead.

So it proved. After preliminary interviews in Bradford I was one of the three candidates who were shortlisted. We were sent to London for a series of psychometric tests and interviews at the headquarters of the college's lead sponsor, the major high street electrical retailing company Dixons Group plc. Shortly afterwards I was offered the post and from September 1989 embarked upon the greatest challenge of my professional career.

I knew that the post would be a high-profile one but I was not aware of the extent of the political bitterness which had been created by the project within Bradford. In fact, the city community had been completely polarised between those who felt the CTC was the 'best thing since sliced bread' and those who believed it was totally unnecessary and would be a 'white elephant'. Worse still, planning permission had been granted by the casting vote of the Conservative mayor in a 'hung' Council but before the college opened local government elections had resulted in a Labour majority – a situation which was to be progressively extended over the coming years. From then on the Council was openly opposed to the new college and did everything it could to make life difficult for it.

Tensions were compounded by the fact that Bradford was one of the few remaining LEAs to have a middle school structure. This meant that, as the CTC was to be an 11 to 18 institution, it would recruit its students halfway through their middle school careers. Consequently there was no chance of any significant liaison with the feeder schools taking place such as had been one of the strengths of the cross-sector provision at Birchwood. It further meant that, no matter what tactics were to be adopted, the CTC was destined to be isolated and friendless within the Bradford educational establishment.

This inheritance led me to be in no doubt that the new college would have to stand on its own feet and 'fight its own corner' from the beginning. It was clear that any mistakes which became public would be seized upon with glee by its many opponents and would be given prominent coverage in the local media. I also realised that we were in a 'no win' situation – if the CTC failed there would be massive criticism from many sources; if it succeeded people would put it down simply to unfair resourcing.

At this time I certainly did not believe that success was assured. When we embarked upon the first student recruitment drive, in the spring of 1990, the college was still completely unproven; it had no tradition, no reputation, few actual members of staff and not even any buildings to show to the prospective parents. At that time the site was still a muddy waste; the province of builders, tall cranes and JCBs.

I have always had a tremendous admiration for the courage of our first parents who, as an act of faith, were prepared to defy these unpropitious portents and entrust to us their most precious possessions – their children. I'm sure that it confirmed in me and my colleagues a strong desire to do our very best for those families at all times.

Major contrasts with my previous post soon became apparent. The overall responsibility for ensuring that the project was completed on time and within budget was given to a project director. As one of his first duties had been to arrange for the appointment of the Principal, it was always tacitly accepted that he was my 'boss' for the duration of his contract. As he came from an educational background himself, having been the headteacher of a new school in the Middle East, there was an obvious and ever-present possibility of him attempting to influence the educational side of the project.

In retrospect, I believe it would have been better all round if the project director had been from a building/business background and had been inclined naturally to concentrate on getting the best value for money from the building contract itself. Although it is true that the project was indeed delivered on the financial basis which had been agreed there was considerable evidence that money had been ill-spent in many areas. The design and finish of the building left much to be desired and was to require a great deal of money to be spent later to remedy the most obvious defects.

The absence of a conveniently situated local authority advisory team was compensated for by the appointment, on short-term contracts, of a group of 'curriculum consultants'. They were operational and had already taken many important decisions regarding the lay-out and equipping of all the specialist rooms in the college. As the building consisted of seven individual teaching blocks, each constructed at right angles to the central mall, this meant that the consultancy team, together with the project director, had decided the location of every subject area as well as the number, size and shape of rooms that they should have. Their decisions were encapsulated on the set of plans which I was given at interview.

It was on studying these plans that my first serious doubts about the project emerged. Not only did the overall dimensions of the site (7.5 acres) seem small for a school of 1,000 students but I found it hard to see where all the functions which I envisaged for such a school could be accommodated within the building plan. I noted with disappointment, though not surprise because the same had applied at Birchwood, that there was no provision for an assembly hall. I knew that the Department of Education believed that such a large space was not 'cost effective', a view with which I personally profoundly disagree. As someone who believes in the value and importance of sport, I was saddened by the fact that there was room on site for only one junior sized artificial pitch, augmented by a sports hall. Coming from a school which was surrounded by high quality natural grass pitches I was to find this minimal provision to be a major obstacle to the development of sports teams of the standard that I wished the college to be associated with. In addition I was amazed at the fact that a deliberate decision had been taken to omit a staff common room in favour of a number of satellite staff rooms related to specialist subject areas. I was also surprised to see the single small music room sited on the ground floor immediately behind the reception desk and finally that the area allocated to reprographics was compressed into a small part of the library.

The decisions taken by the consultants would have profound effects on the way that the curriculum was to be delivered. In particular they had deliberately created huge open-plan areas in most of the blocks, presumably to encourage team-teaching and resource-based learning. While this was commendable in many ways it meant that, by my calculations, the college would be short of at least twenty basic classrooms when fully developed. In fact, over the next few years, each of these open areas was to be 'boxed-in' to rectify the situation. The other impact stemmed from the fact that particular areas had been 'claimed' by each consultant as 'their' specialist bases. It was easy to tell which consultants had been the most persuasive and influential by even the most casual look at the plans. The major victory had been gained by the science consultant: he had 'won' the whole of the largest block in the college! The plans indicated that there were to be no fewer than eighteen specialist laboratories on two floors. I found it hard to envisage how there would ever be a situation where eighteen lessons of science could be going on simultaneously, or that we could ever appoint anywhere near that number of science teachers.

The consequence of these decisions was that other subjects did not do anything like as well. Hard though I searched, I could find no areas allocated to either mathematics or English; not surprisingly neither of these subjects had bene-fited from the presence of a consultant! Clearly this would not do but it did make for a difficult first meeting with the consultancy team when I had to make root and branch criticisms of their work rather than offering the praise which I'm sure they had been expecting. Without question all the consultants had done their best within their respective briefs. The problem was that there was neither a clear overall vision nor an effective co-ordination of the sort that had been provided in Cheshire.

In addition the consultants varied enormously in their backgrounds: this influenced the quality of the advice which they gave. Some were up to date and quite innovative, others had come from a traditional grammar school back-ground and advised accordingly with the result that their areas were not of the style or content that needed to be associated with a school which was expected to be at the forefront of technology. The real lesson is surely that, in any such project, it is essential to appoint the headteacher at the very beginning of the undertaking because, at the end of the day, it is s/he who will be held to account for the success or failure of the entire undertaking. Accordingly, it is vital that s/he is able to influence and direct its major aspects from the outset.

I was aware that the main reason for not following this line at Bradford was the necessity for speed. The construction of the CTC was a prime example of a 'fast-track' project. From the granting of planning permission to completion of the building, work took only eighteen months and all this on an extremely difficult site which was above many disused mine-shafts all of which required locating and capping. Clearly the project team were extremely wary of the arrival of a Principal with the authority to demand major revisions to already agreed plans as this would inevitably slow things down. The consequence was that, once I had succeeded in achieving substantial changes to the allocation of subject areas, I withdrew from the building project in a substantive sense.

However, I did observe the progress of the construction with interest and was horrified to see that all the internal walls were to be of wallpapered plasterboard: the obvious difficulty of maintaining such surfaces in a busy school was all too apparent. In retrospect, this flimsy internal construction method was to prove highly beneficial because it was easy to move walls and box-in areas to remedy some of the problems caused by the original design. I also noted that, while the teaching areas were generally very basic in their construction, much money had been devoted to making 'front of house' areas extremely attractive. In fact a conscious decision had been taken to make the building appear quite unlike an ordinary school. In this the architects were undoubtedly successful. All visitors are uplifted by the spacious mall which forms the central spine of the college; it gives it the appearance of a commercial centre rather than a traditional school. I was pleased by this and believed it would help to create an appropriate ethos.

My separation from the building project did give me the opportunity to concentrate on this ethos and on how best to create it. I can now admit that I had little idea at the time of what this should be. I was satisfied that I had helped to create an excellent school at Birchwood and I knew that the CTC, because of the high expectations of all concerned, had to be even better ... but how could this be done? I also gained the firm impression from my governors that it had to be 'different' and 'distinctive', not only from other schools, but also from the other CTCs. Bearing in mind that each of the other fourteen colleges would begin with the same sort of advantages that we possessed, the achievement of 'uniqueness' was clearly not going to be easy.

The obvious place to start was to appoint some colleagues. Operating in isolation is very restrictive; it is vital to have others to bounce ideas off and to receive theirs. During the autumn I advertised for and appointed two Deputy Principals and a Director of Finance. Although each deputy had specific areas of responsibility, they were to be centrally involved also in all aspects of the planning process. The task of the Director of Finance, besides setting up all the necessary financial procedures, was to invoice and record the countless thousands of items of furniture and equipment which now had to be ordered. All three began their appointments in January 1990 after which the pace began to quicken rapidly.

Throughout the spring we were involved in a range of other appointments. On the basis of a curriculum-led staffing model we decided to begin with fifteen teachers in the first year and twelve members of the support staff. Inevitably all of the teachers had a subject responsibility and as a consequence all had significant teaching experience, with the exception of the head of music, who was a newly qualified graduate. She was to remain the only musician on the staff for the next five years – a marvellous opportunity for someone just entering the profession. We also did forward projections for the next six years to take the college to a steady-state situation. These indicated that by the year 1995–96 there would be around seventy teachers and thirty members of the support staff, a prediction which turned out to be remarkably accurate. Each of the subject specialists was given the responsibility of deciding their respective schemes of work and for ordering textbooks and equipment within agreed budgets. This must have been a difficult task as they were still in their previous jobs and did not start at the CTC until September.

While this process was taking place the first round of student recruitment occurred. It had been decided that 180 eleven-year-old children would be offered places. Given the opposition within the middle schools, it was obvious that they could not be involved in this process. Consequently, a decision was taken to mail-shot every household in the catchment area. As this consisted of the entire city of Bradford it was a major undertaking and an expensive one. In the end information brochures, containing an application form, were delivered to over 90,000 homes. It was not exactly a fine-tuned approach but at least it advertised the existence of the college in a very direct manner.

Finally about 350 families went ahead with applications. The interviews were conducted by a specially recruited group headed by one of the college's consultancy team. A deliberate decision had been taken that I should not be part of this process in an attempt to shield me from the flak which was anticipated in its aftermath. Critics had predicted that only the 'brightest and the best' children would be selected with the result that the college would be in reality a 'grammar school in disguise'. In fact there was never any possibility that this would be so. The college had to adhere to strict criteria laid down by the Department of Education. The first of these stipulated that all applicants must live within a prescribed catchment area (equivalent to the old city boundaries); the second that every intake must comprise a broad range of academic ability, including students with statements of special educational need; and the third that each cohort should be representative of the catchment area in all its manifestations.

Thus, by the stroke of a civil servant's pen, the student profile of the college was established. Unless the letter and the spirit of those who founded the CTC initiative were to be ignored, Bradford CTC would begin as, and always remain, a genuine inner-city comprehensive school with strong representation from the mass of ethnic minority cultures which characterise the city.

To my direct knowledge these regulations have always been followed religiously with the result that the average student, in each year group, has been close to the national average score in the standardised IQ assessment which is given to every applicant on the day of interview. The ethnic minority percentage has always been around 35 per cent; slightly higher than the figure for the city. The residential requirement has inevitably caused problems for those families who have found to their dismay that they live outside it. It is true that the notion of a 'catchment area' is now anachronistic and certainly runs counter to the other central tenet of Conservative education policy over the last decade with its stress on parental choice. However, it is easy to understand why it is applied to CTCs; it is a formidable barrier to an unscrupulous Principal who might wish to select his students from the 'leafy-glades' of suburbia!

Much has been made of the 'selectivity' of CTCs. I would certainly not wish to underestimate the advantages that such a power gives to a school but I also believe these should be kept in proportion. The first point is that no school can be selective in any way unless it can achieve and maintain an oversubscribed situation. Nowadays schools are strongly influenced by market forces, especially the laws of supply and demand. Parents can choose a school to send their children to and also choose to withdraw them at any future time. There was absolutely no certainty that Bradford CTC would begin, and remain, heavily oversubscribed; much hard work has gone into ensuring that this is the case. The second point is that the degree of freedom over selection in CTCs is significantly restricted anyway by the DfEE regulations which were referred to previously. The third is that a considerable degree of self-selection always comes into play. It was always obvious to me that admission to the college did not represent an easy option and that the type of education on offer would not be appropriate to all children.

The sheer logistics of getting to and from the college were formidable. For many children it meant two separate bus journeys each way, each day: one into the city centre and one from there to the college. The day itself was a much longer one than was usually the case elsewhere: a 30-hour week for 40 weeks in the year. The academic year was also fundamentally different; five terms each of eight weeks. This would inevitably cause severe difficulties for families with other children in more traditional schools. Finally, the offer of a place would mean that eleven-year-old children would have to give up the ease and security of their small local middle school, where they were almost certainly very happy and where they would have many friends, for the uncertainties associated with a college which probably meant nothing to them and where they might well have no friends at all at first. During the half day of interview I have always made a point of spelling out these problems to the prospective parents, almost encouraging them to withdraw their applications. It is always a surprise, though a pleasant one, that so few ever do.

The key decisions about the structure of the school day, the academic year, the initial curriculum and so on were all taken within the Senior Management Team (SMT) during the spring and summer of 1990 – several of these were genuinely radical.

It was agreed that the college day would be both longer and more flexible than the norm. After much discussion it was decided that it would begin with a daily whole staff briefing at 8.20 am and end at 3.30 pm. There would be a staggered lunch arrangement and a provision of 'twilight' teaching sessions when the sixth form arrived in order to facilitate their curriculum choice and make the fullest possible use of the accommodation and the specialist equipment. The establishment of a genuine work ethic amongst students of all ages and abilities was a critical aim from the start. To encourage this there were to be no school bells – the students were expected to be at the correct place at the correct time; they would be welcomed into the college from 8 am – with a breakfast service available for those who wished to make use of it; and would be given full access to the library and IT facilities throughout all breaks and lunchtimes and up to 5 pm every evening. The consequence of this pattern was that the working week for students totalled 30 hours – about 20 per cent above the national average for secondary schools.

However, the most fundamental structural innovation concerned the organisation of the college year. I had long felt that the traditional three-term school year made little sense educationally. The annual movement of the date of Easter meant that the lengths of both the spring and summer terms varied widely each year. This made the effective delivery of a curriculum extremely difficult to achieve. The only alternative which had been discussed previously anywhere, as far as I was aware, was the four-term model. Recognising the flexibility which our independence from local authority control would give, I first experimented with this pattern. However, I found that four ten-week terms would not fit well into the annual cycle of school life; in particular staff and students would be expected to be still hard at work during much of the peak holiday period in August.

Discussions with the Principal of the CTC at Nottingham and the DfEE convinced me that there was a better model – a five-term year. I was attracted by the idea of having terms of equal length believing that this would facilitate the delivery of a modular-based curriculum and I could also envisage other potential benefits. Therefore, we decided to 'grasp the nettle' and introduce a genuinely innovative structure. Now, nearly six years on, I can report that it has proved to be a notable success.

As predicted, eight weeks has proved to be an ideal length of time for a school term: long enough to deliver curriculum modules effectively and efficiently without the hindrance of a half-term interruption but not too long for the concentration span of either the teacher or the taught to waver. The five eight-week terms have brought other benefits too. Four of them are separated by a fortnight's holiday – ideal for all concerned to recharge their batteries fully before the next challenge and also providing opportunities for the booking of off-peak holidays in the spring and autumn. Although it is true that the summer break is not as long as is traditional (four weeks instead of the traditional six or seven) many parents seem to regard this as something of a blessing! The other obvious advantage is that the college is in session longer than other schools (40 weeks as opposed to 38). This additional curriculum delivery time must have potential benefits for teaching and learning and has enabled the college to claim that it delivers 'the national curriculum – *plus* . . .'.

Besides taking these key structural decisions we also appointed the twelve members of the support staff who would join the fifteen teachers in the first year. As well as the obvious secretarial and caretaking positions, we had to consider carefully the staffing of the library, which we had decided would be at the very heart of the college and, in particular, the information technology systems and their management. The library situation was easily solved by appointing a chartered librarian who had considerable experience of working in a secondary school. The librarian was given a brief to create a genuine Information Resources Centre which was to be integrally related to the curriculum and which would have the potential to influence pivotally styles of teaching and learning.

Information technology was much more of a problem area. It was clear to me that this had the potential to be the major area of distinctiveness for the college. The main reason for this view was the nature of our main sponsor. Dixons is a company which prides itself on being at the forefront of IT retailing and the college surely had to reflect this. Indeed there was the obvious potential for it to benefit from the advice and purchasing power which the company could offer. The governors had already flagged their support for such an emphasis by taking a policy decision to maintain a ratio of one computer to every four students. I knew that to deliver such a commitment tangibly and successfully in terms of student learning outcomes would not be easy. IT is such a complex area and changes so frighteningly quickly that it would be very easy to make fundamental mistakes with staffing, equipment and systems.

In the circumstances the appointment of a capable 'systems manager' was clearly critical. In the event we could choose between people who came from a teaching background or from a technical one in industry. Finally we plumped for the former and initially asked him to combine the task of IT curriculum co-ordination with the management of the technical systems. Over time this conjunction of roles proved impossible to maintain and we split the functions. However, we were fortunate that the initial appointee proved highly capable and chose to remain with us. He, together with other colleagues, established progressively networks and systems of a quality which kept the college in the vanguard of educational applications of IT both nationally and internationally.

I have a clear concept of the role that technology should play within the college. From the start I told everyone that it should not be used as a gimmick but only where it would genuinely enhance the quality of learning. Also, that it should not be seen narrowly, as a specific subject but as a tool with practical value across the whole curriculum, being as important in subjects such as English and history as in the more overtly technological ones such as design technology, science, and mathematics.

As we could not assume that all our newly appointed teachers would be IT experts we needed to ensure that all subject staff were given a progressive programme of IT training to enable them to become confident and competent in the technical aspects and also that they were made aware of the software which was applicable to their subject. As time passed this training became more tailored to individual needs and became one of the clear strengths of the college.

General pronouncements about the place of IT were only the tip of the iceberg. I knew that my colleagues were naturally looking to me to provide both an overall vision and specific direction and leadership in many other areas of school life. They were right to do so. This is surely what heads are paid to do, especially in a new school situation. I believe it to be crucial that any head-teacher has a clear idea of what management style s/he will employ and is consistent in the way this is enforced. Those who change their approach, especially with regard to the management of people, can cause needless confusion and uncertainty amongst their staff which is nearly always counter-productive. I also believe that it is unwise to attempt to be what you are not: to act a part. It is simply not possible to sustain such an illusion in the face of the undoubted strains and tensions which will inevitably occur.

Fortunately by the time of my appointment to Bradford I already had a very clear idea of my own management style: I was comfortable with neither autocracy nor democracy. Instead a consultative style was what suited me. I liked to seek the opinions of my colleagues on a range of matters and valued the advice which I received but recognised that I had to be comfortable with outcomes. I could never accept a situation where I was forced to adopt a policy, or a course of action, with which I was not in favour. The essential managerial skill lies in avoiding getting into such situations.

The nature of the new school meant that I had to be rather more of an independent opinion-former than I naturally desired but, in a situation where most of my staff were not yet in post, this was inevitable. One of my first decisions was to insist that there would not be the artificial separation between teachers and non-teachers that is so common in schools. To me, all personnel are of equal worth, regardless of their post. My job would be to ensure, to the best of my ability, that everyone could operate consistently at their maximum potential and also had the opportunity to develop professionally in ways that would benefit both them and the college.

As a manifestation of this philosophy, I decided that every day would begin with a morning 'briefing' for the whole staff for ten minutes prior to registration. I found that this provided the framework for an orderly start, gave me the opportunity to address my colleagues on a daily basis and gave them the chance to pass on key messages. It also provided a powerful incentive for everyone to be there on time.

My other core statement was that the children were to be treated with respect at all times. I saw no reason why the college should be a battleground with the staff on one side and the pupils on the other. I believed that it was as much in the interests of the staff as the pupils that they reached their potential. Fortu-nately this ethos became entrenched in the college and brought the success that I hoped for. In over twenty-five years in the profession I have never operated in a school where there has been so little evidence of teachers shouting at children, or publicly humiliating them, or of those children attempting to bait or intimi-date teachers.

Also I have been consistently surprised at how few examples of serious indiscipline have reached my door during my five years in post. This is partly due to the efficient pastoral structure and the willingness of staff at junior and middle management levels to deal with problems as they arise, but it is also a manifestation of the generally calm and orderly manner in which the pupils behave. Indeed to use the term 'pupil' seems strange to me now because, contrary to DfEE terminology, we have only ever referred to 'students' within the college. It might appear strange and pretentious to use the term 'student' with eleven-year-old children but this was a conscious decision. I wanted to give a strong signal that all who gained a place at the college were to take some responsibility for their own learning. There was to be a strong and developing partnership between teachers and learners in their mutual interest.

I was realistic enough to know that the capacity for independent learning was not innate and would need to be developed gradually but my aim was that this would occur consistently by the time that those young people were ready to leave the college for either higher education or employment. I basically wanted the college to be a bridge between the world of the child and the world of the adult and felt that the sooner the students began to think of themselves in this way the better.

This quest was coincidentally given a definite impetus by the physical arrangement of the facilities within the building. We decided to cluster together subjects within similar curriculum areas and to ensure that each major area was reasonably close to a high-density IT base in order to encourage regular usage of IT throughout the curriculum. Beginning with one such area, the numbers were gradually extended to the current situation where there are five, in addition to the Information Resources Centre (Library) plus a network of computers in the sixth-form work area which are reserved for use by the senior students.

The decision to cluster in this manner, rather than spreading computers more thinly across all the teaching rooms in the college, was to have profound effects on the delivery of the curriculum. If the expectation that IT should be integral to the learning process was to be other than a pious hope, students of all ages and abilities simply had to be released from the confines of the classroom to use computers for a variety of different purposes: data research; spreadsheets; CAD; CAM; word-processing; desk-top publishing and so on. The prospect was inevitably greeted with considerable caution by the teaching staff, who were representative of a profession whose basic responsibility is normally seen as being to keep their charges *within* the confines of a classroom rather than encouraging them to leave in order to pursue their learning elsewhere and outside the direct control of the teacher. Nevertheless, this concept was so integral to the college's mission that it was adopted and maintained.

The result has been that any visitor would notice a far greater degree of movement around the corridors than s/he might expect. More fundamentally, it has had a significant impact upon the whole nature of the way students learn and teachers teach; there is less *talk and chalk* and more project and resource-based learning. Teachers have become increasingly *facilitators of learning* and *directors of study*.

There is little evidence of the students misusing the undoubted freedoms which they are given. To the contrary, the fact that the library and the IT areas are healthily full before and after the beginning of the official college day and across both breaks and lunchtimes suggest that this is a style of learning which the students enjoy and take full advantage of. I believe that the ability to work in this manner will suit students of all ages and aptitudes and will be an excellent preparation for the self-directed study which is the norm in higher education.

Mention of higher education reminds me that the final outcomes of the educational process at the college were never far from our minds, even from the early days. It was obvious that the college would be judged, to a considerable extent, by the quality of its examination results. Because we had taken a 13+ intake in our second year, to accelerate the development of the college, the first GCSE results would be due in the summer of 1994.

I have never witnessed such tension amongst teachers prior to the publication of these results. It was obvious that, if they had been disappointing, there would have been a plethora of public criticism and condemnation. In the event they were outstandingly good: well beyond our wildest expectations. Of a totally mixed ability cohort: 68 per cent gained five or more A–C grades. This compared with a national average of 43 per cent and the average for the Bradford area of 27 per cent. In 1995 this standard was maintained with GCSE results over 15 per cent above the national average and over 30 per cent higher than the Bradford average.

At the same time the first sixth-form students to follow GNVQ courses succeeded in reversing the national trend with over 70 per cent completing their studies successfully and within the expected time. At the time of writing the college was awaiting its first GCE Advanced Level results, due in the summer of 1996, already knowing that its first student has been made an unconditional offer of a place at Oxford University.

In the spring of 1995 the college experienced an OFSTED inspection. For a week in April every aspect of its life was scrutinised critically by an independent team of sixteen inspectors. As is the case for any school about to undergo such an ordeal there was considerable anxiety amongst the staff as the inspection date neared. In the event the published report was a vindication of all the hard work which had been put in by everyone over the previous five years. It publicly confirmed that:

> Dixons City Technology College provides a very good quality of education with many distinctive features. Pupils achieve high standards and are well prepared for life in a modern, complex society . . . comparisons between the capabilities of pupils on entry and the performance of the same pupils five years later indicate that the school adds value to pupils' attainment.

With these words the central purpose of the college was seen to be being achieved. The unresolved questions are 'why' and 'how'? What are the magic ingredients which combine together to create higher than expected outcomes? The answer must be a complex one or the elixir would have been found long ago.

From the start I believed that one of the major justifications for the CTC movement was that it could provide part of the research and development function that has been so lacking in our educational system. In that vein the short histories of these fourteen high profile colleges should be looked at closely for messages and clues as to what makes a good school. Such research would show that, despite similar advantages at their births, each college has developed very differently and with very different degrees of success to date. I am obviously qualified only to speak for my own college.

The root cause of our success has been the civilised manner in which we have treated our students and in particular the high expectations which we have had of them, regardless of their academic ability. I firmly believe that if you expect people to fail they will not let you down. If that is a truism then so must be its corollary. I also believe that everyone possesses some talent; it is the task of any school to discover where this lies and then to nurture and encourage it to flourish.

This is not an easy job; it is far easier to knock young people and to destroy their self-confidence and self-respect than to build them up and convince them that they have the potential to become employable and active citizens. However, to succeed is one of the greatest joys in teaching and shows why the profession is still enjoyable and worthwhile despite the frequent adverse criticism which it seems to attract.

The same high expectations must also extend to the staff. In the final resort it is the quality of the classroom teaching in any school which will be the most crucial determinant of academic outcomes. It is therefore vital to devote considerable time and thought to the process of appointment and thereafter to providing a quality induction package followed by an on-going, individualised and interlocking programme of professional development and appraisal.

I am frequently amazed at the cavalier attitude which many schools still seem to adopt to these issues, especially to appointment procedures. How anyone can be content to appoint teachers exclusively on the basis of their performance in a twenty-minute interview I do not understand. As a matter of course, we see every shortlisted candidate for a teaching post in front of a group of children in a variety of formats; we always learn more from this than any other aspect of the interview process. Once appointed I regard it as one of my most important tasks to make sure, to the best of our ability that the new colleague is welcomed into the life of the college and is given every help to ensure that the outcome will be a happy one.

It was because of the importance which we placed on staff development that, in the spring of 1993, the college committed itself to seeking the Investor in People (IIP) quality standard. This was not without misgivings because I was aware that the process would inevitably involve additional work and also that there was a natural feeling within the staff that there would be little in it for them and that essentially it would be an opportunity for senior management to gain kudos and glory. However, I profoundly disagreed with this view and was convinced that simply being involved in the process of IIP would lead to improvements within the college. This view was strengthened when the initial audit required by IIP revealed a number of clear, but previously unnoticed, weaknesses in the area of monitoring and evaluation. Unless we addressed these coherently we would not be successful in our application; if we *did* tackle them effectively it would inevitably improve the quality of our service.

The problem of additional workload was easily dealt with: it was delegated to the Deputy Principal with responsibility for human resources and strategic planning! For her the co-ordination of the application certainly involved considerable time and effort but it was central to her existing rôle and she was both interested in and motivated by the task. As a consequence she did an outstanding job and compiled a massive portfolio of evidence which stood up well to the demanding assessment process. With this one exception there was little other evidence of increased work for colleagues. A vital aspect of IIP is that the institution commits itself openly and tangibly to the concept of staff development. Another is that the programme is delivered coherently and in close conjunction with the establishment's development plan.

Throughout my first headship the term *Development Plan* was unknown. Indeed it was only in 1991 that I first became aware of the concept. After that things moved remarkably quickly with the result that by 1994 our plan was dominating and directing everything that we did! This was an area where our links with the business world certainly helped. The advice that we received enabled us to create a genuine *Business Plan* which was fully costed, affected all tiers of management, and which was used internally as a genuine working document.

We were considered to be ready for the final IIP assessment only twelve months after our initial commitment – a remarkably short period of time. We had kept the staff continually informed of progress and therefore I had no qualms when the assessor requested interviews with a cross-section of colleagues – both teaching and non-teaching. My confidence proved well founded for a month later we heard that we had gained the award. We were only the fifth organisation in the Bradford district to do so and the first school. Although the Local Education Authority grandly announced at the time that they would involve all their schools in the award, it is interesting to note that, by the start of 1996, no other school in the city had yet gained this prestigious award.

I was delighted at this success because it was clear that it had nothing whatsoever to do with funding or resources. The question was: what to do next? We decided that the Charter Mark would be a logical development because whereas IIP had concentrated on the quality of *staff development* the Charter Mark was about the quality of *customer service*.

Again we had misgivings because, unlike IIP, the number of charters issued annually was strictly limited. As a consequence the process appeared much more of a lottery. Nevertheless, we felt that customer service was an area that we were not doing particularly well and one that we really needed to improve. For that reason we committed ourselves to another year's hard work. Once again the co-ordination was delegated: this time to the Director of Finance and Administration, under whose control the 'front of house' staff came. Internal and external monitoring groups were established and every attempt was made to keep the rest of the staff informed and involved. As with IIP, definite and quantifiable improvements resulted from the process. Amongst these were: the creation of a waiting area for visitors, together with the inclusion of a complimentary welcoming drink; a photographic display of all staff in the entrance foyer; name badges for all staff; and the issuing of specific charters for students, parents, staff and the general public. After an exhaustive external assessment which lasted from 10 am to 6 pm, we were delighted to hear, a month later, that we had been successful. We were one of only four organisations in the whole of the Leeds/Bradford area to be so honoured and one of only twelve schools nationally. Having secured these two major quality accreditations, the fact that the college was a high-quality establishment could hardly be denied. This would inevitably stand it in good stead in the event of any future political challenge from either a national or local source.

I have left to the end our relationship with commerce and industry. This is not to denigrate its importance; far from it. To the contrary, I believe that our pro-active relationships with the private sector have been amongst the most interesting and rewarding aspects of my experiences at the college. There is very little understanding of how this two-way relationship operates within the CTC movement but basically the framework has been the same for all fourteen colleges. Before the go-ahead was given for any CTC the government had to be satisfied that 20 per cent of the cost of building and equipping the college could be found privately. In the case of Bradford, where the total project cost around £9 million, this meant that about £2 million had to be found privately.

While in macro-economic terms that might not seem a great deal, in the world of education it represented a quantum leap forward from the situation that normally existed. At Birchwood I had persuaded BNFL, who had their main office complex in the locality, to fund a glossy brochure for the new school. At a cost of around £5,000 this was way beyond our own resources and to acquire it through sponsorship was seen as a major coup. Consequently, the fact that the commitment of Dixons, as the lead sponsor, was £1 million, and that altogether we raised over £3 million in Bradford, shows the extent of the difference.

People assume that Dixons CTC was funded by the state and that the private investment came on top of this and that explains why CTCs were so over-funded. In fact, as I have explained, the state funded only 80 per cent of the project. Therefore, the college cost no more to build or equip than any comparative school of its size. There is also an assumption that the running costs of CTCs are more generously provided for than other schools. In fact the funding is formula-based, as is the case for all schools nowadays. The DfEE looks at a basket of twenty LEAs, all with large inner-city populations, and bases the CTC funding on the average amount spent in the preceding year by those authorities on their secondary schools.

I am often asked 'what was in it for Dixons?' I obviously cannot speak for the company but I am convinced that the reasons for their investment were entirely altruistic. I know that they, like many employers in the mid-1980s, were extremely concerned about the quality of the applicants that they were getting for a broad range of jobs within the company. They believed that not all was right with the education system, especially in the inner cities.

Therefore, when an opportunity arose for them to do something about it, albeit on a small scale, they accepted the challenge. They certainly did not do it for publicity or PR. Indeed the publicity associated with the early years of the CTC movement was largely hostile, to the extent that many high-profile businesses were frightened off. Neither did Dixons seek to have their company name on the college. For well over a year it was known as Bradford CTC. I can now admit freely that the pressure to change the name came solely from me, not from the Company. I felt strongly by that time that Dixons were excellent sponsors and I wished both to celebrate this and make it slightly harder for them to walk away in the future!

Another fear which stemmed from the private sector involvement was that non-educationalists might seek to control the curriculum. In practice at Bradford at least, nothing was further from the truth. For the first few years the governors were almost exclusively concerned about finance. Over that time they established rigorous financial procedures and controls which have served the college well ever since. It was only after they were satisfied that the finances were secure that they became interested in other aspects of what we were doing. Since then I have found the governing body demanding and searching but also fair and very supportive.

So, in conclusion, what is it that has made the college so successful in its early years? I believe that there has existed an especially fortuitous combination of circumstances which offer the ideal recipe for the creation of any securely based school which has the good fortune to be able to start from a 'blank sheet of paper'. In the case of Dixons CTC several of these stemmed from the fact that we were able to operate in new, purpose-built accommodation with the most modern equipment. In addition we were able to appoint a staff from scratch and to recruit children who were clearly educable. We also benefited from enthusiastic support from parents, governors and business sponsors. None of these points should be underestimated. In themselves, however, they offer no guarantee of successful educational outcomes. For that to occur they must be combined with other factors which depend far more upon people and the way in which they interact with each other. In my estimation some of these which have been particularly important at Dixons CTC are:

- an ethos based on mutual respect between students and teachers
- a clear vision which is shared and accepted by all
- a culture which encourages innovation
- successful experiments with the structure of the day and year
- a willingness to be involved in research and development
- clear structures for communication and decision-making
- managers at all levels who are respected and valued
- staff who have a genuine vocation for teaching
- high expectations of students of all abilities
- technology which is used coherently to enhance learning
- mutually beneficial partnerships with industry and business
- a constant search for total quality and continuous improvement.

I am also keenly aware that although it may take a long time to create a positive reputation for any institution it can take only a very short time to lose it. It is one thing to have the obvious advantages of newness: it is quite another to use them to their full potential.

A real danger for any school lies in complacency. To be successful in the longer term there must be an emphasis on continuous improvement and an active desire to seek new challenges and new opportunities. Any school which does not strive to remain in the vanguard of developments runs the risk of becoming 'run of the mill' and mediocre. Because of the circumstances of our formation and the nature of our sponsors such an option simply does not exist for Dixons CTC. The college will always be associated with rapid change; with the willingness to take calculated risks; with involvement in educational research and development and with the provision of high quality services.

I am convinced that a great deal has been achieved over a very short period of time but also that much more remains to be done; the foundations have been securely laid but the superstructure still needs to be finished. Indeed it will *never* be finished because there will always be more to do: some things to amend, some to augment and some to abandon, all in the light of experience.

It has been this fundamental uncertainty; the sudden yet frequent occurrence of opportunities to be involved in genuinely pioneering work; and the constant pressure to achieve and maintain the highest levels of quality in all aspects of the life of a busy and high profile college, which have made my role so exciting and unpredictable. I have felt highly privileged to have been the Principal of Dixons CTC in its formative years and now look forward to guiding it into the complex world of the twenty-first century with all the challenges and opportunities which that will undoubtedly offer.

Commentary – reengineering: whole school approaches

BRENT DAVIES AND JOHN WEST-BURNHAM

These three case studies highlight a number of key issues in the reengineering approach. Each of the schools was set in a different context. Pat Collarbone at Haggerston was faced with the need to improve radically an inner city school that was seen to be under-performing. Richard Wallis was part of a senior management team at Hugh Christie, a successful school which needed to be even more successful in the future and John Lewis at Dixons Bradford City Technology College was creating a brand new school in a hostile local environment.

Each of these educational leaders had rejected incremental thinking and sought fundamentally to rethink their operation to meet their individual organisations' needs. This illustrates the point that reengineering need not be undertaken only in times of crisis but when more radical approaches are needed in a variety of contexts. What comes out of the case studies in this section is that in each of the schools there is a focus on the future environment and on the central rôle of learning in the students' experience. This reinforces a fundamental tenet of reengineering, that of reinventing how work is done. Instead of focusing solely on structures that organise how teaching is delivered, there is a fundamental reassessment and focus on how learning takes place. In Haggerston the rôle of the learner becomes a driving force, especially when it is reconceptualised from the pupils' perspective. In Hugh Christie the increasing importance of technology becomes a driving force for reassessment, while in Bradford the pattern of the year challenges previous assumptions of the organisation of learning time periods.

In each of the schools it can be seen that leadership makes a difference. Leadership clearly comes from the individual headteacher but there is an emphasis on the senior management team and leadership in depth. Characteristics that are apparent in all three accounts are those of proactive and reflective leadership. Hammer and Stanton (1995, p. 58) talk about leaders not being content with the present in terms of 'An inclination toward change that borders on restlessness: a congenital inability to accept things as they are, and a determination to find out what lies over the rainbow.' This need to drive change and be proactive is not based on whim or reacting to circumstances but on a combination of experience and judgement based on a reflective process. This reflection draws on a number of sources. Interestingly, Wallis clearly demonstrates that the school is at point A on the sigmoid curve (*see* Figure 1) and has engaged in fundamental reflection to rethink its future direction.

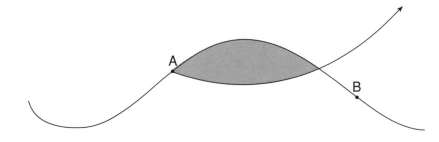

Figure 1: The sigmoid curve

Handy (1994) suggests that most organisations rise and fall or expand and contract in a way very similar to a sine wave. The challenge for leadership in successful schools is to spot when the organisation is at point A and to reengineer so that the organisation does not rest on its laurels when it is still expanding, but takes the risk of moving onto a new sigmoid curve and does not wait to change until it is moving downwards at B. Handy expresses this as:

> *The right place to start that second curve is at point A, where there is time, as well as the resources and the energy, to get the curve through its initial explorations and floundering before the first curve begins to dip downwards. That would seem obvious; were it not for the fact that at point A all the messages coming through to the individual or the institution are that everything is going fine, that it would be folly to change when the current recipes are working so well. All that we know of change, be it personal change or change in organisations, tells us that the real energy for change only comes when you are looking disaster in the face, at point B on the first curve. At this point, however, it is going to require a mighty effort to drag oneself up to where, by now, one should be on the second curve.* (Handy, 1994, pp. 51–2)

Hugh Christie has used an external catalyst, the American Coalition of Essential Schools, to assist in this process of rethinking at point A. This links with Caldwell and Spinks' (1992) work regarding educational leaders being aware of global trends as part of their portfolio of skills as transformational leaders. Similarly, Collarbone cites the Harvard Principals' Centre and the work of Roland Barth as significant influences in fundamentally altering her educational approach. Her establishment of the Haggerston Conference to disseminate these change forces and to involve the whole school community in rethinking its purpose and sense of direction represents a fundamental shift in the way ideas are created rather than reporting research from a second-hand source.

The sigmoid curve is a powerful demonstrator of the need to reengineer not only at point B when the organisation is in a critical state but also at point A when there is the opportunity to rethink different patterns of operation for the future.

In all three schools there is an expression of a shared and clear vision of where the school needs to go in the future. This involves not just the mechanical process of strategic planning but, more importantly, as Wallis describes, it involves creating a strategic intent within the organisation. There is also, as demonstrated by Lewis, a recognition of the crucial importance of staff in the process and of binding them into a common sense of purpose. More importantly there seems to be an establishment of a culture of continuous change where innovation becomes continuous and new patterns do not become the new orthodoxy.

In all the schools there is evidence of a number of influences and approaches that enable the leader to draw on these experiences to formulate their own map of the world. Operating in this reengineering environment is summarised by Hammer and Stanton (1995, pp. 56–57) as:

- Understanding the old process and customer requirements, so as to recognise the weakness of the existing process and the performance demanded of the new one.

- Uncertainty. When reengineering begins, we know little other than that the old process is inadequate and that we need something better.

- Experimentation. Reengineering is an iterative experience. It is impossible to design a new way of working on paper; it must be tried in reality.

- Reengineering's style differs from that of traditional business projects. Those generally start with well-defined goals and a clear project plan. Reengineering does not. It is about exploration and discovery rather than analysis and knowing. It is a journey into the unknown.

These characteristics are well demonstrated in the accounts in this section. In Part Three our contributors look not at reengineering the whole organisation but at one part of the educational process. This shows how, unlike total quality, reengineering can be applied both to the whole organisation and to parts of it.

References

Caldwell, B. J. and Spinks, J. M. (1992), *Leading the Self-Managing School*, London, Falmer Press.

Hammer, M. and Stanton, S. A. (1995), *The Reengineering Revolution – A Handbook*, New York, Harper Business.

Handy, C. (1994), *The Empty Raincoat: Making Sense of the Future*, London, Hutchinson.

PART THREE

■ ■ ■

Reengineering: learning and teaching

4
■   ■   ■

The laptop revolution

PAM DETTMAN

Introduction

We all want schools to be exciting, stimulating places for students and teachers alike. The following is one school's story of how computer technology significantly altered learning and teaching processes, personal relationships and classroom ambience for all those involved, and thereby revolutionised their educational experience. The school is the Methodist Ladies College (MLC), Melbourne, Australia.

MLC is an interesting school. In Australian terms it is well established, being 114 years old, with long-standing traditions and a significant network of former scholars. It is a large school, having a student body of 2,300 students from pre-school to university entrance level. It is a single-sex school for girls and rather feminist in its attitudes. In recent years, it has received national and international attention for its technological innovations. The focus in this account lies on the upper primary group of 210 Year 5 and Year 6 girls, aged between 10 and 12.

A visitor to MLC in 1989 would have seen relatively little evidence of computer technology in use, although there was much discussion to be heard. A visitor now would see every girl aged 10 and above using her own portable computer for most of the day. The young learners might be using MicroWorlds to construct a detailed map of Australia by plotting co-ordinates or to design a walk tour of their local district, highlighting places of interest. Others might be working with LegoDacta to create sophisticated models controlled by input and output sensors linked by the laptop. Others would be down-loading information from Internet or CD ROM without having to leave their desks. A multimedia group would have students recording field trip experiences with scanners and digitising equipment. In short, enormous technological advancement was achieved in a matter of only a few years. How did this happen?

Development of the programme

Background

In 1989, there was a great deal of soul-searching on the part of staff in the primary section. Parents' satisfaction seemed to be at a lower level than usual and it was clear that an upgrading of facilities was necessary. Lengthy discussion about likely futures for the students resulted in the finding that an increase in exposure to computer technology was essential. This, in turn, became entangled in the discussion about renovations, with staff divided about the amount and type of space to be devoted to computers.

It seems strange now that the major developments that occurred subsequent to those discussions could have originated in such a way, but it was indeed the consideration of matters such as the amount of space available, the need to preserve flexibility in all learning spaces and, consequently, the desirability of portability of learning tools, that forced staff to confront a range of alternative actions.

In essence there developed the notion that students might possibly be equipped with a portable computer each. Educationally, this approach seemed sound, but a large amount of research revealed a dearth of evidence concerning the value of such an approach. It was some time before it was understood that such a programme had not yet been undertaken in a major way in any other place. Logically, however, it seemed probable that portability of this learning tool would allow for student use at the point of need, which after all is a major principle of teaching and learning, and, in similar vein, would allow for student use in a range of locations, including the home. On the other hand, the question of financing such a programme was obviously huge, and there were many problems to be faced such as the possible effects of repetitive strain injury (RSI) or of screen radiation and the effect on spelling, creativity and social skills. All of these issues were raised as probable sources of anxiety for parents in addition to the concern about finance.

As staff returned again and again to their preference for laptop computers, to be purchased and owned by students, it was decided to take the matter to the parents. Although this was a private school, with parents paying a few thousand dollars per annum in fees, it was known that most parents took on extra jobs in order to pay the fees and many made serious sacrifices in other ways in order to send their daughters to this school. In the event, although there was serious concern about the financial implications for many amongst their number, and although there were many possible negative outcomes such as the aforementioned, which necessitated some debate, the parent body agreed to participate in this innovative programme provided that a long-term payment system of three years could be devised. Of considerable surprise to the staff at that time was the strength of the parent viewpoint that a school had to be forward thinking and prepare its students for the technological world of the future. Thus was born the original 'laptop' programme.

Philosophy

While the next few months saw a great deal of energy expended in the selection of appropriate hardware, most significant was the nature of the thinking and discussion that underpinned the change process. The sheer intensity of the planned programme, given that every student would have her own computer with her at all times, necessitated deeper discussions than had occurred before, when the focus had remained largely on hardware and software. Staff attention now moved to renewed considerations of the nature of learning with its implications for teaching and for computing in the classroom. Should we even have classrooms? What could the learner's day look like? What sort of time-tabling arrangements would be most suitable and what sort of student/teacher relationships would become most desirable?

As competing schools gave voice to charges of 'gimmickry', and as media attention invited interest in the programme from a range of experts, it became necessary to articulate more clearly the purposes for which such extensive computing activity was regarded as desirable. With hindsight, it would appear that this enforced necessity to grapple for clarity of purpose became fundamental to the success of MLC's programme. Too often, even now, we see developments in computing that are proposed on the basis of a minimalist statement about workforce relevance, if that. MLC staff came to realise that having a good idea of the big picture, the global perspective, helps both to provide a focus for all participants and to satisfy to some degree those who question the outcomes of serious levels of exposure to computers. MLC staff understood that they were better placed to bring about real change if they showed evidence of having read widely and thought extensively about the implications of the proposed actions. In any major change, many potential problems will be raised and answers must be forthcoming.

There are many persuasive arguments in the literature. With regard to technological change, any 'Futures' literature will provide the basis of a suitable rationale for proposing major change in schools through computer technology. *Futures*, an international journal of forecasting, planning and policy, reports in its January/February 1993 edition the results of the WORLD 2000 project, described as 'an international planning dialogue to help shape the new global system'. This massive project aggregates data from around the world in many sectors of life and sets out what the data indicate to be the 'supertrends' of the next several decades. These trends indicate a continued focus on the development of high-tech to serve scientific progress, as in areas related to the mapping of DNA, genetic therapy, robotics and sustainable 'green technology', along with continued development of information technology to create a single global communications network. Significantly, the author concludes that

> *The key to understanding the emerging world view is to see that unprecedented new imperatives have arisen, principally the revolutionary force of IT, which are unleashing powerful new forces to integrate the globe into a unified whole.* (Halal, 1993, p. 12)

This is surely no cause for surprise. The point is that as leaders and teachers we must be able to take part in a global dialogue to justify what we are doing, to explain why computer work feels more useful to students than a great deal that they are exposed to in the classroom.

Beare and Slaughter (1993) also highlight the rôle of computers in the world of the coming decades, but add a warning about the consequence of failing to consider technology's limitations and failing to mediate its effects with human values. In similar vein, Sachs (1993) draws attention to the need to examine both the micro and macro context of computer use and its application. Like Beare and Slaughter, Sachs emphasises the need for the development of a critical language of pedagogy through which schools help students to under-stand the political and cultural underpinnings of the use of technology. Such views can only add further support to the call for enhanced computing programs in schools. Where better than in a school to learn to ask questions about underlying assumptions and likely ramifications, and when better than at an early age to discover that computers alone cannot create the conditions required to sustain the human race.

Another form of justification used by MLC for extending computing in the school concerned differences in learning styles required by the school and non-school experience. Sachs (1993, p. 33) refers to the notion of 'two cultures of pedagogy, one in the school and one in commerce and entertainment', and states that 'there is some force in the suggestion that the latter is more powerful in the educational sense for most young people'.

Coupled with Rowe's (1993) comments on 'technology as a mediator of cognitive development', there is potential significance in this disparity. Rowe discusses a particular theory of cognitive functioning that says (p. 82)

Activity structures involve mediators, i.e. tools and symbol systems which have deep implications for the way in which intellectual tasks are accomplished ... the introduction of new systems and tools into learning (or work activities) can be expected to change the intellectual aspects of these activities.

There are implications here for students who have exposure to a variety of technologies outside of the school and mainly 'chalk and talk' within the school.

Rowe provides several examples of computer-based technologies which not only 'amplify' the human problem-solving capacities, in terms of 'more and faster', but actually change the processes. Crucial to educators is the view (p. 89) that

computer technology has come to provide cognitive power tools which can improve certain cognitive processes in such significant ways that, once the tool is understood and used regularly, the user feels bereft if it is not available. The computer has opened up new possibilities of thought and action without which one comes to feel at a disadvantage. For an increasing number of people computing has become an indispensable instrument of cognitive activity, and not merely an occasional tool.

This discussion of various theories is designed to show the level of discourse which MLC discovered was necessary for a school to engage in if it was to gain commitment of resources, both financial and human, to its computing efforts. While there will always be some staff who will be very positive about computer growth, others are likely to be resistant to, and resentful of, the effects on their own areas of interest. Parents will have a range of concerns about increased access to computers, and these will undoubtedly include the cost, RSI, the effects of radiation, and the effects on spelling, handwriting, creativity and social development? Some assurance is needed in these areas, but to make real progress, educators must be able to raise the standard of debate to the educative level. MLC's experience showed that such debate was crucial to success.

Resources

Once the philosophical issues had been dealt with at MLC, the focus moved to the choice of hardware. With portable computers having been selected, several new problems arose, such as insurance contracts for loss and damage, maintenance agreements, and levels of on-site technical assistance. These required an enormous amount of effort, in terms of research into legalities and tax issues, along with negotiation about turnaround times for repairs and continued manufacture of spare parts, so that the choice of hardware supplier hinged largely on the adequacy of these arrangements. It was also thought that it might be useful for other schools to enter joint purchasing arrangements to improve buying power and to exert pressure jointly for increased awareness of the education consumer's needs.

The selection of software was seen to be dependent on beliefs about learning and teaching. Would software be selected to support as far as possible the normal school curriculum, or would software direct the curriculum? Since co-operative learning is valued highly at MLC, software was selected that would allow students to develop their own tasks for open-ended assignments, allowing them to assume responsibility for many aspects of their learning.

Curriculum

In those early days the main software package to be used was LogoWriter. A Year 6 maths lesson might have seen students designing a LogoWriter program to solve a linear equation such as $4x + 4 = 16$. Animations and music might have been added to the solution. A map needed for a social studies activity would not be taken from a clip-art package but would instead be drawn in a set-position activity using co-ordinate pairs. The students' understanding of mathematics was extended as they were now able to do hitherto unreachable exercises such as tessellations, which needed absolute accuracy, and to construct a range of spatial representations. Most importantly, young minds were no longer held back by outdated technologies. Once the essential concepts of construction of a polygon were understood, for instance, a myriad of examples could be created from which deep understanding was more likely than from two or three shaky examples drawn with a slippery protractor and a wobbly compass, which caused the work to be untidy and the student to lose heart.

It was very quickly evident that the computer, when used sufficiently and effectively, was more than just a tool to aid the teaching of the old curriculum. With the vast array of new activities and functions now available through the laptop, the curriculum became 'computer-led'. Subjects were redefined to provide for more open-bounded fields of learning, and learning tasks were reconstructed to account for the different ways of retrieving, organising and producing information that were afforded by the computer. The nature of assignments was reconsidered to allow students to exhibit their work in a manner appropriate to the dynamic nature of the ideas that they were producing. Working with computers for at least a couple of hours every day, and using the constructionist LogoWriter package for much of the time, students had developed the desire to demonstrate their work as it was created, with movement and sound, which needed to be done by means of a data-show rather than a static printout which could only be stuck on the wall or in a book.

Staffing

With such a rate of change, the need for extensive staff development was continuous over a lengthy period of time. Some schools take the view that teachers with no computing background can start as beginners and learn with their classes. Others prefer to use just one expert person to teach all classes and to leave other staff out of it. MLC took the view most firmly that all staff in the college were expected to develop a high degree of computing ability over a period of a few years and that the college was to focus its professional development resources on this area for that period of time. Several different approaches to professional development were taken. The first was to bring experts into the school, particularly to develop staff expertise in relation to LogoWriter and other software packages. This had mixed success, depending on the nature of the individual instructor. Second, several two or three-day in-service courses were organised, over both school days and weekends, usually in comfortable residential situations off the school site. Again, these pro-grammes were given a particular software focus. While these weekends were greatly appreciated by staff and very useful in terms of outcomes, it became evident that staff were more open to learning when they were free to follow their own individual needs relating to their capacity and teaching activities of the time. Yet another approach to staff development involved several teachers enrolling in a Graduate Diploma in Computers in Education by correspon-dence from a local university, but at the same time organising themselves into a study support group within the school, to work regularly with the senior computing person, discussing theoretical and practical aspects of the formal assignments. At the upper primary school level, this latter alternative became the preferred option for staff, as they were able to gather after school regularly to discuss their progress and did not have to suffer the inconvenience of travelling to an institution for studies. A small study conducted some time later at the school to investigate the relative merits of the various approaches to staff development showed that future activity should be planned better to incorporate certain accepted principles of adult learning. The factors most significant to staff in determining the impact of development activity were the following: ready access to human resources at all times, personal control over the learning experience, relevance to current work, the nature of the activity itself, collaboration with colleagues, location (on site preferred), prior computing knowledge and, finally, the attitudes and actions of school leaders.

Outcomes

It is now six years since those first classes of MLC girls started using laptops. In the meantime, many other schools in all states of Australia have adopted such programmes. While most of these schools are from the more affluent independent sector, many government schools are also providing as many laptops as resources allow. Formal longitudinal studies have not, to the writer's knowledge, been undertaken in any laptop site, but the anecdotal evidence over the years has been overwhelmingly positive.

To a participant in the original programme it was very clear after only a few weeks that there would be no going back. The advent of the laptops had already caused a fundamental restructuring of curriculum and timetable and a radical change in the rôle of the teacher and the teacher–student relationships. The most immediate realisation on the part of staff was that with a computer each the girls were working much harder. There was greater focus on the task at hand, and serious engagement with classmates about the problems to be solved. Students were reluctant to leave their tasks for lunch breaks. What was going on? Were we putting too much pressure on these young people? Observation and discussion showed the reverse. In fact, as was suggested at the time, 'the lid had been taken off the pressure cooker'. Students would spend much time and effort in solving a problem of their own creation, whereas they had tended to give up earlier on teacher-set questions and tasks. With the computer, they were prepared to get something 'wrong' dozens of times, whereas even with the most encouraging teacher, a few attempts would probably have been enough for them. With the computer, anxiety about being wrong gave way to interest in what either worked or didn't work. The escape and delete keys allowed multiple attempts at solutions with no traces of error remaining for all to see. The immediate feedback provided by the computer motivated students to try again and again, and the capacity to provide non-judgemental facilitation allowed the students themselves to be the judges of their own work.

Of great interest was the fact that the girls worked much better with each other than before. Whereas earlier they might have worked in parallel fashion alongside each other and maintained an ongoing discussion about social aspects of life, they now engaged fully with each other about the work in hand. They became eager to share their personal discoveries and learned to ask other people for help and suggestions. The less able students gained in self-esteem and improved their social skills, because the computer allowed them to produce work that looked as good as that of the more able students.

Dependence on the teacher was decreased, with students having more control over the nature of the activities and the rate and level of their personal performance. Actions were guided more by natural energies and curiosities than by a teacher's decisions. The teachers' rôle changed from teaching what they had learnt many years ago, to helping children to access the most up-to-date information and to deal with it in a way that made them feel they could construct their own solutions. The teachers were no longer expected to know all the answers to so-called facts. Students began to understand the changing nature of knowledge and to appreciate that having the most up-to-date knowledge could be significant to their lives. They commented that the information in the ten-year-old encyclopaedias could not necessarily be taken as still accurate. They also began to understand that teachers could not possibly keep up with the rate of change of knowledge on a daily basis and that it was often helpful if they themselves found some new information and passed it on to the teacher.

With information technology readily accessible to everyone, the teachers' rôle changed to one of moving around, helping, suggesting, encouraging and, very largely, learning along with the students. Modelling the discipline of perseverance and the joy of discovery of a real learner became a significant aspect of the teachers' work life. Those who had feared that teachers would become redundant observed that teachers became in fact very much busier. With the curriculum no longer under control in the sense that it had always been, because students could now explore a greater range of topics of their own choice, the teachers had to learn to cross the boundaries of subjects much more frequently. Covering the range of areas in which the students were interested was a much more difficult task than delivering materials selected and prepared by themselves. In short, teachers were required to become, perhaps, 'wise'. The curriculum was now truly individualised in a manner that had not been achieved before and this required the teachers not only to know each child and her strengths and weaknesses, but to know at least the broad parameters of a vast range of subject areas.

Problems

Several problems occurred, although some of these were solved as improvements in technology were made. For example, as time moved on, the working life of a battery between recharges improved. Curriculum issues relating to the boundaries of subjects, the desirability of different computing systems and the continuity of use of software had to be debated and negotiated. The changes in children's learning patterns and styles caused parent interest and questioning. A change for which people were unprepared but which affected many staff was the shift in the school power structure, as those staff with advanced computing knowledge and skills became indispensable to the school's future and, with their inside knowledge as to likely directions and their use of computer jargon, became a rather élite group. All of these issues required extensive discussion.

Technical and related issues

Quickly evident was the need for technical support to be accessible on site. With so much of a student's work programme being conducted in an integrated fashion through the laptop, fast turnaround became essential whenever there was a problem with the hardware. To avoid the necessity for machines to be taken off site for what might be a very small problem or perhaps not a real problem at all, it was decided to maintain two technicians who could regularly check the computers and diagnose any suspected problems. That support centre has now grown markedly in size and there are five full-time technical personnel.

Fortunately, the rate of loss and damage was extremely low. When the programme began, the school had been unable to find any insurance company prepared to underwrite such a programme, so the school had found itself in the position of underwriting the insurance itself. When, however, the early evidence showed such favourable results, insurance companies became more prepared to participate. In 1996 such companies actually seek the business of laptop schools.

Fortunately also, in the same vein, there was no evidence at all of students being harassed because of their portable computers. This had been an early fear on the part of parents who were concerned that once the general public knew about the programme their daughters might become targets for assault. The situation was no doubt aided by the school's clear direction to students that machines should never be carried in a conspicuous manner if being taken home, but should always be packed away inside their bags.

Gender Issues

Late in the third year of the programme, confident about the gender equities being achieved through its technology programme, the school agreed to participate in some case study research, examining the ways in which young adolescents learned gender rôles. The results were very disappointing. A policy of increasing the number of males on the previously all-female staff had overlapped with the appointment of new computer-literate teachers; the result was that a disproportionate number of males had been appointed and that computing expertise had become strongly linked with maleness, even though the girls themselves used computers well and saw female staff doing so. The feminist aims of the project were thus being seriously undermined by the staffing arrangements. Steps were quickly taken to modify the processes and so to alter perceptions.

Conclusion

The MLC project not only continues after these several years; it has grown and flourished. At this point every one of the 2,100 students above the age of ten years has her own laptop or notebook computer along with an Ethernet card to enable her to tap into the school's network from any of many points. MLC is known far and wide for its innovation and the programme attracts a continuous stream of visitors from other states and from overseas. School personnel are frequently asked to address audiences across the country and indeed in other countries as well. Most important of all, however, is the atmosphere of continued excitement about learning that hits one almost physically on entering the MLC environment. Girls, teachers and administrators have an ongoing sense of accomplishment and of self-renewal while parents are grateful to have been able to enrol their daughters at the school.

The lessons learnt about computing were many and they continue to this day, but much was also learnt about the change process, although some of it might be termed politically incorrect.

Of greatest importance is the need to do one's homework in order to be prepared to answer the consumers' queries. Next is the need to select and encourage key individuals to carry out the process, people who have a high level of relevant skills and the strengths to withstand possible criticism. It is important also to remember always that finance is only one of the factors contributing to success; imagination, audacity and hard work are just as vital. The principle of 'divide and rule' is very significant; entrenched malcontents who are never enthusiastic about innovation must be somehow structurally isolated from those who are prepared to take a chance. Finally, perhaps the hardest lesson of all to learn is how to keep the faith, or to believe when times are hard that the change will work.

References

Beare, H. and Slaughter, R. (1993), *Education for the Twenty-First Century*, London, Routledge.

Halal, W. E. (1993), 'World 2000' in *Futures; the journal of forecasting, planning and policy*, Vol. 25, 1, Jan/Feb. Butterworth-Heinemann.

Rowe, H. (1993), *Learning with Personal Computers: Issues, Observations and Perspectives*, Australian Council for Educational Research.

Sachs, J. M. (1993), 'Computer education in Australia: What is the direction of policy?', in *Unicorn*, Vol. 19, 1, March, Australian College of Education.

5

■ ■ ■

Reengineering post-16 courses

NAYLAND SOUTHORN

Profile of the school

Sir John Talbot's School is an 11–19 comprehensive, co-educational day school with controlled status, situated on the south side of the small market town of Whitchurch. As the only state secondary school in the immediate area, it draws its pupils from the town and the surrounding villages of north Shropshire. The full ability range is represented with some very able pupils among the 750 on roll. There are 33 pupils with statements of special educational need. Less than one per cent of pupils is from ethnic minorities and there are none for whom English is a second language.

Whitchurch is in a rural development area. Local unemployment levels are high and 'geographical isolation' demands a community school offering appropriate teaching and learning opportunities for all. Sir John Talbot's operates an open sixth-form policy, encouraging all Year 11 students to continue their post-16 education in the school. In line with the Success Criteria for Secondary Schools in Shropshire, the school has moved 'to develop a curriculum programme adapted to meet the express needs of the community that the school serves'.

Sir John Talbot's School has developed as a Learning Resource Centre for both pupils and the local community. Facilities such as the information technology suites, library, drop-in language centre and the multi-gym have all opened to offer training and re-training opportunities to all local people.

Detailed discussion took place with neighbouring 11–19 schools, the nearest of which is nine miles away, to establish collegiate links for certain sixth-form courses. However, logistical problems proved too great, the nearest FE colleges being in Oswestry, Shrewsbury and Crewe, all at least twenty miles away and difficult to reach by public transport. Consequently, the school presented students with a wide, open choice of courses, responding to demand within the constraints of a teaching staff of fifty-six and the demands of teaching 750 pupils across the 11–19 range. The offer of a vibrant, dynamic sixth form had to be realistic for the whole school community and it posed a particular challenge for the senior management team. Strategic planning was vital if the school was to respond to market demand and to push home its claim to having an open sixth form for all.

The plan being formulated had to be flexible to respond to changing circumstances. In planning parlance, the management team had its eyes fixed on the road ahead but checked regularly in the rear view mirror!

Intentions and demands

The moves toward an open sixth form began in 1993 but several problems faced the school in making such a policy work. We needed to respond to the demands of Year 11 students when they made their post-16 choices. With limited work and training opportunities in an area suffering acute rural unemployment, (1,250 jobs have been lost in Whitchurch since 1980) more students wished to stay on into the sixth form. In response, a wide range of academic and vocational options was offered and this even halted the small, but significant, drain of students to further education colleges in Crewe, Shrewsbury and Chester.

This was all very well but our existing teaching staff were already fully committed in the post-16 sector and could they really be expected to teach new courses? Meanwhile, there were external pressures to run programmes and courses to 'gear up' the future workforce for local employers. We also tried to respond to the trends revealed by the surveys conducted by Shropshire Careers Service and Shropshire Business Centres, particularly for employment in electronics and electrical engineering.

While many students opted for the more traditional combinations of 'A' level and GCSE subjects that the school has operated successfully for several years, other demands were starting to appear. There was a growing demand in the vocational area, particularly to replace DVE in Art and Design, Business and Finance and Health and Social Care. We were being pushed to transfer these subjects into GNVQs, to add Leisure and Tourism, Manufacturing and Engineering and to offer all at intermediate and advanced levels. There was also a good deal of interest for 'A' and 'AS' levels in sociology and electronics with smaller numbers declaring a wish to study psychology, law and accountancy.

Market research

We were prompted to search for ways of servicing this growing and more diverse subject demand. Our research investigated distance learning strategies

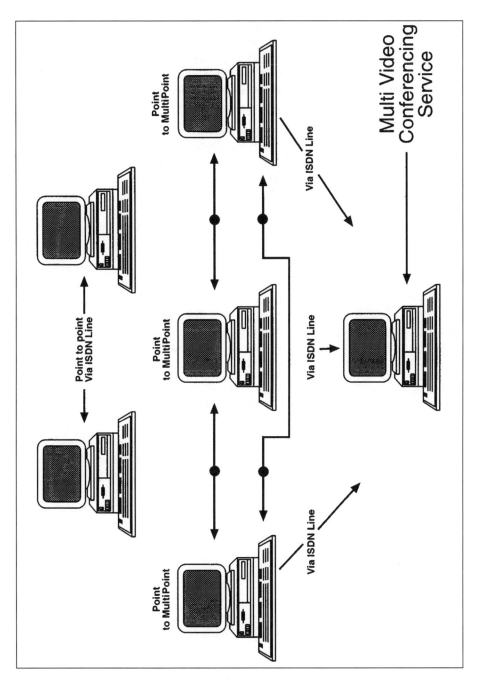

Figure 2: Video conferencing

operating in nearby Clwyd. We visited schools and colleges in Wrexham and Llangollen and discussions took place with headteachers and curriculum managers. These revealed that distance learning in Clwyd was delivered, essentially, by peripatetic tutors. Although a possible way of delivering extra courses at post-16, this approach did not really offer the stimulating and quality teaching and learning opportunities we were seeking.

Meanwhile, there were hints of very interesting developments taking place in Gwynedd which led to contact with the Gwynedd TVEI Centre in Llangefni, Anglesey. Their distance learning set up was based on video conferencing. Tutors in the broadcasting studio in Llangefni were using interactive TV links with receiving stations and rural schools throughout Wales were successfully using the service (*see* Figure 2 on page 81). Visits to the Gwynedd TVEI Centre allowed us to view facilities and to talk and negotiate with tutors and technical staff.

Gwynedd's 'distance learning' 'A' level results, over an eight-year period, were exceptional. Course materials had been evaluated, re-written and approved on several occasions and appeared to be well written and very user-friendly. The teaching and learning strategies that were integral to the Gwynedd scheme seemed highly appropriate, stimulating and closely matched my own beliefs of how flexible learning should operate. There was major emphasis on each student taking control of the pace of his or her learning (*see* Figure 3).

The scheme would be led by tutors from Gwynedd with no teacher input from Sir John Talbot's. The only requirement was for a member of staff to monitor student attendance and to set up the distance learning facilities.

'A' level delivery would take place in half the time normally devoted to the more traditionally taught subjects – 30 minutes video conferencing per week with a further 1 hour 45 minutes timetabled for support work (four periods of a 40-period week) for electronics and sociology. Conventionally taught 'A' levels are allotted 4 hours 40 minutes teaching time (eight periods per week). This is a considerable time saving with seemingly no threat to the quality of student performance. This was a most cost effective option!

Setting up

We were so convinced of the potential of the scheme in Sir John Talbot's School, especially with its proven track record in delivering successful 'A' level courses, that we moved to establish distance learning via video conferencing. A working party was set up to plan a scheme and to produce a document outlining the background, intentions, outcomes and financial analysis of the proposed distance learning programme. This document 'Extending learning opportunities in a rural area using distance learning technology' was produced by early 1994 and distributed to potential sponsors. Back-up negotiation

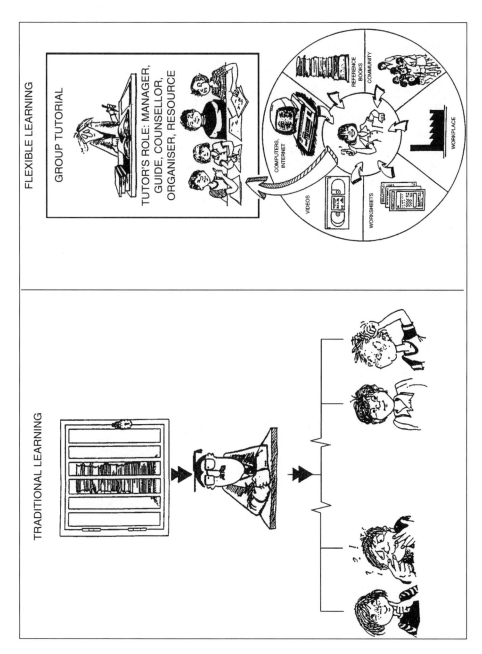

Figure 3: Changes in learning processes

secured financial support from several sources including Shropshire LEA, Shropshire TVE, Shropshire TEC, Keele University, BT and Lloyds Bank.

We maintained close liaison with the distance learning support team at Gwynedd TVEI Centre during the set-up period at Sir John Talbot's. In September 1994, we started to run distance learning 'A' and 'AS'-level courses. Twenty sociology students received a two-hour, face-to-face lecture from their tutor every fortnight, backed up by occasional video conferencing sessions. Five electronics students video conferenced with their tutor for thirty minutes each week. They were timetabled for approximately one and a half hours per week to cover theory work, practicals and assessment. Both arrangements took up significantly less time than that devoted to more traditional 'A' and 'AS' level subjects. Figure 4 shows the cycle of activities which had to be managed within the scheme. The school also became a Shropshire pilot for distance learning.

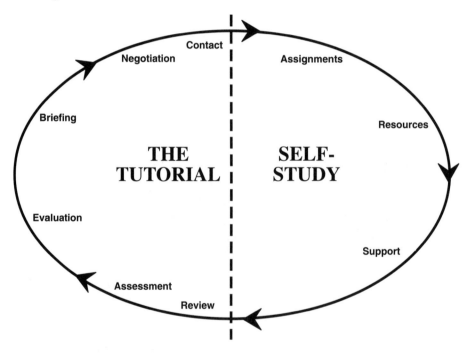

Figure 4: The management cycle

Challenges and successes

The scheme has not been without its teething problems. Students following a package of traditional 'A' levels mixed with electronics or sociology, found it difficult to ally face-to-face teaching and 4 hours 40 minutes subject time with the more irregular contact with the distance learning tutor and 2 hours 20 minutes subject time per week. An early compromise established a weekly video conferencing session for the sociologists.

Initially, students found it difficult to handle video conferencing and the constant tutor eye on them in the studio. Students cannot hide and they are forced to contribute! Staff expertise is needed to set up the distance learning facilities for video conferencing broadcasts. We trained support staff rather than use valuable teacher time. Growing student numbers have put pressure on accommodation and facilities. Further equipment has been purchased and extra ISDN lines networked into larger rooms.

In the light of the success of distance learning and its approach, some teachers have voiced fears about job security. Indeed, electronics and sociology are both cheaper courses to run but we have no plans to extend it to our more traditional subjects. The introduction of distance learning has been gradual and incremental and change, and the perceived threat to staff, have been allayed through consultation and involvement. All stages have been agreed with governors, policy group, academic board and departmental staff.

Eighteen months into the scheme, it is proving to be both popular and highly successful. Numbers opting for 'A' level electronics and sociology are rising rapidly and module scores have been consistently reaching A and B grades. Motivation is a key feature and the 'student control' of their own learning is excellent preparation for higher education and the changing patterns and ways of working.

The scheme enhances student expertise by providing excellent tuition from hand-picked tutors with a proven track record of public examination success. Video conferencing emphasises the tutor–student link and prompts verbal exchange. Tasks are assessed immediately and this appears to be a great motivator and encourages greater efforts.

The Future

All indicators are most encouraging and the scheme will be further developed to meet changing need. The immediate future of the scheme will see continued expansion of distance learning facilities in the school with new courses in accountancy, psychology and law. We will offer further GCSE courses in electronics and 'fresh start' modern foreign languages while further expanding our pre-16 vocational sector for GNVQs. We will also continue our role as a pilot distance learning centre for Shropshire and other similar rural areas.

Summary

The key stages and features of the scheme can be summarised as:

outset → *taking risks* → *innovation capacity* → *outcomes* → *benefits*

Perceived demand prompted the school's management team to initiate change. Distance learning has been introduced, bedded in and continues to grow. Anticipating the potential of distance learning, a risk was taken. Current indications are excellent but back in 1993, along with many other schools, Sir John Talbot's was operating in a turbulent, fast-moving environment which demanded rapid response and 'corporate fleetness of foot'.

Again, as in many schools, there is a liking for stability and a reluctance to change. However, the risk and innovation have taken place, prompting further allied development in a school now quite used to absorbing change. The school will shortly move onto a single site location with an increasing pupil roll and continued growth of community use. This in turn has

> led to an emphasis on the actual implementation of change, to be sure that the changes have occurred and that, having occurred, they bear at least a family resemblance to what we had in mind at the outset. (Huberman, 1992)

Indeed:

> there is an entrepreneurial climate in the school; change is considered normal; and staff are encouraged to put ideas into action. (Jenkins, 1991)

The benefits of the scheme can be summarised as follows:

- wider course options attract more students to the sixth form
- allows expansion of the curriculum programme with no additional staffing costs
- provides first rate tuition with a proven track record of public examination success
- 'A' and 'AS'-level module results are consistently higher in distance learning subjects
- courses are taught in half the time normally devoted to 'A' and 'AS' levels
- teaching materials are regularly evaluated, updated and approved by public examination bodies
- immediate assessment leads to high student motivation
- enhances student expertise and is an excellent preparation for higher education and modern working practices

- traditional teaching methods are challenged and more flexible approaches demand that the student is at the centre of his/her own learning, dictating the pace of progress made
- encourages further subject developments throughout the curriculum
- new facilities and a growing technical expertise will allow quality areas of our own teaching to be offered to other distance learning stations outside the school
- facilities and accommodation are open to all members of the school community
- the scheme puts the school in the vanguard of technological developments in this area and there is no doubt that technology will play an increasingly important part in delivering a quality curriculum.

References

Huberman, M. (1992), *Innovation up Close*, New York, Plenum.

Jenkins, H. O. (1991), *Getting it Right – A Handbook for Successful School Leadership*, Oxford, Blackwell.

Acknowledgement

I would like to acknowledge the contribution to this project of:

David Black, Distance Learning Co-ordinator, Gwynedd Technology Centre, Bridge Street, Llangefni, Anglesey, Gwynedd LL77 7TW, Tel.: 01248 724929, Fax: 01248 724674

Commentary – reengineering: learning and teaching

BRENT DAVIES AND JOHN WEST-BURNHAM

These two case studies by Dettman and Southorn provide excellent examples of how reengineering has been applied to the learning process. Dettman outlines how technology has transformed the learning environment of the school through the use of laptops for all pupils so that computers are totally integrated into the learning process rather than being bolt-on additions. Southorn demonstrates how the range of sixth-form subjects can be extended by the use of distance learning through video conferencing to yield increased student outcomes and completely restructured teaching processes.

Dettman was faced with the central challenge of reengineering, that of knowing that previous practice is inadequate but unsure about the future as there was a lack of research in this new and untried area; in fact she was creating the research. Thus she displayed the leadership characteristics of drawing on experience and using judgement and intuition in order to design new approaches and ways of working. Most importantly, it is having the courage to innovate in this way that is of crucial importance. This particular innovation led her to ask a number of fundamental questions about the processes of learning rather than about the structures of curriculum delivery. The use of computers was not organised in terms of computer labs or scheduled time but in terms of 'students using computers at the point of need', thus paving the way to 24-hour access and the laptop solution.

The reengineering mentality engendered by this change poses a series of other fundamental questions about the organisation of the learning process such as: should we even have lessons? what should a learner's day look like? what sort of timetable arrangements would facilitate the learning process? These questions go back to the original definition of reengineering proffered by

Hammer and Champy (1993, p. 32) 'The fundamental rethinking and radical redesign of business processes . . .'

In the commentary to Part Two we referred to reengineers in schools being aided by staff having a global view of educational changes and developments. This need to read and access information widely is reinforced by Dettman as she details an account of trying to change the culture of the staff to adopt new ways of thinking and operating. The final part of Hammer and Champy's (1993, p. 32) definition '. . . to bring about dramatic improvements in performance' is illustrated by the outcomes articulated by Dettman. These do not relate merely to the technical skills of computing but to more profound learning processes. These are articulated by her as 'students began to understand the changing nature of knowledge and to appreciate that the most up-to-date knowledge could be significant in their lives . . . the teachers' rôle changed to one of moving around, helping, suggesting, encouraging and very largely learning along with the students . . . modelling the discipline of perseverance and the joy of discovery of a real learner became a significant aspect of the teachers' work life . . . The curriculum was now truly individualised.' This is allied to changes in process skills with pupils working better with each other.

While Dettman has given a profound example of how technology has reengineered the learning process on a cross-curricular basis, Southorn shows how reengineering has been applied to a specific sector of the curriculum but with none the less significant results. Facing the challenge of a wide range of student choice for the 16–18 age group and, at the same time, maintaining quality provision at an economic cost, Sir John Talbot's School radically rethought its approach to effective educational provision.

The school was able to draw on emerging practice and to join a distance learning project encompassing a video conferencing approach. Like the Australian example, profound changes to the process of learning have taken place. Foremost is the change in the rôle of the student as learner as opposed to the student as receiver of information from the teacher in the classroom. This requires fundamental changes in the rôles of both student and teacher. Again looking at the definition of reengineering, the process can be seen to be radically changing, reflected by comments such as 'students taking responsibility for their own learning'.

Benefits such as high quality tuition and the material being regularly updated are reflected in 'dramatic improvements in performance', in 'A' levels being delivered in half the normal teaching time, leading to significant cost reductions and increased pass rates. Thus, a fundamental improvement in performance of this key aspect of the school's activity has been achieved by focusing on the learning process and reengineering from there, rather than by reorganising organisational units.

These chapters and the ones in Part Two show how, using a reengineering framework, very significant changes in schools can be achieved. The basis of the remaining chapters will focus on how total quality approaches can be used to significantly change practice.

Reference

Hammer, M. and Champy, J. (1993), *Reengineering the Corporation*, New York, HarperCollins.

PART FOUR

■ ■ ■

Total quality perspectives in schools

6

■ ■ ■

Introducing TQM at Heathland School

GEOFFREY SAMUEL

Introduction

In this chapter I set out the development of Total Quality Management at The Heathland School since 1991 and show how it has led to the adoption of a quality system and the introduction of internal audit. The approach is chronological rather than analytical but concludes with a general description of the present position. The Heathland School is a mixed comprehensive school with a roll of 1,640 including a sixth form of 370: some 90 per cent of the pupils are drawn from ethnic minorities. I opened the school as a purpose-built comprehensive in 1973.

How did it all begin? During the first part of 1991 I became increasingly interested in articles on TQM which appeared in various publications of the (then) British Institute of Management. The senior deputy and I were attracted by the Department of Trade and Industry's 'Quality Initiative' and sent for the videos, the best of which featured Professor John Oakland, Exxon Professor of TQM at Bradford University. The idea of BS 5750 appealed to us. In the summer the deputy head attended a course held at an FE College for schools and colleges applying for BS 5750. He concluded 'I found it stimulating. It was positive and pointed the way to improvement.' He recommended that we begin the process in spring 1992. At the same time I attended a DTI roadshow at which representatives from Royal Mail, a bank and two industrial companies urged us to 'take the total quality route'.

In the autumn we set up a task force to investigate. What could TQM offer to our school? Were its principles even applicable to a school? Should we embark on one or two limited experiments? We threw ourselves into jargon. We read (some of) Deming, Juran, Crosby and the other gurus. We invited a representative of the British Standards Institute to visit us. We followed up every likely lead. For example, Professor Ennals from Kingston University reviewed in *Education* a book entitled *Is Quality Good for You? A Critical Review of Quality Assurance in Welfare Services*. Professor Ennals then visited us to discuss the concepts involved. There were articles in *Home Economist*, a feature in the 'Justice of the Peace' (19 October 1991) on TQM in the South Hampshire Bench and many other professional leads. Customer-orientation, 'get it right first time, every time', zero defects and continuous improvement were approaches that appealed to us – approaches that would lead to school improvement. Our limited experiments led us to devise procedures for a range of school activities which impact directly on pupils such as homework, safeguarding pupils' learning during staff absence and the organisation of an arts week.

By the end of 1991 we were convinced. But we realised that we were mere amateurs blundering in the wilderness. We needed professional help. There was another factor. The original aim of the Bill which was eventually enacted as the Education (Schools) Act of 1992 was that governors should commission their own inspection. The £4,000–5,000 which BS 5750 certification would cost would be defrayed from the inspection budget; more than that BS 5750 would form the core of our approach to inspection. By this time we had understood the key difference between quality control and quality assurance.

Quality control is best exemplified by inspection; quality assurance by an internal system devised and managed by the people in the institution and merely verified by outside inspectors. There is no doubt that quality assurance is the professional model.

The die was cast. We would begin with a mission statement and proceed from there to invite tenders for the establishment of a quality system. My brief for the mission statement conference aimed to ensure that it would

- provide the focus for TQM
- provide the framework for all our policies and procedures
- unite staff (teaching and non-teaching), parents and pupils behind a clear statement
- provide the touchstone on which performance can be tested
- be the focus for our prospectus and all our communication within and without the school
- be our starting point for our SDP.

We were fortunate to have a British Airways (BA) manager at this conference. The eventual format of our mission statement is pure BA. After dinner, when we were all in a mellower mood, a guest who was a university lecturer in business confessed that he hated mission statements. 'But,' he claimed 'I bet we can all remember our old school motto.' We could. And so the lead sentence of the mission statement became 'Committed to Excellence'. Printed on every door label, on every single school document without exception the mission statement really does carry both the understanding and support of every pupil, of every member of staff.

The final job of the task force was to let the tender to a consultant. Unfortunately we did not qualify for any government support. But it is necessary to keep things in perspective. Out of a budget in excess of £3 million we could afford a reasonable amount. Four organisations visited us, asked questions, talked and listened: three sent detailed proposals. We chose Coopers and Lybrand although they were not the most expensive: their consultant seemed to offer what we needed. And so the second stage began.

Coopers and Lybrand

By now we had a Quality Committee. It comprised the four-strong Senior Management Team (all the best books tell you that TQM is dead unless it has the active commitment of the leadership) and two other senior members of staff, one of whom was later to become the quality manager. Our consultant planned to spend several days in school interviewing staff and meeting the Committee before a draft Quality Manual was developed.

Almost at once we abandoned the idea of BS 5750 certification. The government had accepted the amendment to its Bill which gave OFSTED sole responsibility for commissioning inspection therefore any cost would be met entirely from our own budget. But we were also advised that elements of the standard were too inflexible for our needs; we would be better advised to take on board the philosophy and approach of BS 5750 but not the certification itself. Indeed, the more we progressed, the further we moved from the detail of the standard.

But things did not run entirely smoothly. To avoid excessive disruption to lessons, committee sessions were fitted in to suit the timetable, which was not the most effective use of the consultant's time. Nor was every member of the committee convinced of the merits of the 'Quality Manual' approach. A quality system is not TQM – it is merely a contributor to a Total Quality culture. Some colleagues became impatient as the Quality Manual began to take shape. I departed for my summer holiday in 1992 full of doubts.

Two factors changed my mind. The first was that Coopers and Lybrand supplied to me the quality manual of a large firm of solicitors. I saw how they had taken the quality approach, selected those parts which were relevant, discarded the rest and produced a document totally suited to their needs. I was certain that we could do the same. Equally I realised that the school had lost some of its early coherence. When we set up the school in 1973 we had an elegant management structure, balanced, coherent and suited to our needs: in addition a clear, consistent staff handbook. Over the years the coherence had been eroded, the consistency compromised. Here was a marvellous opportunity to have the radical re-think which we had successfully avoided for nearly twenty years.

We had now reached the stage when the consultant handed the real work over to us, acting discreetly in the background as an adviser. We approached the task with relish . . .

The quality system

In essence the quality system is a manual which sets out broad general principles which are then carried into effect by quality procedures. As procedures are the key to the system, we call them 'Key Procedures'. First they are written in a set format (back to consistency!):

> *Title (e.g. Staff Absence); Purpose (e.g. to ensure that pupils etc.); Scope: (i.e. to whom this procedure applies); Responsibility.*

Yes! One of the best features of the system is that responsibility is clearly defined; it cannot be assumed – or fudged. The procedure is then written in clear, concise jargon-free language. No passive voices – the language beloved by all responsibility-shunning bureaucrats! 'Reports are sent home . . .' becomes 'the tutor will send reports home' so that we all know exactly who is responsible for this stage. Strong verbs: virtually everything is 'shall/will', 'must' or 'is responsible for'. Newcomers can see immediately what they have to do! And then, at the end – and the significance of this became clearer as we introduced audit and approached OFSTED inspection – records. In most cases, of course, the records were already in existence – registers, copy letters, mark books, etc. Records are the evidence. The importance was brought home to me when simultaneously with this work we received an HMI visit to a specialist area of the school. The lead inspector asked for evidence: 'I am quite sure' she said 'that as headmaster you want real evidence that this resource is well used but all I have been given is anecdotal evidence . . .' Of course, records of the kind she was seeking did not, at that stage, fully exist.

By late autumn of 1992 the Quality Manual was nearing completion. Most key procedures fall into one of three categories. The first of these covers areas in which our clients (external or internal) rightly demand consistency. If parents ask: 'how does this school approach setting?' they want one answer and not ten or twelve. Similarly I learned that some staff felt unhappy that we approached internal promotions in differing ways: they felt – rightly – that there should be one, clear, consistent approach, applied in all cases. Equally with a teaching staff in excess of 100, pupils are entitled to feel that there are some aspects of teaching which they should experience consistently, irrespective of the teacher allocated to them. In the next category there was a number of potential areas for conflict where a simple series of statements incorporated in a procedure can take the heat out of an issue. Good examples of this are admission to 'A' level courses and public examination entries – issues guaranteed to cause ruffled feathers in the staff room. The final category comprised administrative procedures. Some have a statutory connotation, e.g. every aspect of health and safety (a massive document!) or equal opportunities: others have a local framework, e.g. financial regulations. Finally, a number simply spell out 'how we do things in this school'.

How do you reconcile the requirement for whole-school procedures with the need for local initiative, the *sine qua non* for an enterprising and challenging school? The answer lies in 'local procedures'. In these, individual departments or other sections of the school may produce their own local department procedure or amplification of a key procedure. A department may feel that they need to add some refinements to the school approach to setting: science or PE may feel that they have individual characteristics which require marked additions to the school safety policy. So we set aside two Inset days for departments and year teams to devise their own local procedures which, almost without exception, we merely rubber-stamped. In any job people are more committed to rules or procedures when they have been personally involved in the formulation. To our delight every department save one took to the task with enthusiasm.

We were equally pleased that the office staff asked for a full-day session to draw up procedures for themselves. In fact, one of the leading TQM areas in the school had for some time been the caretakers who had devised a 'defect' procedure for reporting problems and ensuring that the complainants were kept in touch with what was happening. The new quality system – replacing the old staff handbook – was ready for issue at the beginning of the school year in 1993.

The quality committee and the quality manager

An early decision was taken to appoint a senior member of staff as quality manager. The person appointed was a long-serving member of staff on the 'senior teacher' scale. The job description had three main foci. The first, obviously, was the operation of the system (a task soon to be massively increased with the introduction of audit). This is not simply a maintenance job. The whole philosophy of TQM is based on continuous improvement. Gone are the days when the staff handbook is subject to annual, or biennial, review. The system is kept under continual review so that as soon as the possibility of an improvement can be described, it is put into action. The second focus was an oversight of our review and development processes. The requirement to produce an annual school development plan was for us a development, not an innovation. We produced our first 'Corporate Plan' in 1974, our first whole-school evaluation in 1980. But despite this experience – and now six previous SDPs – I can never read our SDP without thinking of ways to do it better! The particular contribution of the quality manager has been to integrate it into existing processes within the school – in particular, our annual evaluation supported by 'Management Information Statistics'. This latter document records in some fifty pages all the facts and figures needed to illuminate the evaluation and to inform future decisions. (As we were later to find, this meant that OFSTED's headteacher's form and associated statistics held no terrors). Third: the quality manager was responsible for all the preparations for OFSTED, the organisation and management of the week and the response thereafter. Quality, in the person of the quality manager, is therefore at the heart of the work of the school.

The Quality Committee oversees every aspect of the system. It now comprises the Senior Management Team (head, two deputies and the bursar), assistant heads and the quality manager. It meets three or four times a year. However, there is one occasional additional member. An early decision was taken to give quality a section in the SDP in its own right (others are: curriculum, pupils, personnel, premises, pupil progress, management, in-service training and the budget). As part of our wish to involve governors more closely in the work of the school, four of these areas are serviced by governors' committees while others have a designated 'Link Governor'. Quality has a Link Governor who happens to be a higher education lecturer in management. His contributions are invariably well received. Obviously, the setting and evaluation of the plan for any year is part of the work of the committee. Audit is now a major concern of the committee as is a review of the system.

The complaints procedure is an interesting example. All schools need a complaints procedure but in our early discussions with Coopers and Lybrand this was one of the procedures which we could not get right. In a school, what is a complaint? A pupil complaining about homework? Do you need a cumbersome procedure to deal with that? Of course not! Our original procedure was burdensome and largely ignored: it involved a complaints form, entirely separate from other approaches in the school. Despite several amendments (continuous improvement dictates frequent reviews of all procedures) it still seemed unworkable. The fifth version just approved by the committee may be more realistic. It recognises that existing informal systems do seem to be effective: e.g. all pupils have a diary in which parents can write comments (complaints?); heads of year have telephone books in which they can record calls from parents and subsequent action taken; satisfaction-questionnaires are issued at all parents' meetings. Provided that the quality manager can see all these records and analyse them, no specific additional procedure is normally needed. The analysis is the most important part. Complaints are an opportunity, not a threat. Certainly a pattern of complaints, for example about homework or examinations or sets is a clear indication that this is an issue which a client-orientated school must address. As an alternative we have a highly formal complaints form – based on the procedure of the court where I am deputy chairman – which must be offered to parents or outsiders. Responses to complaints are one of the ways in which we can show that our quality system results in a positive improvement to the service which we offer.

Internal audit: philosophy and structure

Once the quality system was in place we turned our attention to audit. The essence of quality assurance is that the institution implements its own system to ensure that it is actually delivering what it claims. We went back to Coopers and Lybrand. We heard that two days were needed to train us in auditing: we offered two hours and settled for three.

In the BS 5750 approach the purpose of audit is to identify non-conformance with procedures and to set in train remedial measures. We adopted unquestioningly many of the underlying principles but opted for a wider-ranging approach. The first is that audit must be detached and objective: in other words any auditor faced with the same evidence will come to the same conclusions. We were advised to ensure that the audit process was not too time-consuming, must be scheduled at appropriate times and that there should be clear, consistent audit procedures with an audit check-list. A key issue to be resolved was lesson-observation. This, we knew, would be expected by staff.

Once again, audit was a development, a refinement of existing school practice: every year since 1974 I had 'visited' every department, every year team biennially. For each 'visit' there were foci, lesson observations, discussions with staff, inspections of accommodation and resources and final conclusions and recommendations. Somewhat surprisingly these visits were always well received, with lesson observation a highly approved aspect. Observation, as part of the audit process, could not be inspectorial, that would suggest quality control.

Quality assurance is a much more professional approach, which assumes that the head of department is the professional leader in the school. Observation is therefore not designed to challenge his or her judgement but merely to see whether agreed department (or school) practices and procedures are actually being carried out. Homework is an example. An inspector would be entitled to criticise the task set for homework; an auditor would be debarred from this approach. However, the school procedure lays down that homework shall be set 2–5 minutes before the end of a lesson. (The origin of this is interesting: teachers of special needs often told us that their charges frequently complained that they were not given a fair chance to do their homework as they did not have enough time to write it down). An auditor would be entitled to comment that in five lessons seen the homework was set at least four minutes before the end of the lesson, in the sixth as the lesson change-over bell was sounded. (Note that this comment is purely factual and devoid of emotive adjectives!).

Observation was therefore simply part of the evidence for audit. Whereas in another context an outsider could check the procedures of, for example, the sales department of a car sales showroom through its paperwork, the essential nature of a school requires that lessons are part of the evidence.

Who should audit and how often? We decided on a full audit in the first year, followed by a review year. Departments were to be audited from April 1994 to March 1995, year teams in the following twelve months. In each case the headmaster was the lead auditor, supported by another member of the Quality Committee. At the conclusion of the audit, responsibility was passed to the member of Quality Committee who would be assisted in the review year by another member of staff (often a head of department or head of year) who had undertaken a brief training session. Coopers and Lybrand told us that this approach was the fastest way to break down interdepartmental barriers in an organisation. We have found this to be true to some extent. It is also a way of spreading good practice. Whereas I have tried to be relatively discreet, I have sometimes taken the opportunity of inviting a less well-organised head of department to be assistant auditor to a superbly managed and administered department. It does not always work!

As often happens the quality of the documentation has a marked impact on the success of the exercise. The quality manager devised the forms for our use: they have proved to be fairly satisfactory, but are subject to regular review and improvement. The basic report is contained on four pages of A4. The front page summarises, for example, the additional foci, reports on discussions with staff and refers to the department's records and so on. The second page summarises the lesson visits and particular broad areas such as management and administration, accommodation and resources, assessment (departments), attendance and punctuality (year teams). So far everything is formal and objective. The top of the third page is entitled 'Audit Summary' and value judgements are permitted. There follows 'Action Needed'. This is determined by the auditors. The head of department/year nominates the 'staff responsible' and we negotiate the 'review date'. A final column, designed solely for a tick is headed 'rectified'. The whole of the back page is left free for the review year with the two headings of 'report on action taken' and 'summary of evidence'.

Clearly this format is not suitable for universal application. A completely different form has been devised, for example for the library. Work-related studies have produced an interesting challenge. Here, evidence to be inspected includes pupils' work experience diaries, reports of work experience placements visited and a review of links with industry. A recent decision requires spiritual, moral, social and cultural education to be included in every form. To inform these reports there are individual checklists where the auditors use a structured format to make notes: these checklists are always made available to heads of department etc., but they are not formally part of the audit report. Every department showed its audit report to OFSTED inspectors.

Internal audit action

Has it worked? Of course, if you are amateurs – and we are! – you learn on the job. Continuous improvement is not just an instruction to other people! We began with the audit of a core department. First there was a planning meeting with the head of department. One thing we made clear: time was limited. For the first few audits we laid down a maximum time allocation which we were not prepared to exceed. An average department was given twenty hours, i.e. ten hours for each auditor to include reading time, meetings, discussions, visits. This never proved to be a problem. The planning meeting then settled the entire timetable for the audit. The initial stage involves reading the departmental documentation and holding a discussion with the head of department. This gives the head of department an opportunity to set the agenda for the audit by emphasising certain aspects of the documentation. Most departments have the kind of department handbook that the experts now recommend. But in many ways the most valuable part of the exercise is to discover in one area of the school approaches and methods which could easily be applicable more generally: after all, it is a common OFSTED injunction to 'spread good practice more widely'.

At the end of the first round we produced for heads of department an analysis of those findings and conclusions that warranted general discussion. And the decision was taken, at staff request, that in the regular TQM bulletin the quality manager should print examples of good practice. These included:

- 'documentation gives a clear sense of purpose'
- 'exceptionally well managed department with clear evidence of remarkable progress'
- 'useful lesson planning sheet'.

On the other hand we drew attention to some common problems:

- 'schemes of work patchy'
- 'greater evidence needed'.

The most common areas under the heading 'Action Needed' included the need to develop success criteria, the recommendation that the department carried out a 'value for money' audit and the need to provide evaluation and monitoring of greater rigour.

To me, who has always been, at best, sceptical of the current fashion for in-class support for pupils with special educational needs, the audit provided an excellent opportunity to review what was actually happening; not just the resources devoted to this area of work (I knew that already) but the outcomes produced. I personally examined 167 records of in-class support under the headings of target pupil/group support given and progress made. In addition we ran a support unit in the school: every use (468 in all) was recorded. The consequence of this, our most rigorous audit, was that it was agreed to determine and define the use of the unit more closely and to monitor it more effectively: but simultaneously we agreed to increase the overall staffing for special needs.

The end-of-audit report for departments included eight examples of good practice which they might wish to consider. This included: 'A number of departments are filing and analysing letters to and from parents. We wish to encourage this practice.' 'One department includes in its documentation the syllabi of feeder primary schools.' There were seven areas of concern, e.g. 'Not all departments include in their lesson planning the role of the support teacher and therefore the means to evaluate success.' In conclusion there were four areas for the management of the school to address such as timetabling and accommodation issues. It is most surprising that most departments found this process demanding but constructive. The next section gives the reason . . .

Audit and inspection

In October 1994 we received from OFSTED the familiar envelope with its news of an impending inspection. The target date was autumn 1995. Whereas OFSTED maintains, with some justification, that it has reduced its demands on schools in terms of documentation, there is no doubt that a school aiming for a good report will produce far more than the minimum. At an early stage we realised that there was a considerable overlap between preparing for audit and preparing for inspection. Even at its lowest level departments found that the degree of rigour imparted to the audit process was a useful starting point for their preparation for OFSTED. In fact the checklist for the audit covered most of the areas of concern to inspectors such as delivery of the curriculum (schemes of work, differentiation, progression), lesson planning, financial planning, assessment, equal opportunities, attendance, staff development and sixteen other headings. When this was supplemented by lesson observation and interviews with the head of department and other staff, the overlap with inspection became even more obvious. However, the main difference was that auditors, unlike inspectors, did not trespass on the subject-orientated professional judgement of the head of department.

For the quality manager also the overlap between audit and inspection was helpful. Part of her job involved preparation for inspection. It was her task to master the framework and tell us what to do! It was also her role to ensure that every piece of documentation was fully in place and her responsibility to ensure that the headteacher's form was completed accurately. Although this was a formidable responsibility, audit had ensured that most of the document-ation was already in place. One decision which she took was not fully in the spirit of a quality system. This was the simultaneous up-dating and re-issue of the Quality Manual. Its re-issue enabled us to emphasise to staff their responsi-bility to master its essential features. After all, neither inspectors nor parents would be pleased if they discovered that there was a school policy on bullying – but that some staff were not even aware of it!

Inspectors were suitably impressed. They wrote: 'Many innovative steps have been taken to ensure a focus on quality. For example, the management structure itself unusually features a quality manager with a responsibility for maintaining a focus on quality, as well as maintaining the quality assurance procedures.' In other areas of the report are found frequent references to the excellence of documentation and records, e.g. 'clear policies for assessment, recording and reporting', 'curriculum planning is fully documented' and complimentary references to the rôle of the procedure in promoting genuine equality of opportunity. 'The administration and day-to-day organisation of the school are exemplary with a key procedure for all aspects of its work.' After this report, even the sceptics feel that it has all been worthwhile.

Quality and school improvement

But a quality system is not TQM although it contributes to it. There is so much else to do. Our most important related initiatives are Investors in People and School Improvement. The Total Quality culture of Texas Instruments includes as part of its operating philosophy:

> There is probably no greater waste in industry today than that of willing employees prevented by insensitive leadership from applying their energies and ambitions in the interest of the companies for which they work.

TQM gurus often state that no one goes to work with the deliberate intention of doing a bad job or, more generally, that most quality failures are management failures.

It was therefore inevitable that TQM should lead at some stage to Investors in People. The seeds were sown on fertile ground. Since the late 1970s the school had an extensively developed programme for staff development with an annual staff course, an annual staff lecture and specific programmes targeted at individuals. In 1981 (some eleven years ahead of a national scheme) we introduced staff appraisal. Various considerations led us to believe that there is an inextricable link between appraisal and staff development. It is somewhat unprincipled to discern a weakness in an employee unless you have the wherewithal to produce a remedy: at the same time it is only through appraisal that you really discover the training needs of staff. As Dr Hargreaves has said: 'In this country we have the provision for in-service training, but no policy'.

In 1993 we made the decision to apply for Investors in People. This was a school decision, totally unrelated (like everything in school) to anything that the LEA did or recommended. Working through the TEC we appointed a consultant of our own choice. Like the Coopers and Lybrand consultant, he began with a series of structured interviews within the school: similarly he presented us with an action plan. Three aspects of Investors appealed to us. First was the training needs analysis: this accorded with our previous approach. Second was the insistence that development planning for the institution carried the understanding and commitment of everyone who worked with it. This has been our aim since school development plans became a requirement. Finally – and I suspect that we were not the only school who were weak in this respect – we needed better to integrate our teaching and non-teaching staff. The outcomes of greater staff commitment, a more highly qualified staff and school improvement were all part of our goal. In November 1994 we became the twenty-first school in the country to be awarded Investors in People certification.

School improvement is in itself an intended outcome of both Investors in People and TQM. We addressed it as a specific issue. It is the *raison d'être* of TQM as 'continuous improvement' is a specific TQM aim. We chose two main, two minor issues as the foci of our school improvements projects. One of these has been both overtaken and confirmed by our inspectors when they enjoined us 'to continue to raise the expectations and achievements of boys by extending good practice already developed in some subjects'. Once again we find that both the philosophy and practice of TQM have prepared us for national initiatives in education.

Other basic elements in TQM remain in the forefront: 'zero defects' was a concept that aroused considerable scepticism – sometimes downright hostility – from staff. This was somewhat of a misconception. Ask any intending mother whether she would book into a maternity ward whose declared aim was to deliver 98 per cent of babies safe and sound and you have the key to the concept of zero defects. But it is the follow-up that is the most useful and ties in so well with the audit process. The route to zero defects requires you to analyse existing defects and take the most effective means of bringing improvement. Just as a cricket coach will study a batsman's dismissals and often realise that the elimination of one particular fault will bring about 50 per cent improvement (a variation on Pareto!), so an analysis of parent questionnaires after a parents' evening may lead you speedily and effectively to the one or two improvements which will give the greatest satisfaction to parents.

Customer orientation does not sit easily in some schools. 'After all', says the typical teacher, 'you do not question the doctor's diagnosis or prescription.' I wonder. But, at the very least, the trend of policy in the last fifteen years –

so-called open enrolment, parent governors, league tables and so on – has been (justifiably) to tilt the balance in favour of the customer. For us an interesting dispute on the presentation of national curriculum attainment targets results was settled by interviews with parents. Did they want a single figure? (comprehensible, but basically flawed) or a figure for each target? (accurate and reliable, but difficult for a layman to appreciate). Overwhelmingly, they chose the former.

The future

TQM, they told us, is a five-year process. We began in 1991. What have we gained? At heart a philosophy which suits our parents and our school. We have, as most outsiders note, a greater degree of internal consistency and coherence than most schools of our size. Above all, we have a mission statement which is not just a form of words, but a statement of our ethos and values which drive our development plan, our governors, staff, pupils and parents. Inspectors reported that the Heathland School was 'underpinned by a school ethos in which tolerance, respect, the important of self-esteem, traditional values and the commitment to academic excellence are the driving principles'. In addition TQM led us to Investors in People. Equally, it saw us through inspection. As I wrote in July 1994: 'TQM rejects inspection as inefficient, ineffective and fundamentally negative. Inspection denies the basic tenets of trust in people and empowerment.' The answer, I believe, lies in schools committed to TQM, implementing quality assurance and subject, at regular intervals, to outside monitoring and evaluation. But in the meantime the work involved in preparing and introducing our own quality systems was the finest preparation for OFSTED.

Although a quality system is but part of TQM, it is the most visible and concrete expression of our commitment. Its value is considerable. Speaking at a recent post-OFSTED training day our curriculum deputy told the staff that we had a clear-cut value system introduced and accepted by all; Investors in People to ensure the on-going commitment of our staff; a comprehensive quality system to guarantee consistency in our processes and procedures and to remove any obstacles to concentrate on our real work. Without the need to waste time on administrative and organisational matters, we were in a strong position to give overriding priority to classroom practice. And that way lies school improvement.

7

■ ■ ■

School improvement – translation from theory into practice

CHARLES SISUM

Introduction

This chapter traces the evolution of the author's progress into the fields of school improvement and his subsequent attempts at the practical application of principles of Total Quality as a way of working towards the implementation of a strategy for improvement in the effectiveness of his own school.

It outlines the influence of various external catalysts to his own thinking and sets the practical implementation of school improvement in Wisewood School into the context of post-OFSTED action planning and dealing with budgetary problems of the first order.

The context – place

Wisewood School is a co-educational secondary school of 670 pupils on the north-western fringe of Sheffield. It serves a distinct catchment area within a stone's throw of Hillsborough stadium, the home of the Owls (Sheffield Wednesday Football Club). The community surrounding the school and from which 95 per cent of the pupils come to Wisewood, is a socially stable area. Many grandparents and some great-grandparents of our pupils went to the school when it was built in 1934. The area is not wealthy but neither is it deprived, having only one small council estate where problems of a socio-economic nature are significant. The school is the secondary partner of a small pyramid containing three main contributing primary schools, though children do come in small numbers to Wisewood from another five or six primary schools in the same north-western part of the city. The Wisewood area is not an area of major unemployment but many families have experienced short-term unemployment over recent years as Sheffield city has seen a major collapse in employment in the steel industry, despite actually manufacturing more steel now than at any time in its history. Most people in our community work in 'blue-collar' and manual occupations. Few families have experience of university life and the parent body contains very few people in professional occupations.

On the whole the Wisewood area gives the impression of being a community at relative ease with itself. This character in some ways has been a significant contributor to the nature of the task of school improvement as perceived by me in ways which will be referred to in more detail in later stages of this chapter. Suffice it to say here that some of the prerequisites for school improvement such as the belief that there is room for improvement and the desire to make an improvement, were not immediately apparent in this school community at the outset of this saga. Furthermore I do not exclude myself from that accusation for this is a story first and foremost of self-realisation.

The context – time

In May 1991 the inspectors came to call! To be more precise, Wisewood School was subjected to a full school inspection by Her Majesty's Inspectorate of Schools. This inspection came towards the end of the era of HMI school inspections. OFSTED had not yet started to function though dark mutterings could occasionally be heard amongst the team of ten inspectors in Wisewood and the object of the conversations was not just the management style of the headteacher.

The conclusions (Department of Education and Science, 1992) on our school were quite positive but there was clearly room for significant improvement. In the period since my arrival at the school in 1986 we had engaged in considerable curriculum innovation as a TVEI pilot school. The success rate of our pupils at GCE and CSE levels was improving but from a rather low base level. Where only 12 per cent of the cohort had obtained GCE pass/CSE Grade 1 in the 1986 results we had progressed in 1991 to a success rate of 20 per cent. We had little real knowledge about the ability profile of our pupil intake and hence no clear view of any value-added (or subtraction!). Our monitoring and evaluation work was almost non-existent and although we professed to be a caring school it was difficult to justify this claim in terms of our effectiveness at raising children's levels of attainment. Like many schools at that time

Wisewood was very proud of the pastoral support systems we had in place. Teachers, pupils and parents (and the HMI team) commented very favourably on this aspect of our school operation. What we didn't really know was whether this pastoral support system was really leading to any tangible benefit in terms of learning for our students. At the same time we were a school with a long and distinguished history of mixed-ability teaching across the whole curriculum from Year 7 to Year 11. (Wisewood ceased to be an 11–18 school in 1988 when Sheffield education system was partially reorganised along tertiary lines). Despite our espousal of mixed ability grouping we had not made any lasting attempt at monitoring the teaching and learning process in the classrooms in order to satisfy ourselves that all was well and that our students were learning to the limits of their potential. We were relatively happy to accept the received wisdom that mixed-ability grouping was socially and educationally a more optimistic environment for learning.

The experience of the 1991 HMI inspection was to prove to be a professional turning point for me and for Wisewood School though at the time we would not have considered such a statement to be likely when this phase was to be later viewed with the advantage of hindsight from 1996.

Before moving on, however, to the subsequent development of the Wisewood improvement story it is worth reflecting on the general context of our school and the inspection process at that stage in 1991, particularly in the conceptual landscape and language of Total Quality Management.

The HMI inspection had reinforced a view in us that 'quality' was a characteristic that was inspected into the organisation from outside and that it was a judgement to be made by the professionals, certainly not the consumers. We did not feel any ownership of the process. We were not involved. Indeed it is almost strange now to reflect how little we knew of the processes and criteria for the judgements laid upon us at the time.

Apart from the headteacher's form and the 'shopping list' of documentation required before the inspection we really knew almost nothing about the rules of engagement. We would discover at the end of the game what the rules had been and what the score was but at the time we were playing in the dark.

It is also interesting to reflect how distant the LEA officers and advisers were to the whole process compared to the current system where, if they are not actually doing the inspection, they will take a close interest in supporting the school in the pre-inspection phase as well as being more heavily involved in the post-inspection action planning period.

We may complain about the bureaucratic and at times almost checklist mentality of the current OFSTED system but at least, if we are going to try to 'inspect-in' quality, it is useful to have made some attempt at defining the basis of judgements to be made and the process through which the school community will pass. I well remember listening to a governor of Wisewood School attempting to seek clarification from the reporting inspector of a judgement on classroom practice. The governor's ever-increasing frustrations at lack of clarity were simply met by the response that 'we've been doing these inspections all over the country for many years and we know quality when we see it'.

The strength of the former HMI inspection regime however did become apparent in the post-inspection phase. Unlike the OFSTED system our HMI friends did return to help us with the post-inspection work, and would have continued so to do if the demise of the old system and the removal of the few remaining HMIs to run OFSTED training programmes had not prevented it!

A further area of reflection on the state of the 'Wisewood nation' at the time of the inspection in 1991 reveals our almost complete lack of any knowledge or understanding of process. It was to be another three years before my own experiences of Total Quality outside the world of education were to lead me to an appreciation of the importance of processes in any organisation. Schools are awash with processes. Now it is self-evident but back in 1991 I did not realise the significance of this view: much less did I have any insight into the importance of measurement in attempting to understand and subsequently manage the processes.

Although in 1991 we were about to enter the brave new world of league tables, and perhaps indeed because of it, those of us who worked in schools were very sceptical about any notion of measurement. We took the view that 'you could not measure the aspects of school that were really important'. Along with many colleagues I would be quick to point out that there was a danger that 'the only aspects we would value would be those we could measure'.

In 1991 any notion that state schools were engaged in providing services for customers would have received very short shrift. We were the professionals. We knew what was best and the pupils and parents were kept at a playground's length on any matters to do with the educational functioning of the school. Yes, we had a PTA but inspection of committee meeting minutes will reveal that the topics discussed were of a social and fund-raising nature. Yes, we had a students' council with an annual budget but they were not allowed to encroach upon the territory of learning and teaching quality. Yes, we had a governing body but in truth for many years the business and outcomes of the meetings were decided in advance of the once-a-term meetings by the headteacher and the chair, the latter strongly influenced by the former. Yes, we were a school community with several groups of people each contributing in their own way to the running of the organisation but any idea that we were all customers of each other offering services within the whole school operation was unknown.

In summary, at the end of the summer term in 1991 Wisewood could have been described as having the following characteristics:

- large proportion of apparently contented and happy children
- large proportion of staff who seemed equally content

- strong pastoral system
- no clear view about the main aim of the school
- gradually improving examination results
- lack of proper approaches to monitoring and evaluation
- no real involvement of community members in discussing educational matters
- dislike of the concept of measurement
- little knowledge of process
- no obvious commitment to increase the current pace of improvement
- increasing problems of budget due to formula funding weightings.

The Wisewood HMI inspection report, published in January 1992 (DES, 1992), concluded that 'the school is aware of the many factors currently restricting improved achievement for pupils. It has plans already in hand for some and the willingness to tackle others. There is every reason to expect success.'

Following the publication of the inspection report we were expected to prepare an action plan to respond to the main findings of the HMI team, although the timescale was less clearly defined than in the current OFSTED framework. The inspection process had persuaded us that there were significant areas of our school organisation requiring improvement. Now began the search for an approach to this improvement activity.

The Total Quality strand

As we searched for a strategic framework within which to set our improvement activity we became aware that the Cutlers' Company in Sheffield was offering an opportunity for three secondary schools to take part in a Total Quality Awareness Raising programme. We knew nothing of this concept of Total Quality Management but gathered that it was an approach to organisational improvement activity and hence expressed our interest in becoming one of the pilot schools in this education/business partnership.

The Total Quality induction course was organised by Royal Mail North East and Avesta Steel. Twelve teachers, a governor and a member of the support staff attended. During the course of two days we were introduced to the basic principles of Total Quality Management, now well known, but at that time still relatively new ground for those of us who worked in the education sector. We were introduced to the concepts of quality, as defined by the customer or 'fitness for purpose'. Process improvement became an expression with some meaning and the use of measurement to help control and manage processes was examined. The idea that if you want to improve a process you should involve the people who do the job came to some of us for the first time! The benefits of self-review were explored and through this process we were introduced for the first time to the organisational model used as the basis for the European Foundation for Quality Management (EFQM) Award Scheme (1995). Finally we were introduced to a whole range of tools and techniques associated with quality management facilitation. The terms force field analysis, mission statement, Ishakawa or fishbone diagrams, critical success factors and many others came into our vocabulary.

Our group returned to school fired with enthusiasm to spread the word. A steering group was set up, consisting of the initial group plus a number of other interested staff. Discussion on the approach to the involvement of the pupils ranged far and wide but in the end it was decided that we would wish to adopt the use of Total Quality approaches to the improvement of our school via the staff and plan to involve pupils through classroom activity at a later date. In hindsight this was probably one of the most serious mistakes we made. Total Quality approaches require the involvement of all from the start. A failure to do this means the undermining of the values of the statement of purpose (mission statement) and the considerable weakening of the sense of common purpose, so important an ingredient for a successful outcome to the whole improvement venture.

We arranged awareness-raising meetings for staff and governors, organised a curriculum training day devoted to the introduction of the total quality concept and waited for everything to become perfect. It didn't! Some progress was made in that we involved parents, pupils, governors and staff in a large group exercise of producing a revised statement of purpose for our school. The process was facilitated by the TQ Steering Group using facilitation skills, tools and techniques learned at the awareness-raising course. There was a common sense of purpose while working on the new statement and it was accepted by all staff, parents and pupils. The school still works to that statement.

The failure of this initial period was based on our lack of real understanding of the principal concepts inherent in the Total Quality approach and a mistaken belief that Total Quality was just about the mechanics of processes rather than the underlying principles and values of involvement and customer-focus. We also underestimated the resistance of our colleagues to the language of Total Quality, which they perceived as being too business-orientated. The argument that 'education is different to business and you cannot translate ideas and processes from one world into the other' was to become very commonplace. This last point is one to which I will return towards the end of the chapter as it is a critical obstacle to progress which continues to need addressing by all those who work at the interface of business and education organisations.

Wisewood School thus continued on its way, attempting to pursue the post-inspection action plan. Wherever it seemed useful to use Total Quality approaches to help to facilitate improvement activity, those of us who were brave enough to try would so do, despite some colleagues who expressed an opposition to Total Quality Management, almost as an act of faith, in no less a manner than some of the proponents might seek to convert the doubters!

Total Quality Management meets school improvement!

During 1994–95 I was fortunate to be granted a secondment to the Headteachers into Industry programme, based at Warwick University. The secondment was sponsored jointly by Royal Mail and Sheffield Training and Enterprise Council. The majority of the year was in fact spent on a placement as a quality manager with the Quality Directorate of Royal Mail North East, based in Leeds. Through this secondment I was able to further my own understanding of the Total Quality movement, its historical background and present development as well as receive further training in the processes of facilitating continuous organisational improvement. I was also expected to contribute to Royal Mail's Quality Team work in leading some examples of business process improvement activity within the North East Division.

At the same time as my secondment work was progressing I had been able to continue my involvement with Sheffield LEA's School Improvement Group (SSIG), a consultative body involving headteachers from all sectors, officers and advisers of the Authority and representatives from the Sheffield TEC. As part of SSIG's internal programme of awareness raising on the topic of school improvement a successful bid was made to the Central Bureau for Teacher Study Visits for funding to enable a small representative group to visit a series of schools in Baltimore, other parts of Maryland, Washington and New York which were deemed by academics and school improvement *cognoscenti* to be examples of world best practice in school improvement. I was granted leave of absence from my secondment by Royal Mail, who also supported the study visit with further sponsorship.

The study visit proved to be an inspirational experience. The common factor of all the schools visited within the two-week stay was that they had been identified as schools who had previously been deemed to be failing their students but who, through a very rigorous and single-minded approach to improvement, had succeeded in raising the level of attainment of all their students to a significant and measurable degree. All the schools were facing the challenge of raising levels of achievement against a background of considerable socio-economic deprivation but such a situation was seen as no excuse or reason why success could not be achieved.

A full report of the study visits has been written elsewhere (Machin, Sisum, Tomlinson and Waxman, 1995) but for the purposes of this paper it is useful to record the main findings as they were to have a major influence on the processes of school improvement which we were subsequently to develop within our own LEA in Sheffield and within Wisewood School in particular.

The conclusions of the visit, stated in the full report, included the following comments:

- there are many routes which lead to school improvement (*processes*)
- different routes are unified by a common set of principles
  - high academic standards (*right first time/continuous improvement*)
  - strong and fair accountability and the use of measures to check progress (*measurement to control and manage*)
  - teaching and learning strategies which ensure high level acquisition of fundamental skills, including thinking and learning skills (*process improvement*)
  - continuous professional development of teachers and staff which was focused on learning and teaching strategies (*process improvement*)
  - service to, and strong support from, the community and parents (*involve and listen to the stakeholders*)
  - school autonomy to design its own route (*those who know best how to fix it are those who do the job*)
  - integrated use of technology to enhance the performance of students, teachers and staff
- entrepreneurial broad partnerships are the key to success (*involvement*)
- success is enhanced by a district framework for school improvement (*involvement and process improvement*)
- all children can learn: socio-economic factors are no excuse for under-achievement (*heroic goals – set high targets for improvement*)
- many successful school improvement strategies can be effectively replicated or adapted without significant injections of additional funding (*most improvement comes from re-designing the processes of the organisation, not by forcing everyone to work harder or to always spend more money*).

The italicised sections above have been added by me to the original conclusions as the latter seemed to demonstrate time and time again that real success was being achieved in these schools by the rigorous application of total quality principles to the single but clearly stated common purpose of raising pupil achievement. There was a sharing of belief in the school that they had problems to face but that together they could achieve success. They all had very public statements of purpose or mission statements and these were in constant use as focal points to shape policy and practice for students, staff and community alike. The school improvement teams, which represented all the *stakeholders* in the school communities in pursuing the strategies for raising standards of learning, were conversant with the language and ideas of total quality but this knowledge was subservient to the main educational aim of raising achievement.

This last point seemed to me to be the key to success. In these schools there was a clear commitment to improve, a belief that they could improve and a very rigorous and professionally challenging attitude towards seeking ways of improving the focal processes of teaching and learning. In the words of Deming, *they had driven out fear*. They were engrossed in the task of improving the *process* of learning together. They did not have overt inspection systems for they were engaged in constant self-review.

The application of lessons learned to Wisewood School

I returned to my headship at Wisewood School in the autumn of 1995 pondering how I might set about using my experiences of the previous twelve months to build upon the work currently being undertaken in the school. The task of post-secondment re-entry can be difficult and at times a rather frustrating time. One arrives back into the school, invigorated by the secondment experience and keen to divest one's new-found insights onto colleagues who are ploughing on with the reality of the daily round of teaching and learning, break-time duties, wet Friday lunchtimes and mountains of marking and report writing in the evenings. In the case of the returning headteacher the dangers of upsetting one's colleagues with the over-enthusiastic espousal of new ideas and the imposition of 'yet another initiative' are even greater.

My secondment experiences and the benchmarking visit to the United States had persuaded me that there were two main areas in which I wanted to concentrate my work and in which I believed I might have a real contribution to make. Fortunately in the context of Wisewood School the two areas of interest were to overlap to a significant degree and both had the added advantage of matching the school's needs over the ensuing months.

First, I was keen to find ways of focusing the attention of the school community back onto the central function of a school, that is raising the standards of achievement of the pupils. For a variety of reasons, both internal and external, I believe we had rather lost track of the fact that this was the central rôle of the school. I had rediscovered that central belief in my benchmarking visits. I had also seen that the management structure and processes in the best-practice school improvement projects in Maryland were designed to naturally concentrate the minds and energies of the whole school community on the tasks of learning and teaching. They were concentrating in teams on process, using a significant amount of measurement to check progress and maintaining a high level of classroom monitoring and evaluation to seek ways to raise their effectiveness as schools. How could I develop the Wisewood structures and processes towards this end? The answers to the last question were not difficult to find in terms of an action plan framework. They could be summed up in two short phrases:

- the need to address school budgetary problems; and
- living through an OFSTED inspection process.

The successful implementation of the plan might prove to be a little more problematic!

Budgetary problems – restructuring for involvement and focus on learning

On returning to Wisewood I was aware that I would be facing the problem of a likely budgetary overspend for 1995–96 of £70,000. This was the outcome of a situation which had been developing over several years and which, despite reductions in staffing of 30 per cent compared to eight years previous, still remained obstinately with us. Over the same time our pupil numbers had stayed virtually constant. There were obviously other factors at work and supported and abetted by the LEA we set about the process of identifying the causes of some of our budgetary problems so that we may then start to plan a strategy for improvement.

The practical nature of the task was inevitably quite complex and at times rather taxed my own grasp of statistics, but in essence the work was simple in concept. The school became involved in a pilot study to map out the distribution of its spending plan in relation to the main functions of teaching, non-contact time, management structure and management time. Once this work was complete we could begin to match the data against other information such as average teaching group size at Key Stage 3 and Key Stage 4. From the initial pilot study of six schools it became apparent that certain trends in the profile of our spending plans were leading us to ask certain pointed questions about our management decision-making processes, e.g. the proportion of management non-contact time as opposed to the proportion of basic curriculum non-contact time and the level of staffing required for the school when matched against basic curriculum non-contact time.

It became apparent that we needed to develop this work into a proper benchmarking exercise in order to obtain a more balanced view about our six pilot schools and other schools in the city. The work was therefore repeated across all secondary schools in the city, under the direction and leadership of the Authority's senior secondary inspector, Phil Budgell. Wisewood clearly had historically chosen to spend higher proportions of the staffing budget on basic curriculum non-contact time and the responsibility structure than most other schools, at the same time spending relatively lower levels of the budget on management non-contact time. This work had begun to suggest that if we were to reduce the cost of our responsibility structure and change the balance of non-contact time we could make significant in-roads into the budgetary problems we faced.

It has to be placed on record that these conclusions were only part of the wider picture. There were other conclusions which arose from this work and other detailed analyses which suggested that secondary and primary schools in the city were generally underfunded when compared to other metropolitan areas. These latter points were not specific to Wisewood however and as such will not be developed within this case study.

The attempts to *measure* inputs and outputs within a *benchmarking* exercise had highlighted some questions about the *process* of decision-making in our school. It had suggested that all our attempts to work harder (remember the 30 per cent staffing cuts!) would indeed come to nothing. We had to reexamine the system and find a more effective approach to running our school and spending our money. We had to remember Deming's rule about the majority of improvement coming from systemic change rather than by working harder.

The scene was set to reexamine the management and responsibility structure of the school and within that work to reappraise some of the roles and processes. The imperative for the change seemed to the casual observer to be one of finance but for me the financial problems and challenges were providing the opportunity to address the second and more fundamental area of realigning the school's focus back to the central aspect of learning and raising levels of achievement. Changes to the responsibility structure provided the way in to the process, the OFSTED inspection was to offer the chance to build a culture of continuous improvement upon the new infrastructure.

The restructuring of staffing has removed the curriculum faculty structure, taking more decision-making power and responsibility down to the level of teachers responsible for national curriculum subjects. It has also increased the senior team from three to four so that the strategic management responsibilities of the school can be properly discharged. The senior team increase also contains a reduction in the number of deputy headteachers from two to one while making a strong bid to increase the focus of our work on teaching and learning by creating the post of teaching and learning facilitator at senior teacher level. This latter rôle was a feature of the way in which the Maryland schools had raised their awareness of the teaching and learning processes. The facilitator rôle is to work with colleagues and students on the continuous search to improve our effectiveness as teachers and learners.

As a school we intend to focus our work on appraisal but to make that focus the appraisal of the process of learning. Evidence from recent surveys into the effectiveness of appraisal to raise standards in the classroom suggests that the appraisal of teachers has not been a success story. Our rationale is that by concentrating on the *processes* of teaching and learning, including the proper monitoring and evaluating of the classroom activities we will be able to appraise teachers but within a proper, positive and collegial pursuit to improve learning. Further comment on this aspect will be picked up again when the post-OFSTED action planning process is considered a little later in the chapter.

The description of the restructuring procedure in a single chapter cannot do justice to the welter of detailed consultation, paper writing and redrafting, meeting time and nervous energy that in reality goes into the task. Colleagues currently in post feel threatened, governors need time to accommodate ideas and sort out their own views, officers and advisers of the LEA are consulted and offer much needed support, teacher associations are involved and all of this is taking place alongside the usual daily functioning of the school. In the case of Wisewood we were also working our way through this gestation period while preparing for the arrival of the OFSTED inspection late in the autumn term. Some of my colleagues were not slow to tell me that, in their opinion, my timing was not good. In my own mind I knew that if we were to survive at all as a school we simply had no choice but to face the financial problems and work out a strategy which would position our school more favourably for the future. I was also keen to drive the school to a point where it could build positively for the future when faced by the onset of the next financial year and at a time when we would be into the *process* of post-OFSTED action planning, the latter being my second major strand for school improvement in Wisewood.

School inspection 1995 – action planning for improvement

By December 1995 the governors of Wisewood had progressed in their informal consultations with staff on proposed changes to the responsibility structure. We had lived through some very difficult times as I had sought to convince colleagues that my reasons for proposing change were not solely budget based but once it was agreed by governors that they would offer salary protection to colleagues currently in post then the wider educational and management arguments began to prevail.

At this time, December 1995, the school was inspected by an OFSTED team. Although the previous inspection had been carried out by an HMI team, the December 1995 inspection was our second inspection in four years. We hoped we were about to benefit from the experience of the second inspection having a base line from which to work in terms of measuring our progress since 1991.

In many ways we were not disappointed. The report reflected on the school as they had observed it within the framework for inspection but also referred back to the findings of the 1991 inspection. The report (OFSTED, 1996) concluded that

> *Wisewood is an improving school and has raised standards following the report of Her Majesty's Inspectors in May 1991 ... Standards of achievement have been steadily improving over five years and the number of pupils achieving five GCSEs at Grades A–C has risen from 20 per cent to 38 per cent of entries ... The quality of education ... is characterised by responsive and participative pupils and hard-working staff. Both co-operate to provide an environment in which good quality learning and teaching can take place.*

Comments such as these were very gratifying but, as always, there were still areas for improvement. The key issues listed in the report included:

- resolve the budgetary problems of the school within a planned timescale in order to provide a secure and stable basis for further development
- to further develop strategies to raise the standards of achievement of all pupils but particularly the attainment of boys
- to prepare a new development plan for the school which has clear achievable short, medium and long term objectives, together with success criteria and costings.

These three key issues were very convenient for the next stage of the process of moving towards the improving school as they, in turn, gave further impetus to the need to press ahead with the restructuring work in terms of the financial savings required, as well as allowing our post-inspection action planning process to be heavily concentrated on the tasks of development planning in a more clearly defined way. In particular it supported and encouraged us to move ahead on the plans to focus our improvement activity on the teaching and learning work of the school. It also suggested that the decision to rearrange senior and middle management responsibilities to accentuate the importance of this work was vindicated.

It was at this point that I was able to call on my secondment experience with Royal Mail for an approach to the production of the action plan. From the point of view of the OFSTED inspection process it may seem that the requirement to produce an action plan within forty working days seems an effective way of committing the school to become involved quickly in the improvement process ('improvement through inspection'). The reality for most schools is that the timescale for the production of the plan provides very little scope for proper consultation and involvement of the pupils, staff, parents and even governors. Without a proper planning process mapped out, a balance struck between consultation and direction and major efforts to keep all informed of their part in the process, the post-inspection action planning period can become a period of confusion and disillusionment.

Charged with the task of producing a development plan within the action planning process we decided to concentrate on the response to the key issues of the OFSTED report as our first priority. Within the planning process for producing a new development plan we then scheduled the 'non-key issue' work for later in the spring and summer terms. The process in itself was generated by the senior team taking proposals to a joint meeting (middle and senior management group) to work up a suggested plan to take to governors and which, in fact, the latter group were happy to accept. The governors were attached to the curricular and pastoral areas in order that the former might consult with the latter over the inspection findings and begin to develop a 'feel' for the direction in which the action plan should go.

After the initial consultation meetings between governors and staff it was agreed that the optimum way of striking a balance between consulting with colleagues and also keeping to the forty-day schedule was to use the school's fortnightly joint meeting agendas to lead brainstorming sessions in order to develop lists of success factors which were felt by the groups to be important if success was to be achieved by the implementation of the action plan. Senior team members led the brainstorming sessions. The ideas were then list-reduced to arrive at the critical success factors for each key issue. In turn each critical success factor was discussed in relation to actions which should be followed in order to achieve success. Thus for each key issue we developed:

- a description of the current state
- a 'fishbone' diagram showing the key issue summary statement (Level 1) and the critical success factors (CSFs) (Level 2) identified for attainment of success in relation to the key issue
- a series of Level 3 actions necessary to achieve each of the Level 2 CSFs. Each Level 2 statement was provided with criteria for success, targets, timescales, costings and monitoring responsibilities.

Hence our action plan was developed along the lines of a business process map, at differing levels of detail. Development plans tend towards 'wordiness'. We were keen to produce a document which could become a work-book and to which people would refer frequently to check progress, hence the format shown which enables the user to record progress through the stages.

The action plan included the task of producing a revised development plan. This involves a framework which results in whole school issues continuing to be pursued through departments as well as individual departmental matters being introduced. At the departmental level we have restricted ourselves to a maximum of six major action points. Better to attempt fewer actions and to give yourself a chance of success! We are currently (July 1996) working up the departmental level development plans having spent some meeting time to discuss process lessons learned in the earlier stages of the action plan.

Total Quality approaches to school improvement strategies: an evaluation of the story so far

When one lives so close to a project it is difficult to be objective but I do feel that we can already identify some of the more obvious outcomes and lessons learned from our attempt to marry the approaches of Total Quality Management to theories of school improvement.

School improvement is more likely to occur when there are real threats to overcome. In the case of Wisewood School we were facing financial oblivion. Failure to act was not an option for us. We had to do something.

School inspection does not, of itself, bring about improvement. What it does do is to act as a catalyst for change and provide incentives and support for improvement activity. It helps to develop the realisation that improvement is needed.

Planning processes for improvement is a relatively neglected area (OFSTED 1995). Without the background to Quality Management principles and approaches we would have found it very difficult to manage the complexities of action planning within the relatively tight timescale allowed by OFSTED. It is important that the action planning process for schools is supported by the LEA and OFSTED themselves. At the moment schools are left largely to their own devices, unless they are identified as 'failing'. Such an enormous investment in the inspection process is in danger of being squandered if the deployment of the action plans is not supported and monitored. Wisewood School was fortunate to be included in the first tranche of schools to receive extra GEST monies to support the implementation of the action plan. The provision of extra resources to spend on the implementation of the plan makes it potentially a very powerful mechanism for improvement but only if there is a guidance and monitoring system to support schools in the planning process.

At Wisewood we have made progress with our action plans but still have much to do. Successful action planning will only come about if schools are realistic about workload and do not try to achieve too much too soon. It is important to prioritise the areas for action, to give realistic timescales for action and to set challenging but attainable targets. Heroic goals are fine but we should accept that there are limits. The phasing in of the development plan by working on the action plan first has provided a mechanism to learn as we go and to allow feedback from those involved in the earlier sections of work.

Measurable outcomes?

As yet the outcomes of our work are still in embryonic form. Change is taking place in the classrooms but measurable outcomes will take some time to appear. We have taken part in the Keele University Attitudinal Surveys of parents and pupils and consequently have considerable data from which to measure future progress. For the same reason we are currently engaging in pupil and parent focus group discussions in the areas of raising attainment and reporting to parents. We also have, unofficially, the outcomes of the OFSTED Parent Survey conducted prior to the inspection. The 1996 results to Key Stage 3 tests and GCSE will be with us shortly but given the shortness of the time since the inception of the action plan work we would be surprised to see obvious trends at this early stage. For the last few years since the 1991 inspection Wisewood has seen a major improvement in GCSE examination results while the ability profile of the year groups has remained broadly similar. We appear to be more effective as a school. The real test will come as we see if these improvements continue to show a steady upward trend of the averages.

On the financial front we have worked through our restructuring consultation process to the point of implementation. We now know that we have addressed the financial problems to the limits of what we currently think possible, commensurate with the continued effective operation of our school. When combined with the income derived from actual and projected rising numbers of pupils on roll, Wisewood will be back in the black within two years.

The discussions around the educational arguments for restructuring combined with a supportively challenging OFSTED report on raising standards of learning and achievement has certainly brought about a more rigorous climate of conversation and analysis within the development planning process. We have a much more positive approach to monitoring and evaluation, and colleagues are much more accepting of the idea of measurement and asking the educational customer for their views. There is a genuine desire to look outside the school and to benchmark against good and best practice in other schools.

The general climate within the LEA for much of this work has been improved significantly by the creation of a Sheffield Centre for School Improvement, which is a broad partnership of support for school improvement activity involving the two universities in the city, Sheffield TEC, the tertiary college, the Cutlers' Company, private business and the City Council. The work of the Centre is co-ordinated by the Local Education Authority under the direction of a senior officer of the Authority.

The next steps?

The work described in this chapter is unfinished. The next steps for Wisewood are to continue the deployment of the action plan, taking care to facilitate and guard the quality process. We may give ourselves permission to take different directions to the ones in which we set out, provided that they make sense in the light of new evidence or experience. As always in schools we must strike the balance between keeping to our agenda for improvement as originally conceived and being responsive to the ever-changing context in which we have our place.

At a recent talk on leadership given by General Sir Michael Rose, former UN Commander in Bosnia, he expressed the view that one of the ingredients to successful leadership was the ability to take decisions. He proffered the view that it seldom made any difference *what* the decision was as long as *a* decision was taken. To decide whether to go left, right, backwards or forwards was not crucial. The main objective was to move and avoid getting shot! Sometimes I wonder if that strategy is equally applicable to school improvement.

References

DES (1992), *Wisewood School – A Report by HMI*, London, Department of Education and Science.

EFQM (1994), *Self-Assessment Guidelines – European Quality Award*, European Foundation for Quality Management.

EFQM (1995), *Self-Assessment Guidelines for Public Sector: Education*, European Foundation for Quality Management.

Machin, P., Sisum, C., Waxman, D. and Tomlinson, H. (1995), *School Improvement in the USA – Report of an LEA International Study Visit*, Sheffield Education Services.

OFSTED (1995), *Planning Improvement: Schools' post inspection action plans*, London, HMSO.

OFSTED (1996), *Report on Wisewood School, Sheffield LEA*, London, OFSTED.

Commentary – total quality perspectives in schools

BRENT DAVIES AND JOHN WEST-BURNHAM

These descriptions of the decision to adopt and then to implement Total Quality raise a number of significant issues in the relationship between theory and practice in school management. In all three cases there was a perceived need to find a mechanism that was going to support increased effectiveness or improvement. The pressure for schools to become 'better' has been a consistent theme of the past ten years. How that process of improvement is to be carried out is less clear. In many cases the response has been to work harder. Professional integrity and commitment has been the basis of many of the strategies adopted. While this is an essential component, it is not a substitute for a coherent, integrated and holistic approach to the issues facing school leaders and managers.

For many commercial and public sector organisations Total Quality provided just such an approach. Both as a theoretical construct and as a bridge between theory and practice Total Quality appears to offer a packaged solution. Yet, as the case studies make abundantly clear, the first step in the process of adoption was investigation and adaptation. There is no monolithic construct called Total Quality, or if there is it only appears in academic texts. Rather there is a range of principles and practices which have to be understood, interpreted, defined, applied and then modified to suit a given context. Samuel and Sisum place great emphasis on the process of translating the range of theoretical perspectives into a model that has coherence in a specific situation. In both accounts it is the process of assimilation which helps to create acceptance and understanding.

This approach helps to develop a response to the concern that Total Quality is an alien construct as far as schools are concerned. As exemplified in the texts or practised in a commercial organisation it probably is. But it is very difficult to think of any educational theory that is not modified, adapted and sometimes corrupted by managers and teachers in schools. This is the way in which meaning is created and the process outlined in these case studies parallels exactly the experience of many commercial organisations.

Another significant feature of both studies, and a potential concern in professionally staffed organisations, is that the decision to investigate Total Quality was taken by the headteacher, thus giving it an immediate significance and status. Although Samuel and Sisum both describe how they immediately sought wider involvement, the question remains: to what extent was Total Quality imposed? Both writers in this section are very honest about tensions and concerns associated with the introduction of a new paradigm. This concern is reflected in all organisations who have sought to introduce Total Quality. Without proactive and confident leadership the change is unlikely to occur, the negative corollary of this is that collegiality and commitment may be sacrificed, but they then have to be recreated.

What appears to have happened in both schools is a process of rapid involvement, incorporation and shared learning. It is highly significant that the case studies refer to the involvement of all staff and students and full use is made of a range of learning and developmental activities. In other words the process of understanding and implementation becomes a Total Quality activity in its own right.

A further characteristic of the case studies is the use of external advice, support and consultancy. More significantly that advice was expert and able to draw on a range of practical experiences. For many schools, obtaining appropriate, authoritative and valid advice is a problem. There is no shortage of those willing to offer (and charge for) help but as Samuel shows such help has to be mediated and implemented on the school's terms. Consultancy on Total Quality is very expensive but this is balanced by the social commitment of many Total Quality companies who are willing to share and enter into partnerships with schools. In this sense Total Quality has been a significant catalyst for creating genuine and focused links between schools and business.

Both examples are secondary schools and clearly the strategies they describe may not be available to smaller schools. However, it should be noted that the first educational organisation to obtain BS 5750 (now known as BS ENO ISO9000) certification was a primary school and that many primary schools have developed a response to Total Quality which is appropriate to their size and needs. It is worth reiterating that Total Quality only has meaning in a specific context where the principles have been translated into appropriate practice, i.e. have been made 'fit for the purpose'. One of the important points to emerge from Samuel's discussion was how the application of quality techniques helped to improve and refine that which was already being done. The issue of consistency is a real one for schools but, as Samuel shows it is possible to apply techniques which increase confidence in the consistency of student experiences and simplify systems and processes.

There is an obvious danger of bureaucracy in all this. Quality assurance in particular offers a wonderful opportunity to those who delight in the design of forms as a significant professional activity. However, as has been demonstrated in the case studies, this concern is mitigated if any system or process is contextualised by values and a sharp focus on the core purpose of the school–student learning.

Both examples refer to the process of externally imposed inspection by OFSTED. For many in the quality movement in England and Wales OFSTED's mission – improvement through inspection – is a classic oxymoron. As a means of demonstrating one type of public accountability OFSTED may have a rôle. As a means of supporting improvement it is much more problematic. Certainly, as Samuel and Sisum demonstrate, the use of quality techniques can pre-empt many of the OFSTED requirements. Equally the inspection report can provide useful corroborative data but in the context of Total Quality the OFSTED process is artificial, disruptive and disproportionately expensive.

This highlights the experience of many schools in the USA; the development of Total Quality in an individual school can be constrained by the political and accountability environment in which it has to operate. If the prevailing culture is one of control then it is difficult to envisage how a school could develop a Quality Management system which has integrity. Educationalists might look at business concerns with some envy; superficially at least they appear to have autonomy to devise and develop their own management philosophy. The truth is very different; an organisation like the Royal Mail has to work within government requirements with regard to policy as well as the common context of employment law, commercial practice, etc. Total Quality offers a means of creating an appropriate management culture and of responding to the demands of the external world.

Schools are very different in spite of a decade of central government imperatives; there are still significant opportunities to develop uniqueness. All the evidence we have indicates a wide variety of responses to the central issue of how schools are to be managed. These case studies show the response of schools using the same broad principles but interpreting and applying them in different ways. Perhaps the most important message is that they see themselves as embarking upon a journey, a process, rather than having found a neat packaged solution. In each case the leadership and management of the school is being determined by an evolutionary model based on a view of student learning rather than spurious notions of efficiency or the institutionalisation of pragmatism and reactivity.

PART FIVE

■ ■ ■

Quality strategies

8

■　■　■

Leadership – for the few, or for all?

ALAN MURPHY

The senior management kettle

Let me start with a true story. The scene is an open area next to the head's and deputy's offices of a primary school in the south of England. There is a work-top, sink and kettle. A teacher is wilting at the end of an exhausting day with her little darlings. Having been on duty at morning break and having grabbed a sandwich and apple at lunchtime – while updating a display – she reaches for the kettle. The door of the deputy head's office opens. The deputy looks aghast. 'What are you doing?' 'Putting the kettle on.' is the rather obvious reply. 'But that's the senior management team kettle!' cries the horrified deputy. The teacher slinks off to the staffroom; she knows her place in the order of things.

Believe it, or not, that exchange did happen. Let us now rewind the tape and suggest an alternative response to the tired teacher from the deputy head. 'Kathy, you look all in – let me make you a cup of tea.'

Making a cup of tea can be a significant act of leadership

The simple act of making a cup of tea for a colleague can be a greater act of leadership than many competencies that you might find listed in a handbook of management. Even if we consider my example so outrageous that it could never happen in your school, it has to be said that the SMT kettle is the metaphor for a myriad of other status symbols which increase the divide between 'senior management' and the 'footsoldiers'. For the SMT kettle, read SMT non-contact time, SMT comfortable offices, and various other actual or perceived privileges. Remember that perceptions are all and even perceived privileges can become bricks in a wall which divides a school community.

A community without walls

The opportunity which a new millennium gives for fresh starts, clean slates, new ways of thinking should be taken. We may not have much choice; in an era of greater and greater accountability we are being asked to contribute to significant increases in the achievement levels of young people; challenging national targets are rightly being ratcheted upwards. It is not enough to stand still; we have a duty to our young people to help them to realise their gifts for their benefit and for the benefit of society in a fast-changing world.

The present model of school organisation is a serious limiting factor

I would like to argue that the present model of school organisation is a serious limiting factor preventing the unleashing of the potential of the young people in our care. We have to accept that, in the minds of the opinion-formers, our schools turn out more 'failures' than they do 'successes'. We may try as hard as we can to point out how valuable D, E, or F, GCSE grades are, but it is simply not accepted by Joe Public. Josephine or Joseph Public look for A–C grades, and at least five of those, as the indicator of educational success at the end of the years of compulsory schooling.

As fewer than 50 per cent of the school population is currently achieving that modest goal, we are in a weak position to defend the case that our schools are not failing the majority of our young people. We can all list the other, non-GCSE achievements, that schools help young people to attain but politicians of all persuasions will continue to measure us against a simple yardstick, no matter how much we may protest. Some might argue that even the five+ A–C yardstick is too low and too narrow in a fast changing world. So let's stop protesting and start improving the lot of our young people.

The hierarchical model of organisation, in which most of the power and influence is in the hands of a few staff, may have been suitable when the school itself settled for helping the few to succeed, while the majority were abandoned as failures. For new levels of success we need new models of organisation. We need a model in which genuine responsibility and accountability is devolved as close to the learning process as possible. The principle is not new. The movement towards flatter management structures and supporting those 'close to the customer' has been the trend in industry and in education throughout the 1990s and indeed well before.

Too often, however, the change to a flatter model has been inspired by economics rather than by the search for a more effective way of working. Too often the move has been half-hearted and half-baked. If in schools you simply reduce the number of deputies, but do not change the culture you may save a few thousand pounds, but you will not necessarily improve the performance of the organisation. Ill-thought out restructuring can weaken an organisation, rather than turn it into a more effective learning community.

A new model?

What type of model do we want if we are to organise ourselves to meet the challenges of the new millennium? There is no one model: the circumstances already in place in your school will determine what the starting point is and probably where the end will be. Good human resource management is not about morale-sapping purges which take out layers of people without thought for the individuals involved. However, we must remember that the most important individuals in a school are the students; the key is to get the balance right. We wanted evolution rather than revolution, but evolution on fast forward rather than freeze frame.

The head of a secondary school is responsible for anything from 50 to 150 or more teachers and support staff. Most of the teachers will be highly qualified and well-trained graduates. Support staff will also be intelligent and potentially creative colleagues. They may be less qualified purely because of circumstances, perhaps because their schools were among those geared for the success of the few rather than the many.

Let us use a nice round figure – 100 staff – teachers, support staff, which include classroom and administrative and technical assistants. The annual salary bill will be close to £2,000,000. Can one person – a headteacher – ensure every one of those 100 people works to his/her full potential? Impossible, especially when the head has one or two other things to be keeping an eye on as well. For example, managing that £2m+ budget and ensuring that there is enough in the pot to ensure that the roof leaks are plugged and the latest health and safety regulations are complied with. Not forgetting the small matter of the curriculum, or handling the latest crisis caused by an aggressive 16-year-old with even more aggressive parents!

The traditional solution to coping with a huge range of responsibilities is the 'senior management team'; perhaps two or three deputies and possibly a couple of senior teachers in a larger school with up to 150 staff. In my opinion, such a team may well manage a school very well, but will have little chance of releasing the full potential of the other 95 professionals who belong to the school community.

Teachers harbour extraordinary leadership qualities

Roland Barth, Professor of Education at Harvard University and formerly a school principal, accepts that during his years as a principal he underestimated the potential of his colleagues. He used to think that he shared leadership but accepts that he fell well short of achieving a 'community of leaders'. In *Improving Schools from Within*, Barth (1990) writes:

> *Teachers harbour extraordinary leadership capabilities, and their leadership is a major untapped resource for improving our nation's schools. All teachers can lead ... Leadership is making things happen that you believe in or envision. Everyone deserves a chance.* (p. 124)

I would add that the 'everyone' should include support staff who, given the right support, can become very significant leaders in their own right. If the leadership is perceived – and don't forget perception can be everything in human resource management – to be the sole preserve of the SMT, two problems can result. First, the 90 per cent of staff who are not part of the SMT will, consciously or subconsciously, be less inclined to exercise leadership roles and second, the SMT are likely to be so stretched with *management* tasks that they are unlikely to be able to devote sufficient time to *leadership*.

In the worst cases, these two problems interact to produce a spiral of decline. If a school is having a difficult time, the staff put the blame on the SMT and the SMT blame the staff (or individuals among the staff) for the problems they are having to firefight. In how many 'failing schools' is this the scenario? So how do we involve more in management and leadership?

The cliché 'every teacher is a manager' has been around for a long time. Let us tell the story of Ernest. The staff have gathered in the staffroom for a meeting at which the head is to unveil the new management structure for the school. On arrival all are given a handout; a good tradition in school meetings. Papers are issued at the meeting to ensure no one has time to give any thought to them! The paper has a diagram that looks like the web of spider on speed. All find their place on this new management structure except Ernest, who looks up and down every line, but he cannot find his name. Assuming a mistake has been made he quietly points this omission out to the head as the baffled staff disperse. 'Oh no, Ernest, there is no mistake. If all the rest of us are to be managers, you become the key person in the organisation – the managee – we will all need someone to manage', explains the head as he dives for the shelter of his office. Acknowledgements to Ted Wragg who told the story in one of his enjoyable Friday pieces in the *TES*.

St Edward's school – 'learning together'

The aim of this chapter is to put forward an alternative model for school management and leadership – a model which is actually being put into practice in a comprehensive school in Dorset – St Edward's School, Poole. It is a case study based on more than five years of development. Our aim was to build a learning community in which not only the students reached their potential but the staff did as well. As well as aiming to be a community of learners, we aim to become a community of leaders.

Perhaps at this point I should provide a definition of leadership. There are many definitions, but one I find helpful is described by Dr Paul Taffinder (1995), a consultant with Coopers and Lybrand.

> *management is complex, fragmented, its activities brief, opportunistic, predominantly verbal; leadership is more so. Management reacts. Leadership transforms. It makes a difference.* (p. 37)

In a school where all staff are managers, much will be achieved, for as you see from the above definition, the difference between leadership and management is a subtle one. In the community of leaders, the school moves from achievement to transformation. Eventually, all are involved in the vision, all play an active part in transforming the organisation, not simply managing it. It takes time, it does not happen overnight, but as the community of leaders matures, more and more become involved and this includes all involved in the school, the governors, the parents and most important of all the students.

Where does one start?

Starting with the 'end in mind' is one of Stephen Covey's *Seven Habits of Highly Effective People*. We can all feel that there are too many obstacles in front of us which deter us from thinking afresh. Stephen Covey (1992, p. 42) argues that leaders must have a sense of purpose:

> *I have created the future in my mind. I can see it, and I can imagine what it will be like.*

Towards a community of leaders

In our case, there were two elements to develop if we were to become a community of leaders:

1. **Mission** – to involve all in the development of the vision for our school; the defining of our purpose. The mission statement would try to bring together core values and key aims. It is the combination of these which would make the school distinctive.

2. **Teams** – to organise all people within well-led coherent teams. To these teams would be devolved responsibility. They would be accountable but would be strongly supported as they worked to fulfil their responsibilities.

The two aims described above interact with each other. Without a clearly defined purpose, the teams created cannot be expected to work towards a common goal. Without coherent teams it would be very difficult to ensure that all work in harmony.

Mission – where are we going?

A good mission statement should be brief enough to be memorable, but challenging enough to make one think. It will provide a clear framework, but there will also be scope for creative interpretation. It will not be a rigid dictum seeking compliance, but it will harness commitment.

St Edward's was granted a change of character in 1991. From being a small Catholic secondary modern school, it would break away from the town's selective system to become a comprehensive school. As the school had, for many years, welcomed Christians of other traditions into the school, it seemed the appropriate time to also become one of the few joint Roman Catholic – Church of England schools in the country. The town would be offered a comprehensive and pluralistic alternative to the selective system but the school would specifically aim to serve the church communities of the town. The mission statement had to reflect that.

As we would be trying to develop a comprehensive school within a selective system, it was important that we worked with our principal feeder schools; they had to be an integral part of our mission, if we were to hope to attract the whole ability range into our school. They had to be committed to us and so we had to be committed to them. We decided to work together to draw up a shared mission statement.

A task team was formed comprising six people, two from each of three schools. None were members of 'senior management'. They were given very simple terms of reference.

- To produce a statement that would cover no more than one side of A4, but which would encompass the values and aims shared by our schools.
- To consult and involve all in our communities in the drawing up of the statement.

The only rôle for the heads of the school was to resource the project, i.e. provide non-contact time to enable people to meet. The status of the project would have been devalued if staff had been required to hold their meetings at the end of the teaching day, apart from the fact that at such a time they are unlikely to be at their most creative. The process took about six months; team members would attend full governors' meetings at all three schools, attend PTA meetings, consult colleagues and students, drafting and redrafting on the basis of comments received. This was the final statement:

Mission statement – St Edward's School

> *Jesus says – Where people come together in my name,
> I am with them.*
> Matthew 18: 20
>
> As a Christian learning community, which promotes the value of family life, we support the parents as primary educators of their children. We challenge every student to strive for the highest standard of personal, social and intellectual development, and aim for excellence in all they do. We recognise that all children are unique and aim to guide them along their personal Journey of Faith. During the day to day life of our school and in all aspects of the curriculum we promote Gospel values.
>
> We provide opportunities for every member of our community to experience prayer, worship and reflection.
>
> *My commandment is this – Love one another just as I love you . . .*
> John 15: 12

This is, of course, a statement very specific to a church school, for if a church school does not offer something distinctive and is not rooted in the values of the churches served, what justification is there for the existence of such a school? The statement fronts every scheme of work, each year's prospectus and information packs provided for staff appointments. We have not gone as far as one school which has a copy on the inside of each staff toilet door. While arguably an ideal place for a few moments quiet contemplation, one suspects that if all the staff come to associate the school's core values with that particular location, the school may be about to go down the drain! No suggestions that they will be heading for the bottom of the league tables, please!

Back to our mission statement which has become a living part of the school and indeed spawned a few offspring. We have taken two slogans from phrases within the statement. *'Learning Together'*, in two words, reminds us of our commitment to comprehensive education, of the fact that fellow Christians learn together, and that staff and students are, together, members of a learning community. *'Aiming for Excellence'*, is used on reports, certificates of achievements and above noticeboards to remind all of the challenge that we have set ourselves. Carefully chosen slogans can be a very valuable way of bringing statements of core aims or values into every day use. Translate them into Latin if you wish to forget them!

A final point to make on the issue of mission statements is to suggest that the actual words you finish up with matter less than the process followed to achieve the statement. Getting everyone to discuss the values of the school can take some doing. Suggest that a mission statement would be a good idea and you will get reaction right away – the discussion has started.

Towards teams

Developing a mission statement is the easy part of restructuring a school. The other essential element, that I argued for earlier, was the development of coherent teams whose responsibility would be to put the mission into practice. This is more of a challenge. The apocryphal story, *'If I was going to Cork, I wouldn't start from here'* springs to mind. Whenever I explain the development of our new structure, three responses are common. Some suggest that you need timely retirements, or even redundancies to produce significant change. Others suspect that the only motive is to reduce costs and the third group fear that such changes – downsizing in current business jargon – will lead to the deputy head becoming an endangered species.

There is some truth in all three responses. A retirement can facilitate a rethink, but it is by no means essential. Yes, you can save money restructuring the way we did; is it a bad thing to move more money away from management and towards the students? Endangered deputy heads? Not necessarily, although any deputy not prepared to rethink his/her role in these fast-changing times is likely to find life very frustrating. Those willing to move from administrator to leader of people are likely to find life far more rewarding, although no less stressful!

I will return to the rôle of head and deputy head in a little while; in the meantime to justify why our management structure is team based I will quote from Katzenbach and Smith (1993, p. 15)

> *In any situation requiring the real-time combination of multiple skills, experiences and judgements, a team inevitably gets better results than a collection of individuals operating within confined job roles and responsibilities. Teams are more flexible ... because they can be more quickly assembled, deployed, re-focused and disbanded ... Teams are more productive than groups ... Teams and performance are an unbeatable combination.*

The reasons for the success of TEAMS:

- TEAMS bring together complementary skills and experiences that are greater than those of any individual. Teams can call on a greater portfolio of resources than any individual and are more responsive.

- TEAMS are better at communicating and can respond with greater speed, accuracy and effectiveness.

- TEAMS 'provide a unique social dimension' developing trust and confidence which facilitate performance.
- TEAMS 'have more fun'; they are good places to be and foster personal and collective pleasure.
- TEAMS encourage personal growth and development and create a capacity to respond to change because they 'motivate, challenge, reward and support'.

Bowring-Carr and West-Burnham (1994, p. 105) argue that

> *Teams can act as a powerful antidote to the inherent tensions and artificiality of organisational life by creating a sense of encouraging and measuring performance.*

They also suggest (p. 104) the gain for the school that is able to develop effective teams:

'Effective TEAMS will:

- take less time to produce high quality decisions
- make fewer mistakes
- consistently improve their performance
- meet targets and deadlines
- incorporate externally imposed change
- enhance the performance of individuals
- distribute stress and pressure.'

Managing for excellence

St Edward's has adapted Total Quality Management, keeping all the principles but making the language more school friendly. We have called our model 'Managing for Excellence'.

Below is how the policy is described in our staff handbook.

MANAGING FOR EXCELLENCE

St Edward's management philosophy is based upon 'total quality management'; a management process adopted by many leading industrial companies. We have adopted the philosophy for the needs of a school and termed it 'Managing for Excellence'.

Key elements of the philosophy are:

- Excellence is defined as meeting the needs of those the school serves: students, parents and the wider community. We provide opportunities for those the school serves to express their wishes for the school.

- We work towards excellence by continuous improvement.

- In some aspects of our work, we accept that 100% success is the only standard worth aiming for – e.g. in the elimination of bullying.

- All staff – teachers and support staff – are equally valued and achieve success through effective teamwork.

The prime responsibility of team leaders is to provide the support and encouragement that team members need as they strive to achieve excellence for the students.

All teaching and support staff are encouraged to develop leadership skills, to consult colleagues as appropriate, but also to act decisively as the circumstances require.

Our collegiate management structure provides opportunities for responsibilities to be shared widely for personal, professional and career development and aims to ensure staff are properly rewarded for the responsibilities they carry.

Our Mission Statement, shared by our family of feeder schools, sets out our values and our aims. Each year we agree priorities and specific objectives to be achieved within the framework of the Mission Statement.

Let us now explore two of the key phrases from this policy.

Meeting the needs

'Meeting the needs of those the school serves' in TQM jargon would be described as 'delighting the customers'. The TQM jargon may be off-putting to school professionals but few would disagree with the central premise; we exist to serve students, their parents and the wider community. We take seriously the business of listening to those we serve. Any letter of complaint or concern must be followed up, not defensively, but to find out why a parent or other party is not happy.

Effective teamwork

Occasionally when I explain our team-based staffing structure which has all colleagues working within teams no larger than eight people, it will be suggested that this can only be achieved because we are a small school. St Edward's is small for a comprehensive school, but I have to admit that the organisation I took the idea from employs 40,000 people – Rank Xerox. This huge company is organised on a team basis. No employee is in a team of larger than eight members and equally important no one is a member of more than three teams.

At Rank Xerox your base team is known as your 'family group'. You will be a member of a second team and perhaps a third team. One of these may be a 'cross-functional' team perhaps bringing together sales, design and engineering specialists but, importantly, these project teams are not committees.

> The chief difference between a team and a committee is dependence. Team-mates have to depend upon each other. Committee members 'represent a point of view'. Peters (1989)

Let us now explore how the Rank Xerox team model works in practice at St Edward's School. We have brought together the traditional model of school organisation, with a more carefully structured and planned arrangement, which tries to ensure that the teams are not teams in name only, but are autonomous self-managing teams able to act in a very effective way.

'Curriculum' teams

Bowring-Carr and West-Burnham (1994) agree that all staff should be organised into teams of six to eight, but argue that 'family' teams should not be subject teams, even in a secondary school. We felt that there were a number of advantages in evolving from our traditional subject based faculty structure rather than starting from scratch with a new approach. The faculty mix of subjects is less important than compatibility of prospective fellow team members. We joined our small PE department with the Science Department. There are some curriculum links, e.g. health related fitness, but it was important that the PE team felt they were part of a larger family to which they could relate well. The team leader, the faculty head could support them in a number of ways, e.g. scheme of work, development planning, budgeting, timetable requirements, but in many ways they are a self-managing team within a team and we see no problem with this as long as they accept the responsibility that goes with self-management.

Bowring-Carr and West-Burnham (1994, p. 108) ask a series of questions to test any new 'flatter team structure' against hierarchical tendencies. They suggest that if you answer 'YES' to their questions you are working in a hierarchy. Let us test our new structure against some of these criteria:

Does a minority of people have a higher level of personal resources (offices, clerical support, etc.)?

NO. A new comfortable staffroom was designed by the staff and includes an attractive well-furnished working area, with networked computers available. Each faculty also has a base, most of them larger than the head's or deputy's office. All staff have equal access to high quality clerical support. No reserved car parking for the head!

Does the majority have to obtain approval or permission from the minority?

NO. Capitation and INSET budgets are delegated to teams who make decisions as to how they should be spent or saved against team development plan priorities. One colleague of another local school has taken things further than we have by giving the teams the choice of spending money on responsibility allowances, support staff, non-contact time, or additional capitation. Financial constraints have, to date, limited our development along these lines but the principle is spot on.

Also note the clear statement in the 'Managing for Excellence' policy. '*All teaching and support staff are encouraged to develop leadership skills, to consult colleagues as appropriate, but also to act decisively as the circumstances require.*' Some heads get offended when they find out that an event has been planned that they know nothing about. I am delighted! Yes, of course, this has some risks but then risk-taking is part of strong leadership. Peters (1989) recalls a useful metaphor from the late Bill Gore, founder of the company which makes Gore-Tex products. 'You can try anything as long as it is above the "waterline" . . . If you want to drill holes below the waterline' (p. 264) he'd add the equivalent of 'check with your team leader'. A colleague organising a skiing trip does not take risks on safety and follows every county safety guideline to the letter, but they choose how to organise any fund-raising activities and so on. Teachers do not take risks with GCSE examination entry procedures but decide themselves how best to maximise the number gaining 'C' grades or above. Extra revision lessons after school; up to the team. It works. Professionals know what is 'above and below the waterline'.

Take away constraints and you liberate creativity, build 'permission' barriers and you stifle development.

Are there posts and meetings with the specific purpose of co-ordinating and liaising?

I have to answer YES to this one without apology. I believe we do need a special needs co-ordinator who leads a team – it would be called 'cross-functional' by Rank Xerox – who ensure that policies are developed which have support from all curriculum and pastoral teams.

Are there graduated levels of responsibility and access to information?

YES and NO to the final question. Our 'collegiate management structure' does not aim to be totally flat; if someone takes on additional responsibility, for example, as an examinations officer, he/she should be paid for that. The aim is to make the pyramid flatter but not flatten it. NO to restricted access to information; open access 'above the waterline'. The metaphor in this case could apply to the graphic details of a child abuse hearing. If access was too open it could hurt a child and thus be 'below the waterline'. The guideline in a situation like this is that the person/s closest to the child needs the information; it does not relate to seniority. That person, no matter how 'junior' is trusted to handle such sensitive information correctly.

Pastoral teams

For over twenty years, pious statements have been made by secondary schools that there is no pastoral and academic divide, but traditional structures have made it very difficult to truly empower the form tutor who should be the key pastoral person – she or he is the person pastorally closest to the child. The year tutor/head of year/head of house and so on should be a team leader, supporting the tutors in carrying out pastoral work. Our form tutors do function as the prime pastoral person supporting each student. I would suggest that there are a number of reasons why this has been achieved:

- The title of year tutor is chosen – language is important. Head of year implies a hierarchical approach.
- The year tutor is not given significantly more non-contact time than the form tutor; she/he may have less non-contact time. Who can blame an overworked teacher being reluctant to take on time-consuming pastoral problems if the head of year has a half-timetable.
- The year tutor gains only one responsibility point – for the team leadership responsibility not for the pastoral responsibility.
- Teams of tutors with their team leader stay together with their forms as they move right through the school up to and until they complete their GCSE course. From induction to congratulation! This also helps to identify and clarify responsibility. Of course there are problems from time to time. It is up to the team to solve them, with support if necessary (see role of the central support team below).
- The year teams together form the tutorial faculty, so that most staff belong to two faculty teams.

Central support team

The school has no Senior Management Team. Many staff carry responsibilities that could be considered part of 'senior management' roles, but they are 'dispersed' across the school. Most team leaders will also carry a significant whole school responsibility. What people who work in a community such as ours do need is support. That is the prime role of the headteacher. My rôle is primarily to provide the resources needed by colleagues who work more directly with the students than I do.

I cannot provide this support alone; I do not have the necessary range of skills and expertise so we have a central support team. The single deputy head (reduced from two under the previous structure) is also a member of this team, but also currently acts as team leader of the faculty heads, giving them appropriate support and ensuring that their needs are brought to the central team. Support staff (we never use the demeaning negative term 'non-teaching staff') have key rôles in this team. The bursar manages finance on a day-to-day basis. An admin. officer oils the wheels. Previously acting only as the head's secretary, she now carries out a wide range of 'senior management' responsibilities, including managing all staff cover arrangements, still traditionally the preserve of a very highly paid deputy head in many schools.

One team within the central support team is the 'school maintenance team' which is composed of the bursar, caretaker, assistant caretaker, and myself. We meet half-termly to review progress and to agree and set new targets. If you say you value all staff equally, the caretaker deserves equal treatment with the same real coffee and chocolate biscuits that we make available to teachers who choose to meet in our attractively designed meeting room. Note: the staff choose if they wish to have meetings; there are many different ways to communicate and consult. Many schools are constipated by a fibre-free diet of endless meetings.

A team approach to monitoring and evaluation

'Monitoring and evaluation' is the key phrase as far as OFSTED is concerned. The new 1996 framework places responsibility for the quality of learning squarely on the shoulders of the headteacher. It rightly takes the line that leadership and management need to be looked at in terms of what is happening in the classrooms. Where does this leave a school that actively devolves responsibility away from the centre? How can the head of such an organisation monitor and evaluate the curriculum?

The chief executive of Rank Xerox is no doubt responsible for the quality of every photocopier produced under that brand name, but that does not mean she or he checks every one, or that the CEO even knows how a photocopier works. The head of a 1,500 student comprehensive told me recently that he had spent the last six months going from department to department, sitting in on lesson after lesson, to 'monitor standards'. Is this the right response to OFSTED's emphasis on monitoring? How long could such a programme of mini-inspections be maintained? Where does this leave the standing of the team leader of a department where weaknesses are exposed? Would anything new be found? Most good heads have a pretty good nose for problem areas no matter how large the school. Would those six months not have been better spent working alongside the curriculum team leaders, supporting, coaching, encouraging; acting as a critical friend, perhaps covering their lessons, while the team leader spent time in colleagues' classrooms, working with them to agree points for development.

Roland Barth (1990) suggests that direct formal evaluation can become a meaningless ritual and that it has little impact on teachers' growth and development *'or even worse, it becomes a recurring occasion to heighten anxiety and distance between teacher and principal, and competition between teacher and teacher.* (p. 56)

The team-based model should lead to more focused and more constant monitoring and evaluation as it becomes a way of life to discuss successes and problems.

The self-monitoring team

To help kick start the self-managing – and by definition self-monitoring – process at St Edward's, each team was given a day off timetable to draw up their own 'success criteria'. The team was asked to follow a programme that would enable them as valued trusted professionals to determine the characteristics of a lesson which met our mission statement demand that 'we challenge every student to strive for the highest standard . . . and aim for excellence in all they do'.

There are three stages to the process. We will use the work of the English team as an example:

- A brainstorm which allowed all team members to contribute their ideas as to what the indicators of a 'challenging' English lesson were.
- From the initial ideas, some were looked at in greater depth, e.g. use of language in the classroom, good questioning techniques.
- The outcome of these brainstorms being displayed, the team then tried to reach consensus on how each indicator of good practice should be classified against four criteria:
  - true for all of us all the time
  - true for all of us, some of the time
  - true for some of us some of the time
  - rarely seen.

Those indicators which the team agreed merited only the last two classifications were prioritised and targeted for development. Three years later, this list still fronts the English scheme of work and is arguably of a great deal more value that checklists imposed from outside.

The head of science remarked to me how open and frank colleagues in the science meeting were throughout the day. Would they have been the same if a non-team member had been present?

Outcomes

Our way of working has been evolving for nearly ten years. 'Managing for Excellence' was introduced five years ago and our team-based structure reached its present arrangement three years ago. Our first comprehensive year group (this first year group, still creamed to a degree by local grammar schools) took their GCSEs in 1995, the school achieving 63 per cent with five or more A–Cs. This placed the school only one percentage point behind the top comprehensive in the county and ahead of a number of other long-established and excellent comprehensives. The English team, three years after they analysed the 'challenging' classroom and implemented their own targets for improvement, entered the whole ability range for both English language and English Literature and achieved 74 and 76 per cent A-Cs respectively. Of course, 'league tables' are not everything, but they are a reality and they do provide a useful benchmark for a school trying to establish itself.

Final thoughts – crucial components

We still have much to do, but we now have a strong model which will, I believe, stand up well to the challenges of the coming years. I would like to conclude by suggesting a few additional key components that are needed if one is to achieve a community of leaders.

Appointing staff

Excellent staff appointments are crucial. The following procedures are common to all our appointments:

- We spend as much time as is necessary to make the best possible appointment to every single school position. We do not rely totally on conventional interviews and we are very wary of bland unstructured references. We reach our own judgements.

- All who express an interest in any appointment are sent a very full information pack. The key thing is to be quite clear and explicit about the values of the school and about the way we work, including our commitment to Total Quality Management and our no smoking policy. Better for people who do not share these values, or who are cynical about this way of working, to select themselves out at this stage and decide not to apply.

Communication

If the teams are the organs of the healthy school, good communication systems are the arteries and veins carrying information to and from the teams. Communication systems which are over reliant on paper are likely to be slow and liable to thrombosis, if one can stretch the metaphor a little further. Our daily, full staff, ten-minute briefings are purposeful, dynamic, interesting and often good fun. We save hours of dull formal meetings by having a forum for quick exchanges and at which ideas can be thrown up for comment, or for shooting down.

Staff development and leadership training

Good staff development is vital. We have achieved a lot, but we do need to spend more time considering what further leadership training is necessary and how we can further develop coaching and mentoring, which are important features of successful team based organisations.

What next? – students as leaders?

Roland Barth (1990) again: *'Being entrusted with important school-wide responsibility, brings forth (in students) leadership, maturity, and learning.'* (p. 126)

Students: not prefects, but partners – the next challenge.

References

Barth, R. S. (1990), *Improving Schools from Within*, San Francisco, Jossey-Bass.

Bowring-Carr, C. and West-Burnham, J. (1994), Managing Quality in Schools – A Training Manual, Harlow, Longman.

Covey, S. R. (1992), *Principle Centred Leadership*, London, Simon & Schuster.

Katzenbach, J. R. and Smith, D. K. (1993), *The Wisdom of Teams: Creating the High Performance Organisation*, Boston, Harvard Business School.

Peters, T. (1989), *Thriving on Chaos*, London, Pan.

Taffinder, P. (1995), *The New Leaders*, Coopers and Lybrand, London, Kogan Page.

9
■ ■ ■

The team solution

SUZANNE TAYLOR AND IAN McKENZIE

Background to the school

Eumemmerring Secondary College is the largest State (Government) School in Victoria. There are four campuses three of which are Year 7–10 and the fourth is a Year 11–12 campus, catering for the two years of the Victorian Certificate of Education. The college is situated in the South Eastern growth corridor of Victoria and has a student population of 2,600.

In recent years The Endeavour Hills Campus along with the rest of the college has undertaken a complete review of its curriculum and teaching and learning strategies, resulting in a refinement of our educational practices and policies. One of the results of this review was to examine closely the transition of students from primary school (Grade 6) to secondary school in Year 7. We felt that this was a good time to look at the gulf which seemed to exist between our Year 7, first year of secondary education and Year 6, the last year of primary education. Our college has some fourteen major feeder schools, with children coming to us from diverse social, economic and educational backgrounds.

The teachers at our campus felt that the creativity and imagination with which the children came to us from primary school was very soon snuffed out by the industrial revolution model of schooling that we were imposing on them. We were tending to ignore the skills and knowledge with which they were endowed and attempting to start anew.

Our initial response to the diverse background that the children were coming from was to 'start afresh in Year 7' with very little consideration given to previous learning. As a result there was considerable repetition of previous work which took away the excitement and challenge of secondary education. Students in primary school are used to having a home room with one teacher and perhaps one or two specialist teachers. Yet when they came to us, they were being confronted by a range of teachers, often up to nine when you consider some of the elective subjects. In addition, there were the issues of losing old friends and making new ones, new and often bigger schools, and moving from being 'top of the tree' to being the 'juniors'. Our expectations of them were unreal and had no sound educational foundation. We did not acknowledge the anxiety and trauma that some of our pupils were going through. This was turning students off and we felt we were not adding value to them.

At the same time our campus was involved with the Victorian Department of School Education's '150 Schools Project' which was later to be named the 'Quality Schools Project'. This project 'aimed to identify key factors which consistently affected the students' progress in English and mathematics, as well as those which promote a positive school climate'. The project tracked the same cohort of students over a period of three years, (1992–94). This project also demonstrated what we as teachers suspected all along; in reading and spoken language there was in fact a dip in the rate of progress of students in the first year of secondary schooling. Students in primary school had strong positive attitudes towards schooling whereas this was less favourable in secondary schools.

A survey we conducted among our Year 7 parents revealed to us that their initial anxiety on day one centred around the single most important issue to them and their children, which was whether or not they would be issued with their 'lockers' on the first day. A moment of truth on which we did not deliver. We wanted to bridge the transition gap, to make the students comfortable on arrival at our campus, and so we began to visit our primary schools and talk to the Grade 6 teachers to understand the children a bit better. We also decided as a staff to reduce the number of 'new' teachers the students had to face, and to develop the home room principle. This led us to introduce the development of the team/small group model, as practised in Germany (see below).

For many years now, educators have been attempting to address the question 'Are our kids really learning?' The result has been that many more questions are raised than answered. As we teachers struggle to adapt to the changing needs of the community, industry and more specifically future employers of students, the messages have been getting more and more confused. Which methodology do we choose from the vast majority that we are presented with? A closer look at the functioning of various organisations has shown that the majority of them rely on the co-operation of its employees for the successful operation of its workplace. Our rôle in the future welfare of our students is undeniably that of preparation – but preparation for what? The workplace is constantly changing, its needs are changing and the jobs themselves are changing. Jobs that existed ten years ago may be gone in another decade and so too will many more be created. Our rôle then changes focus slightly – we must give our students *skills* to cope with any situation, placing less emphasis on content.

One visionary, Klaus Winkel, based in the Saarland in Germany, has embraced the idea of providing students with an environment in which the learning that takes place addresses their individual needs. He referred to it as Social Learning. In response to the Minister's direction, Dr Winkel moved from the rôle of a consultant, to that of head of the in-service training programme, readying teachers for a classroom with a different structure. The structure he advocated and played a key rôle in developing is referred to as the Team/Small Group Model (herein the TSM model). Two aims which led to the development of the TSM model in Germany were:

- to diminish the isolation that students traditionally feel in a large school
- to develop an institution which could enable students of different abilities and backgrounds to reach their potential.

The teachers in this model work with each other in a team which is responsible for students at one year level. The teachers follow these students through from Year 5 to Year 10 delivering all the curriculum to them. They teach as few students as possible and teach them as many subjects as possible. These teachers meet regularly to discuss a range of issues relevant to their own and their students needs.

The international study of schools by Kevin Piper for the 'Effective Schools Project' has highlighted that two important dimensions are required in an effective school. They are:

- a climate conducive to learning
- an emphasis on learning.

We have to change from the teacher/subject driven model to the student-centred model, which the TSM so aptly addresses. We know from research that continuity of instruction and teaching strategies across the learning spectrum from Prep to Year 12 is an important factor for the development of the student. Bill Stringer of the University of Melbourne sees it as a continuum: integration of knowledge at prep to the specialisation of knowledge at the final year of schooling. He believes that the early years should be spent on skills development with the latter being discipline-based. This continuity and consistency leading to stability is achievable in the TSM as the teachers follow the students for at least two years.

Because of the team approach to teaching that the staff are placed in, teacher collegiality is increased; they discuss problems that arise, deal with issues that are of importance to them and provide support for each other. This model steps beyond the token gesture at collegiality, largely anecdotal, to the more sophisticated and useful form of professionals treating each other with respect, and developing meaningful, practical solutions to challenges that are faced by the team. Teachers now discuss students in their care rather than subjects and content.

The students also work in teams. The classroom is structured in a way that allows three or four students to sit around a table and work on a given task, using the skills of each team member to complete work. These students have the opportunity to experience success, through working co-operatively and sharing their unique knowledge with others in a structured situation. Co-operative social behaviour is taught and developed through a range of experiences and exercises. Students get to know themselves and the expectations of others. They also understand that a team approach to problem-solving or assignment work is often more valuable than independent work as there is a richness in the quality and quantity of ideas. The pupils take on the responsibility for their own learning, the teachers become facilitators of this learning. The traditional student/teacher relationship is broken down into 'colleagues in learning'. The teacher becomes a fellow learner, and is not the centre of all learning.

The team model provides the opportunity for all members to experience a sense of worth. As the model evolves and the individuals begin working as a team and not just a group, the individuals begin to recognise that all have something to offer in a wide range of situations; there is no longer the situation where one person knows all. Furthermore, there is an adult modelling of what is expected of students. The social and emotional needs of students are very well catered for in the team group model. Here is an opportunity to share with and support fellow students. A climate 'conducive to learning' is created. In such a climate students are willing to take risks and each student is also willing to invest himself or herself in the team in order that the team may accomplish its tasks.

A working example: Endeavour Hills Campus of Eumemmerring Secondary College

By adopting the philosophy of the TSM, the staff at Endeavour Hills campus have attempted to give students and staff the opportunity to develop the skills to work in teams, to share their knowledge, their resources and their ideas with the whole group thus removing the sense of 'competition' in its current sense.

The staff

Some staff at Endeavour Hills have embraced the ideology of team work. Recognising the benefits to themselves as professionals, such as:

- An increase in meaningful collegial relations as staff take time to discuss the progress of the curriculum, making changes as necessary, and the progress of students. Who is performing well? Who would benefit from further assistance?

- Team management, as they take control of the welfare of a small group of students. Recognising that the students will remain within the realm of the teaching group and no longer referring problems on as they see this would defeat the purpose of the teaching team – to be able to deal with any situation that arises using the strength of collegial support.

- Tackling integrated curriculum issues, by meeting regularly and developing links between subject areas. The students can then have access to a curriculum that is relevant and has clear applications in life – no longer segregated pieces of information that often seem totally unrelated and irrelevant.

- The realisation that the students begin to take more responsibility for their learning as they become much more critical of the work they are required to do and question the need for it. The students also begin to ask questions of themselves and their team members about the work they are doing such as: why are you right? what is wrong with my answer? These students are no longer content to accept given solutions to problems; they are questioning those solutions and trying to find out *why* they are wrong.

- The sense of belonging to a team and making a difference beyond the single classroom as all team members contribute and discuss ideas to the benefit of the whole. There is also much more opportunity to try something new, with the knowledge of a team behind you to provide the support structure so necessary when dealing with something different.

The current situation at Endeavour Hills is that all Year 7 students are taught by two teams. The teams are made up of five teachers who deliver the majority of the curriculum to three classes of Year 7 students. The teaching teams are scheduled to meet every fortnight to discuss the relevant issues. The students themselves are in teams also. They remain in these teams for most of their classes where they are gradually being taught the skills necessary to begin working as *teams* rather than *groups*.

The staff who are following the model closely are being rewarded by the quality of students' work. These teachers have seen these students moving from unco-operative group members to productive team members. By meeting regularly to discuss the philosophy of the team model and to tackle problems, the staff are able to gather new strength to continue in their work and new ideas of dealing with specific incidents that occur. New staff at the campus have taken advantage of the opportunity to discuss classroom management and curriculum with their peers, easing their acceptance into a new school.

Those teachers involved in the TSM have had many opportunities to reflect; with their peers, the students, and also with senior management. Many have commented that there are markedly less discipline problems with the students in teams than in the traditional 'rows' of seating.

The classroom atmosphere is also markedly different. There is more time for the teacher to move around the room and discuss work with the students and hence there is much more opportunity for the teacher to reward students quickly for good work. This is so often difficult in the traditional classroom as the teacher struggles to maintain order and get around to assist the sea of students' hands constantly demanding attention.

The teacher's rôle in these classrooms has changed. They are no longer the instructor from the front of the classroom, but rather the facilitator as the students make the change from passive to active learner. This means that the teacher must be prepared to relinquish control, trusting the students to work productively, relying on each of the team member's resources more as they realise that each of them can contribute something of value and between them they can come up with solutions to a variety of problems.

This does not mean, however, that there is no longer a place for the traditional teaching style. Some knowledge is still imparted via traditional means, but the team methodology ensures the knowledge becomes something tangible, useful and relevant to the students. One of the rewards of having team work across the curriculum areas is that work done in one subject area is carried across and utilised in others. The teaching teams allow this to occur with relative ease and the enthusiasm often present in these meetings is infectious and can carry people away.

One important aspect of the TSM model is that we find that teachers are spending more time reflecting on their teaching practice. There is a rediscovery of curiosity, imagination and sensitivity which is almost numbed out of existence during their years of teaching. Collegiality supports this new focus and it soon spreads to other members of staff.

Since we believe that adult modelling is an important aspect of the programme, our campus has initiated and developed links with the Royal Automobile Club of Victoria and has shared in their staff team development programme. We felt that as we were embarking on a team-based pedagogy we should be involved in this programme to put ourselves through the experiences and situations that we were expecting of our students. Middle management staff and Assistant Principals were involved with the Club in their professional development. We anticipate that this will be an ongoing programme with the Club sharing its resources with our Campus. The opportunity to become involved with a service club and to be given the opportunity to become involved with the 'real world' has had enormous benefit to our staff participants. They come back with their batteries charged and their energy levels high. They are forced to work through the various stages of team formation in a contracted period of time as well as performing two or three of the team rôles as outlined by Belbin (1981). Like any team, teacher teams also go through the stages of team formation.

The students

Students in these classes are taught that the strength of the group can overcome many problems they are likely to encounter; that many minds are better than one. This is not to say that the individual is undermined in this model. From experience we find that one member of the team may excel in English while another may excel in technology. There is ample opportunity for individual success and individual work. The TSM stresses interdependence and independence.

The teams are mostly made up of two boys and two girls, with the odd single sex team, depending on the class. The teams were created on the first day of school, with the students being randomly placed into their team, through such methods as height, date of birth, favourite colour and so on. They remain in these teams for all their subjects for at least a semester.

There are a number of stages to building successful teams and each requires a great deal of time and effort, but the rewards are enormous. The stages are :

- Forming
- Storming
- Norming
- Performing
- Disbanding.

The *forming* stage is more than simply putting the students into their groups. They are given a range of experiences and circumstances and the teacher leads them through the team solution process. This is done through using rôle plays and games. An example would be 'Noughts and Crosses', using chairs and people instead of paper and pen. This game is played in silence and the students have to work together to make decisions before the game starts. The strategy they decide on will make a difference to the outcome.

There are many problems in this stage, as the team struggles to deal with reforming and the changes that come with it. There are changes in power and influence, based around experience, gender or any of a huge range of factors. The goal is to give the team members contact with each other in as many circumstances as possible, not just the typical work-based classroom but through social occasions, where the students learn to work together and appreciate each other in different situations.

The *storming* stage is a time when individuals begin to test their influence and power. Problems arise when individuals do not view the differences as normal and healthy. Disagreements will arise concerning the how, why, when of any number of activities or tasks, leading to friction and dissatisfaction. As the team members work their way through this phase, they vie for team power and influence, creating potential situations of conflict.

Individuals can respond differently to these situations, some respond in a 'tough response' mode by adamantly refusing to conform, or insisting upon their own methodology, seeking support from the rest of their team for their ideology. Those taking the 'tender response' will form alliances and conform, often for self-protection. They also tend to withdraw or become indifferent and are generally anxious and frustrated. It is important at this stage to ensure that tasks are of such a nature that complaining and refusal to co-operate do not become entrenched in the everyday functioning of the team.

The storming stage is unavoidable and if there is an attempt to control this through authority, the dissatisfaction, anxiety and frustration will remain. The team needs to be given the skills and the opportunity to deal with the problems, through listening to each other and experiencing success through producing team work.

The *norming* stage is where the procedures to deal with conflicts, make decisions and communicate effectively are put into place in such a way that all team members agree. Skills building needs to occur here; such things as feedback skills, sharing and testing ideas. A team spirit is developed and high performance is encouraged.

Performing is the most rewarding of the stages, as the team members work closely together, providing support and encouragement and constantly striving to improve on previous work. This is the best time for evaluation to be introduced to provide recognition for the students involved, potential rewards and also to ensure that the team remains dynamic and constantly renews itself. This is also the danger time. It is too easy to become comfortable and fall into a rut. It is essential that individuals are exposed to new ideas and people and changing work focuses.

The final stage, that of *disbanding* occurs as people begin to withdraw their energy from the team and its tasks, often seeking new challenges. It can be a time of sadness, if the disbanding arises from conflict and is premature. It is also a great opportunity for the team to reflect on their work, their work practices and their individual development.

The students at Endeavour Hills have a team book in which they may write about their experiences in their teams. These reflections may be about the actual work, comments passed or their feelings about their team or themselves. In these books are also the rules that the teams themselves have decided upon and the consequences for breaking those rules. There are a few classroom rules set down by the teacher, but most of the rules for the functioning of the classroom rely on the separate teams. This means that most teams have different rules and that these rules and consequences change as the team develops and recognises the need for different work practices. This is real evidence that these students are taking more responsibility for their own learning and are indeed becoming 'professional learners'.

The future/vision

'We must hasten very, very slowly.'

For the entire staff at Endeavour Hills to make the change to the TSM there is a desperate need for funding to ensure that all staff receive adequate INSET, that there is adequate time for discussion of the model and that all staff may have the opportunity to take the change on in their own way. As with any change or innovation, this is proving difficult. There are the staff who claim they have tried this before, those that tried it once and had a bad experience (so will not try it again), those that state they have no need for such a teaching style as theirs is already perfected and those that claim it is not relevant for their subject area.

Those staff that have been involved from the early days of the introduction of the TSM are striving to overcome the negative feelings from other staff members, yet fortunately, they are rewarded by their experiences in their teaching teams. The aim is to have staff who would follow their students right through from Year 7 to Year 10, where they then go to the senior campus.

Summary

As a staff we now are constantly evaluating and reviewing our curriculum in order to make it more meaningful to our students. We have developed a curriculum at Years 7 and 8 that may be called an integrated curriculum, which at times takes a thematic approach. We have done this to remove the repetition and overlap between subjects.

While not all teachers have embraced the Team/Small Group Model, co-operative learning strategies are being tried in their classrooms. There is also continuous dialogue now taking place between our primary schools and us, centred around teaching and learning strategies. There is a natural progression in place from the co-operative group learning of the primary school to the team model of the secondary school resulting in a smoother transition.

There is little doubt that what we are trying to achieve has much worth. The collegiality, the work produced by students and their increased interest in their own learning are rewards in themselves. Nevertheless, the path is littered with obstacles that need to be removed to enable the staff to embrace the model as a whole. The students are learning to work with others, they are discovering their own self-worth and are challenging much of the knowledge that is given to them and endeavouring to learn and discover it for themselves. The teachers are gaining new insight into the workings of the learner's mind – a key to successful and relevant teaching. The future looks bright as we define our rôles and modes of operation more clearly, learning from our mistakes and perhaps, most importantly, taking the lead from the students themselves, who without realising it have become the teachers in a far more powerful way than we will ever be theirs.

What we are doing at the campus has attracted quite a bit of attention from the education institutions in and around Victoria. We are members of The National Schools Network who support and finance our professional development workshops. In order to support our work in the area of documentation and to review our work periodically we have established links into partnership with Deakin University. They provide our campus with the resources of a professor to act as a mentor and to guide us in our measurement of value added to our student and teacher teams. This form of support goes a long way in establishing the credibility and in legitimising the programme. It also affords us the opportunity to reflect on what we are doing and to have a critical friend to guide us along the way. We are in partnership with Deakin University for three years and we hope by that time to have fully established the programmes across Years 7 and 8 and have done enough evaluation to formulate policy.

Also, since team-based teaching and learning requires a flat hierarchy and is akin to the principles of Total Quality, we also include elements of Deming's philosophy in our classrooms. This takes many forms from 'driving out fear' and so encouraging risk-taking in students to ensuring that student teams do not proceed to the next task until the previous task is completed to the satisfaction of all team members (usually 80 per cent on a graded scale) and this may be measured through a project, research assignment or test. In addition we have developed a partnership between the Australian Quality Council, the local Technical and Further Education College (CASEY) and ourselves to produce a programme called 'Quality Uniting Enterprise, Schools and TAFE' through which we offer a one-week interactive module of work for our students to experience the effects and demands of quality in the workforce. Students are placed in a service or manufacturing firm for one week, and are given a 'real' problem to solve using the tools of Total Quality Management. The students are given a one day training session in the tools of TQM and their previous experience of working in teams is recognised and built upon. During the week the students investigate solutions to the problem by visiting various sections of the company and by interviewing employees and employers. At the end of the week the team of students presents its findings to the board of executives of the firm.

A study (Lou, Abrami, Spence, Poulsen, Chambers, d'Apollonia, 1995) clearly demonstrates that students placed in co-operative learning situations achieve better results than those in non-grouping placements. The results further improve if the size of the group is between three and five. A group size of six to ten in fact has a zero effect.

META-ANALYSIS OF WITHIN CLASS GROUPING

Grouping versus not grouping	+0.20
Homogeneous grouping versus not grouping	+0.18
Heterogeneous grouping versus not grouping	+0.23
Group size – pairs	+0.13
Group size – small (3–5)	+0.26
Group size – large (6–10)	0.00
Method of instruction – co-operative	+0.27
Method of instruction – other	+0.04
Ability of students – low	+0.37
Ability of students – medium	+0.16
Ability of students – high	+0.28
Subject area maths/science	+0.24
Subject area reading/language arts	+0.14

[Lou, Abrami, Spence, Poulsen, Chambers, d'Apollonia, 1995, unpublished]

References

Belbin, M. (1981), *Management Teams: Why they Succeed or Fail*, London, Heinemann.

Lou, Abrami, Spence, Poulsen, Chambers, d'Apollonia (1995), unpublished.

10

■ ■ ■

The child as client

CLAIRE TROTT

Introduction – context and history

Mereway Middle School is a 9–13 purpose built middle school of some 430 pupils on the south side of Northampton. The school was opened in September 1990 after an intensive period of preparation. 'Excellence and Enjoyment in learning' was agreed as the motto.

Those of us involved in the setting up of the school had varied professional backgrounds but we were united in the desire to set up a child-centred organisation. This primary purpose was not to be clouded by the trappings of institutional systems, the expectations of unhelpful educational traditions and the pressures of external legislation and the market economy. The children were always seen as our clients and our aim was to provide an exemplary service to those clients. In trying to achieve this we would strive to work in various important partnerships with others, the key partnerships being parents, governors, LEA, community, outside agencies, other schools, our link inspector and Northampton Inspection and Advisory Service.

Establishing positive relationships between all those in the school was a priority which formed that backbone of much of our early work. It informed many decisions including our commitment to using first name terms for all those involved with school. We wanted to avoid the hierarchy created by systems where certain people use titles while others are called by their first names. We felt that in the 1990s in a caring, learning environment which equally valued each individual, we should all use first names, adults and children alike. This reflected our belief that true respect is earned and not demanded and that all relationships should be mutually respectful. First name terms was accepted by almost all staff and everyone's commitment had been gained by the end of the first year. Before we opened, a whole staff conference focused on the vision of the school as a place where children felt secure in supportive relationships where we were working towards the same ends. Positive relationships have remained the foundation of all we do in school, for it is upon this that we feel most able to build 'excellence and enjoyment in learning'.

Opening a new school is an excellent opportunity to reassess some fundamental issues to do with schooling. It is a chance to shed some of the assumptions that are often made. We chose to appoint staff at their current allowance level, with the commitment to review during the first year. In this way our staffing structure could evolve in response to our needs and the qualities of the staff appointed. We set up a supported class teacher system to deliver a thematic curriculum to all year groups. Little teaching in school involves a specialist taking over responsibility for the class. To support this system we have subject co-ordinators who are involved in rigorous topic planning with the production of detailed forecasts of work. We also make use of teachers' specialisms to develop each others' practice, arranging for staff to work together for particular topics. In order to facilitate the above developments, staff were given working time in school. This involved the use of senior managers' time and, most significantly, the establishment of a system where non-contact time was not an automatic right. Where our limited use of specialists allowed for non-contact time this was generally used for forecast planning, the support of children, review meetings and professional development. This pattern has continued and it has assisted in the development of teaching and learning partnerships for professional development, a curriculum audit cycle involving all teaching staff, NQT mentoring, appraisal mentoring and the establishing of 'Enhanced Education Plans' for some of our most able students.

Although we have only been open for five years the school has made many changes during this time. This positive approach to change, and our belief in responding to the organisation's needs both short- and long-term, has led to us making school structure changes every year since we have opened. We have found that changing the structure releases energy. This has particularly been the case in a recent staffing development. A responsibility point is now attached to the managing of a specific school initiative rather than the management of a curriculum area. The idea for an initiative can be proposed by any individual or group in school. The initiatives, which can be related to any aspect of school life, have clear objectives, success criteria and are for a specified period. These responsibility points are therefore action-related and allocated on a temporary basis for the duration of the project. Those wishing to retain responsibility points after the completion of a project can apply to manage another initiative if they so wish.

We have always tried to ensure that changes bring us closer to achieving our core purpose, while responding to the continuously changing world that we live in. This, I believe demonstrates our commitment to quality improvement. Efforts are then taken to quality assure so that the base level of service given is agreed and adopted by all.

As a senior management team, in the initial years, we had no conscious awareness of the quality movement and its application to education. However, when we met and came across the work of John West-Burnham and others writing in this field, we immediately saw it as being compatible with our ways of thinking. It gave us a practical and theoretical framework upon which we could hang much of our client-centred philosophy. Thinking and speaking about our work using the terms introduced by the quality movement brought a clearer direction, in some cases, and greater rigour and consistency. It also encouraged us to continue these developments and relate them to the world outside education. As with most organisations that have considered total quality we have done so through a process of adaptation and assimilation. In this chapter I will particularly focus on our interpretation and use of some of the key quality concepts and terms.

Culture and philosophy

One of the things I believe that Mereway Middle School is known for in the Northampton area is having a distinct culture or ethos which emanates from a strongly held philosophy. There has developed a Mereway Middle way of doing things and many who have come to know us would be able to predict accurately our attitude or approach to something, even if it would not be their own. Our corporate culture is clearly reflected in a number of key aspects of school life, some of which have become a form of cultural symbol for us. Our use of first name terms is perhaps the most obvious. The way we view and treat our clients, the children, is key to the kind of service that Mereway Middle School provides; we want to be partners with our clients. We have involved them directly in managing aspects of school life, their classroom environment and their learning. All groups in school were involved in formulating a school mission statement recently. This served as a way for us to check and further develop our understanding of the school philosophy. It involved us re-building our original school aims and redefining our shared values. The school mission statement applies to all in school. We are increasingly consciously working to use our mission statement, and the corporate culture from which it emerged, as a sounding board or reference point for all that we do. Children are seen as partners in learning. We are all learners and are actively striving to make the school a learning organisation. Whole school efforts are being made: for instance the focus of this year's school development plan is action research based improvement projects.

The importance given to the school environment and classroom displays is another area often cited as part of our school approach. People have commented that we are an unusual mixture of the modern and the traditional, i.e. we have first name terms and friendly relationships but insist on high standards of behaviour, respect for the environment and we also have required

165

school dress. For us this is about each decision being made on the basis of what has seemed most appropriate to Mereway Middle School. For many years I have explained our approach to relationships in school as relaxed, not to be mistaken for casual. Our school ethos is dependent on such subtle distinctions. We have always maintained that we are creating a school for the vast majority of us who consistently work positively to achieve 'excellence and enjoyment in learning'. In the minority of situations where this does not happen we firmly intervene and work with those experiencing difficulties. A phrase often used by staff in school when questioning a particular response to a situation is 'do you think that was appropriate?' The use of this phrase emphasises that in school there is a strong sense of what *is* appropriate in the context of our school and that we are all in a position to recognise appropriate and inappropriate action, retrospectively if not always at the time. In this way we hope that our school ethos directs us all in our work and interaction with others where we are relying on our own judgements. Along with others I often find myself thinking I know what Allen, (the headteacher) would say, because we share a characteristically Mereway Middle School response to many situations.

Agreed understanding and common mission contribute to a feeling of a developing confidence. It is in a climate of confidence and clear purpose that experimentation and development are most likely to occur. This is clearly important in an organisation which has said in its mission statement that 'We will continue to be a forward looking, innovative school, proactive in our pursuit of excellence and continuous improvement.' We hope that our continuing commitment to translating our vision into practice in school will increase the climate of confidence and openness necessary if innovations are to prosper.

Other culturally identifiable aspects of the Mereway Middle School organisation include some personnel issues. We generally have a noticeably young teaching staff and have appointed many newly qualified teachers over the years. This is not a matter of policy: teachers have always been appointed, and also promoted within the organisation, on the basis of achievement and future potential within our school. Age or experience is never seen as a barrier. We have also consistently given public recognition to vital rôles in school that do not involve teaching. Most notably this applies to our campus supervisor and admin. manager. Their importance to the whole school operation is reflected in a variety of ways, for instance the creation of the school name board and headed paper; their participation in staff conference events; investment in their professional development and the nature of their management and leadership roles in school. This year we have furthered this approach with our admin. manager becoming a full member of our Senior Management Team of four.

Client care and satisfaction

Whether what we provide at school is quality is primarily determined by the clients, *their* achievement and level of satisfaction, not the teachers, the organisation or that of some outside body. Our intention is to continuously improve in meeting and exceeding client needs and expectations.

Finding ways of listening and responding to young people is an increasingly vital ingredient in our work in client care. In order to do this we must find ways of discovering our clients' needs in order to ensure a curriculum which is 'fit for purpose'.

Increasingly we are giving young people opportunities to tell us what they know, have learnt and how it was learnt. This can be useful before a topic begins, during a topic and before we move on. Our attempts have included open questioning and specifically designed activities. In mathematics work a process of mental mapping has been used. This is a method of brainstorming children's existing knowledge and understanding of a specific area and their grasp of mathematical language related to this area. The children begin brainstorming individually or in pairs, share with a group and then share their combined understanding with the whole class. The teacher's rôle is to observe individual and collective understanding, help with focusing on the area and extending the contributions of children through careful questioning. This work provides individual and group information which can be used to help make decisions about the work to come.

In our newly designed forecasts/schemes of work we are increasingly building in such opportunities in order to try and find out the young people's needs. These core activities are then followed by learning opportunities/activities which are targeted at differing needs and levels of understanding. Later in the forecast, opportunities are being built in to enable children to demonstrate what they now know and to transfer that learning to different contexts.

A number of us at Mereway Middle School have become increasingly interested in the notion that individual learners have preferred learning styles. As part of in-service training sessions we have tried to analyse how we have learnt things and the ways in which each of us choose to learn when we are able to make a choice. We discovered that our preferred learning styles varied considerably. Some of us dived in at the deep end and learnt through doing, others preferred following instructions or structured steps, others benefited from reading around a subject, watching a video or using a computer. Some staff enjoyed listening to others, others preferred working alone. Not only did we have preferred learning styles but many of us have a developed understanding of the ways in which we find it most difficult to learn. We believe that this is also likely to be true for children and their learning. Children need to be given opportunities to discover and tell us the ways in which they best learn or learn least well. This information should be taken into account when planning and individualising the curriculum. We are now beginning to look at ways of finding out and recording this information.

Preferred learning styles was covered in a recent survey to discover more about young people's attitudes to the learning experiences that they have in school. Year 8, led by Strategy Group member, Gaynor Crute, devised and circulated a questionnaire to all students in the year group. A database was then prepared in order for staff and students to analyse the results and produce some generalised statements which could be acted upon. A number of questions provided interesting feed-back for the teachers. For instance, it was possible to see if the range and the degree of use of particular learning and teaching styles matched the children's preferences.

Now we have such information we must respond to it by making appropriate adjustments. It is also important to provide the support and in-service training necessary to make desired changes. Here our Year Team Co-ordinators' rôles as professional tutors for their team can be useful.

The Year 8 questionnaire provided some information for our science co-ordinator. It emerged in the survey of 185 students that 40 per cent had a negative attitude to science. Only 11 per cent thought science was excellent (*see* Figure 5). This was a surprise to the co-ordinator, Josie Kaal and the Year 8 teachers. An immediate response was necessary.

Q18. I think SCIENCE is . . .

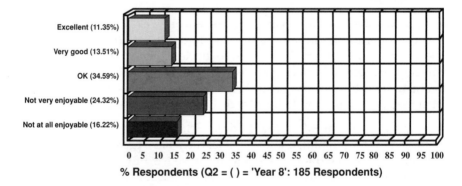

% Respondents (Q2 = ( ) = 'Year 8': 185 Respondents)

Figure 5: Year 8 attitudes to science

168

The next day Josie produced a follow-up questionnaire. The questionnaire contained fifteen open and multiple choice questions, its aim being to define the nature of the negative attitude. Two particular areas emerged as the foci for students' negative attitudes:

- the structure of some science sessions – particularly CASE sessions (Cognitive Acceleration through Science Education)
- the way in which science learning was recorded, particularly the use of traditional science write-ups at the end of each piece of science work.

As a result of the survey, the structure and delivery of science sessions, particularly CASE work, are being reconsidered. Josie has proposed that work be undertaken to amend some CASE activities to encompass a more explorative approach, in line with the school's stated aims for 'investigative science'. This would include more selective use of worksheets. At the same time, alternative methods of recording some science-based activities are being tried. One method involves the children writing in detail on one or two aspects of the traditional science write-up, rather than superficially covering all aspects. The aspects identified are then those that are assessed. Another method being tried involves children, after a practical activity, being asked to produce evidence of what they have learnt. This can be provided in any format that they like: it does not have to follow the traditional write-up format. Since this original survey a further survey of students' attitudes has taken place. This occurred about three months later. Small improvements can be noted: we are hoping that this is the beginning of a trend.

Student and staff questionnaires are increasingly being used by subject co-ordinators during curriculum audits. Curriculum audits are designed to regularly monitor the learning and teaching in school and give us an opportunity to listen to the learners, both children and adults. There are three audit cycles which take place in school. Cycle one audits are conducted in order to provide an overview of an area in school. Cycle two audits concentrate on one or two areas thrown up in cycle one. They focus on children's learning and the teaching styles used, formulating action points based on evidence gathered. Cycle two audits often lead to identified Teaching Partnerships. Teaching Partnerships between school staff occur in order to provide in-service training to a teacher on a specific aspect of his/her work. They can be linked to the school appraisal and mentoring programme. Cycle three audits revisit action points and reflect on actions taken, evaluating their impact in terms of children's learning. Co-ordinators are thus being encouraged to measure their own effectiveness through evidence of children's learning in their particular area of the curriculum.

This year's cycle two mathematics audit enabled us to learn more about the children's learning in this area of the curriculum. It looked in detail at some issues which had emerged from the cycle one audit the preceding year. The main issues chosen were the match between teaching styles used by staff and the needs of the children concerned, and some emerging gender discrepancies relating to the older children's attitude towards their own abilities. In a school paper 'Monitoring and Evaluating Mathematics' Dawn Wilson described the process undertaken in the following way:

In order to understand the feelings and opinions of children in school towards their mathematics work and assess the issue of gender, a questionnaire was developed entitled 'Student Mathematical Survey'.

The questionnaire was brief and designed only to give a snapshot of the present situation. In order to gain a greater insight into some children's perceptions of maths in school, four able children from each class, two girls and two boys, were also asked to fill in an evaluation sheet suggested by Heather Scott, Mathematics Inspector for Northamptonshire Inspection and Advisory Service.

To involve the staff in the audit process and to gain greater insight into where they felt they were at the moment, a questionnaire was put together entitled 'Teaching Strategies Survey'. Having decided to focus further on Year 5 teaching of maths, further investigation was required. It was therefore decided to use interviews and observations to fulfil this.

Although the samples used were small, the second cycle audit threw up some interesting issues worthy of follow-up. For instance, although both male and female able mathematicians seemed accurately to see themselves as being good at maths, the boys who considered themselves good more often placed themselves at the top of the class when asked where they saw themselves in their class. On the other hand, the girls who considered themselves to be good more often placed themselves in the middle of the class.

A recent whole school survey on children's attitudes to subjects of the curriculum and ways of working has raised some other gender and year group differences. In this case we were dealing with larger amounts of data generated by all children in school completing the survey. As the graphs below indicate there is a dramatic drop in attitude to maths between Year 7 girls and Year 8 girls. For the Years 7 and 8 boys the gap is much smaller.

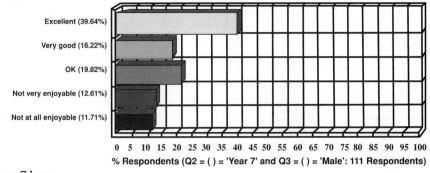

Year 7 boys

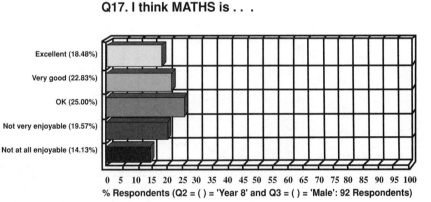

Year 8 boys

Figure 6: Attitude to maths (boys)

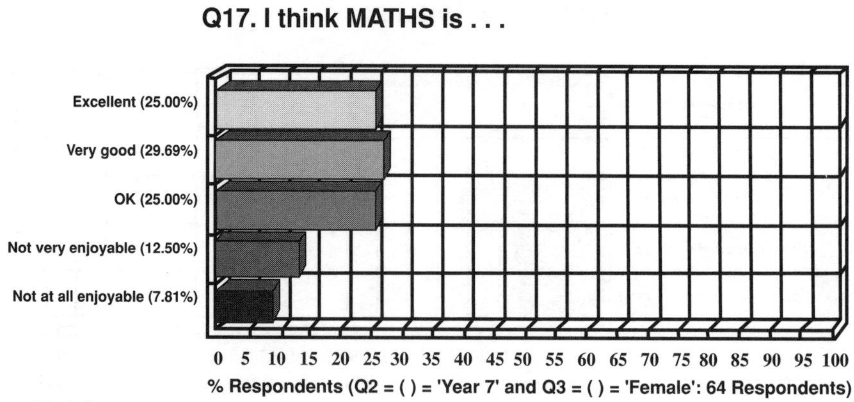

Q17. I think MATHS is . . .

Excellent (25.00%)

Very good (29.69%)

OK (25.00%)

Not very enjoyable (12.50%)

Not at all enjoyable (7.81%)

0 5 10 15 20 25 30 35 40 45 50 55 60 65 70 75 80 85 90 95 100

% Respondents (Q2 = ( ) = 'Year 7' and Q3 = ( ) = 'Female': 64 Respondents)

Year 7 girls

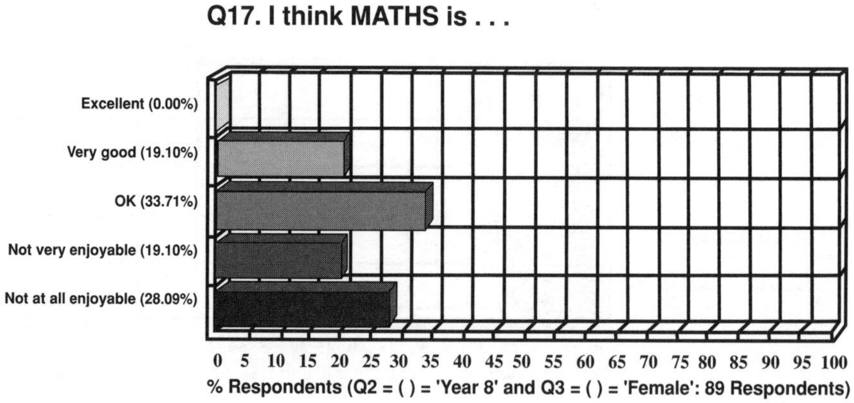

Q17. I think MATHS is . . .

Excellent (0.00%)

Very good (19.10%)

OK (33.71%)

Not very enjoyable (19.10%)

Not at all enjoyable (28.09%)

0 5 10 15 20 25 30 35 40 45 50 55 60 65 70 75 80 85 90 95 100

% Respondents (Q2 = ( ) = 'Year 8' and Q3 = ( ) = 'Female': 89 Respondents)

Year 8 girls

Figure 7: Attitude to maths (girls)

The information gathered from the maths audit and the attitude questionnaire has directed us towards a need to improve girls' confidence in maths and, in particular, to work on the less positive attitude towards the subject in Year 8 girls. In order to improve these things we will need to listen even more to what our clients have to say and let them lead the way to improvement.

The work of these surveys has served to raise teaching staff's awareness of students' views of our work. We are now finding ways of responding to these views.

In other areas we have provided structured opportunities for students to express views and to participate in managing school life. For instance since the school opened, children have been in the majority on the library committee. They are listened to as the major clients of our school library and the main participants in the school's Book Week. Four children are also members of our Challenge Centre Committee and make significant contributions to this advisory group. As a result of the success of such endeavours, children are increasingly becoming involved in school working parties alongside governors, staff and other members of the community. Most recently they have made a major contribution to a working party on developing a school drugs policy and our approach to this work. We are also hoping that a group of particularly able speakers and listeners will be able to present children's ideas of ways of improving the cloakroom situation in school. The group has been asked to make a presentation to our Senior Management Team. We hope that in listening to our clients in this way we will hear new insights into some everyday problems that concern us all.

'Moments of truth'

Inevitably at times we get it wrong, our customer service breaks down. These occasions are our 'moments of truth'. Usually they are relatively small issues but small things matter. For instance the quality of a child's experience of a school day can be significantly affected if information in a note or phone call is not passed on to the appropriate person, or special needs information is not taken account of when setting up a learning activity. However good a learning experience has been, our clients may well feel negative if their coat is trampled on the floor in the cloakroom that day. The fact that a school has a well-developed and understood 'Positive Approach to Behaviour' pales into insignificance for the child who is bullied, however occasionally this happens.

Trying to understand the everyday school experience of Mereway Middle School children is important. In the early days, and periodically since, staff have put themselves in the shoes of our clients by doing such things as joining the end of the lunch queue, sitting on the floor in assembly, lining up in the rain or using the same toilets as a hundred and twenty others. In some cases our understanding has resulted in changes or adaptations to our practice. Where this has not been possible it has still resulted in greater empathy and appreciation.

Consistency and monitoring

Consistency is a feature of a quality service. In the context of school life we have interpreted this as meaning that children have a right to expect consistency across staff and teaching sessions in terms of the following: behaviour and work expectations; attitude shown towards them; assessment and record-keeping issues. Consistency also means day in and day out. Consistency in the context of teaching does not, we believe, mean providing exactly the same service to each child, but it *does* mean providing a consistently high level of service, taking account of individual needs.

Quality assurance

The concept of quality assurance is based on the principle of prevention through definition which can then be assessed in order to ensure the consistency of experience for every pupil. In order to ensure this consistency, the school has taken a variety of measures. School policies, the staff handbook and the induction and mentoring of new staff lead to clarification of our school approach to things. School policies are created and developed over a number of years, the process involves various combinations of staff, governors and children. Policies are discussed and reviewed in various forms but, until any changes have been agreed and published, we are expected to follow established school practice. We can all expect to be pulled up by others if we move away from agreed policy. Recently we have recorded our 'Positive Approach to Behaviour' as a policy document to be followed by all those who have direct contact with the school. The document was produced from the work of staff, governors and children. It is written to apply to all of us, whatever our rôle in school, and can be referred to, by adults and children alike, as a marker against which we should measure our own behaviour and the behaviour of others in school. The policies in school have also ensured greater consistency in other areas, for instance: evaluating and responding to children's work; homework; staff development.

In order to ensure that all children within a year group have access to similar learning experiences, whoever their class teacher may be, half-termly forecasts or schemes of work which cover all key subject areas within a topic are designed. These forecasts and the production of a target bank for student use have ensured that staff and student expectations are clear.

Monitoring performance

In order to ensure consistency and provide feedback on our service, the school has put into place various monitoring systems. Without these systems it would be difficult to know if consistency was being achieved. School meetings have always provided opportunities for the sharing of good practice and reminders about agreed school policies but we have found that this approach could lack sufficient rigour therefore we have, this year, instigated more rigorous management monitoring of various aspects of teaching and learning.

All staff are curriculum managers. In this role they are required to undertake an audit for their area. We have developed an audit cycle where each half-term one national curriculum core area and one other subject is audited. We have provided in-service training on auditing methods and staff are now using a wider variety of ways of monitoring their area throughout the school. Some of the audits have been used to inform action-research projects and are beginning to have a significant impact on practice in school. We are now hoping to extend the use of audits more widely to cover other aspects of school life.

As senior managers in school, the headteacher and I believe that we have a responsibility to monitor regularly what is going on in school and to act on inconsistencies. Our work to date involves us each alternately taking an aspect of classroom practice and gathering relevant data. The raw data is then fed back to staff. Year teams are encouraged to interpret the data that relates to them and, where possible, draw some conclusions from their findings, attempt to verify them and act on them. Where the practice of an individual appears to deviate from what is expected, then this is directly taken up with the member of staff concerned and appropriate clarification, support or action is taken. The areas that have seemed suitable for this type of monitoring include: children's work books, teacher and children's record keeping; classroom displays.

Mereway Middle School has also instigated a variety of child and parent surveys. In most cases we have used questionnaires to find out information, attitudes and levels of satisfaction with aspects of the school service. At present we are analysing data from our 'Learning About Learning' questionnaire filled in by all children in school and our 'Service Quality Questionnaire' for Year 5 parents which focused on gathering responses about our entry year's first term and a half in school. We have previously made use of computer programs such as 'FileMaker Pro' to help us interrogate our data. However, our recent acquisition of EasiQuest has made much more detailed and informative analysis possible. This package has further convinced us that for schools today it is not only important, but also increasingly easy, to become a data rich school. We believe that by the time we are next inspected we will have a considerable amount of data collected from our own ongoing monitoring systems to offer to an OFSTED team, information which, I suggest, may well have a value above and beyond that which it is possible to collect during a week's inspection.

Outrageous goals

These are goals that challenge the school to try things which it thinks might be beyond its current capability. The adopting of 'outrageous goals', which are clearly and strongly vision-related, is a way of making a strong commitment to improving the service for our customers. This year, one of our 'outrageous goals' formed part of our Year 5 reading initiative. It was stated that it was our declared goal that at the end of the year no Year 5 child, who is not at present receiving extra special needs funding, would be reading at more than a year behind his/her chronological age. Our results to date are encouraging but not yet outrageous!

Delighting the customer

Customer/client satisfaction is an acceptable base line for our work in school but our aim is to go further than this, we desire to delight our customers. In order to do this, it is important to be reflective and self-critical. As a learning organisation we are working at continuous improvement in all areas, trying to detect weaknesses before our customers detect them. This was our approach in our recent work on again reviewing our system for reporting to parents towards the end of the academic year. Under the comment bank system reports were very long, detailed and used some educational jargon which we felt might at times carry little real meaning to our children and their parents. Within the amount of complex detail it is possible that the heart of the report may have been lost and that parents may well have completed reading a report still feeling they did not have a clear answer to the question 'how is my child doing in school?' We sought some feedback on the reports but the picture was not clear. We wondered whether parents were accepting what they were given on the basis that the teachers had put a lot of effort into the reports, they sounded knowledgeable and what more could they expect anyway?

With this in mind, over the last two years we have attempted improvements. We have tried to go beyond traditional expectation, our aim being not merely to satisfy our parent customers but to 'delight' them. We now have a front cover with general information about topics, curriculum aspects covered and curriculum enrichment activities undertaken by the child. In the centre is a double-page spread which provides national curriculum attainment information grouped around a scanned in photo of the child. In order to make up this page the teacher simply selects the level the student has attained in teacher assessment in each of the national curriculum areas. A paragraph which is standard to that level appears with, in the case of English, mathematics and science, the level the child is now working towards printed above. The back page provides space for the teacher to personalise the report with comments on attainment and non-national curriculum achievements. Guidance is provided in terms of what type of things should be included on this page but it is composed by the class teacher. The combination of a standardised element and more of a personalised, free writing element has, we hope, allowed the best of both systems to come through in the final document. We are now looking into practical ways of reporting more regularly to parents.

The reporting system described above has also significantly reduced the work load for teachers. For those who were particularly conscientious the letter style reports and the use of the detailed comment bank led to many days' work. We always felt that the work involved was, in many cases, disproportionate to the value of the report in terms of informing parents and leading to greater future achievement for the child. The purpose of the new style reports was to make things better for parents and children, not to reduce teachers' workloads. However, this additional consequence is welcome for it gives teachers more time and energy to devote to providing quality planning and teaching to the children during the report writing period.

Customising client services

In order to provide a customised service, a quality company should adjust or fine tune its service to match its customers' expectations. A perfectly customised service would require the service given to each individual to be a creation from scratch not a judicious adaptation of a programme developed for another client.

It is expected and required that all state schools will provide the national curriculum but, unfortunately, following a generic national curriculum designed for all children of a particular age does not allow teachers and children to start from scratch in designing tailor-made programmes. Even in the area of special needs, where excellent practice has resulted in the creation of highly personalised programmes, the national curriculum blueprint still needs to be adhered to in all but the most exceptional of cases, while it should be adapted or differentiated in order to try and accommodate individual needs. Where schools may differ is in the way that they meet or indeed exceed this expectation. At Mereway Middle School we have made a commitment to providing a customised service to each child. We have adopted a number of different approaches to ensure this, the most notable being target setting and the development of our challenge centre.

Target setting

Two years ago a target-setting approach was introduced in school as a way of addressing the need to help children to find their own personally appropriate routes through the curriculum. The targets presently used are, in most cases, child-friendly versions of national curriculum programmes of study or statements of attainment which have been put on a computerised database. Targets are set up each half-term, their number and choice is personal to each child. Children's target sheets contain their individual learning objectives, both academic and social, for a half-termly topic. The individualised sheets then become part of a child's Record of Achievement and a basis for teachers' further planning. This approach has been adopted and is being fine tuned by all teachers in school. Its use has radically changed a number of teachers' approaches to planning. Daily plans are now focused more clearly on children's individual needs.

Some teachers have achieved particular successes with this approach, with significant impact on their teaching and the children's learning. In describing the approach in more detail I will be using information and direct quotes from four teachers working in different year groups. These members of staff are continuously developing their use of targets with the children in their respective classes. As Ros Burman, senior teacher and Year 6 co-ordinator explains 'The constant factor I have discovered with target setting is that, every time, I have approached it slightly differently. Each time there has been a reason for me to reflect on my practice and think "yes, it would be better if I tried this or that . . .".'

In Year 5, teachers begin the process of identifying learning targets with a team approach. From the key questions provided by curriculum co-ordinators for each half term's topic, the Year 5 teacher team identifies the times in the study when each key question will be addressed. Using the suggested activities and learning opportunities, appropriate methods of differentiation are discussed and the learning process for individual children or groups of children is planned. The team also considers how the product produced by an activity will show a child's current level of achievement. Alison Hawkes the Year 5 co-ordinator supports the client-focused approach explaining 'For each key question and related activities we identify the most appropriate target which could be achieved. We then use our prior knowledge of our classes to identify the children who are most likely to be working at each level. Thereby we create personalised learning pathways through the forecasted work and individual target sheets for each child.' Thus a balance between entitlement and differentiation is attempted.

In Year 6 Ros begins the identification of new half-termly targets by focusing on her teacher evaluation of the child's present level of attainment. In a way similar to that used in Year 5, the most appropriate learning opportunity for each child or group of children is considered.

Individual children are then directed towards the targets from which they can select in each of the core subjects. A wider freedom of choice is offered in the Foundation subjects, with children being encouraged to choose from targets at the level they are working towards or a target which is consolidating a level previously achieved. This pattern results in the majority of children having approximately twenty national curriculum targets for a half-term. Those children who have been identified as having special needs will have fewer national curriculum targets but their list is supplemented by targets identified in their Special Needs Programme. Additional personal or social targets are agreed upon, these go beyond the national curriculum and reflect particular strengths and weaknesses.

Gaynor Crute the Year 8 co-ordinator ensures greater student involvement by the older children in agreeing their own targets. They are actively involved in customising the curriculum for their own needs. She explains:

All children in my class are aware of the levels they are generally working towards and have previously achieved in each National Curriculum Attainment Target. Before a new half-termly topic begins, children are given a sheet which indicates the focus for learning, key questions and the range of targets at different levels within each subject. They select their targets with another child of similar ability who acts as their critical partner. They then use the target database to input and print out their own selected targets. At the beginning of each teaching session, the key question and a range of relevant targets are put on the board. At all times, children have their individualised target sheets in front of them.

In all of the year groups at the beginning of most new pieces of work the children write down the key questions relevant to that learning opportunity and the target or code from their selected targets. Targets are reviewed regularly. Gaynor details the processes used in her Year 8 class saying:

At this stage of individual reflection, each child notes down on the target sheet the title of the work which provides evidence for the achievement of each specific target. Working with their critical partners they look at the work they have done and discuss their understanding. A dialogue takes place to agree if each target has been achieved. When both the child and the critical partner are confident that a target has been achieved, they initial it. It is then the child's responsibility to show the teacher the evidence of achievement which the teacher then initials.

Vanessa Lee, a teacher in Year 7, is using a somewhat different method. 'At the beginning of activities the class are made aware of the key questions, objectives and the range of suitable targets and what needs to be understood in order to achieve each target listed. The children do not self-select at this stage but they are aware of what they need to be working towards at each level.' When Vanessa is evaluating and responding to children's work, she 'puts on the end of the piece of work any target which I believe a child has achieved at any stage in the activity not just in the outcome. In practical subjects, if we video a session the children will evaluate their own work against the targets, this is then discussed and a level agreed.' The children then use the target database retrospectively to update their achievements. The printout provides a running record of the child's achievements in each curriculum area.

When identifying the strengths and successes of the target system used Alison says it has helped make differentiation her priority. 'It causes us to consider in depth the individual needs of every child in our year group. We endeavour to create activities which give each task an element of excitement, challenge and uniqueness. With the key questions acting as the umbrella overhead, the differentiated learning opportunities feed off each other. The children's desire to show others what they have been doing seems to help ensure there is little or no element of hierarchy of ability. They show an interest and learn from each other regardless of ability.' Other strengths and successes of the target-setting approach are identified by Ros and Gaynor as being:

- it causes reflection on individual achievement
- children feel secure and purposeful in knowing what they are working towards, they see the relevance of their work
- children set themselves ambitious targets, more ambitious even than teachers would have been likely to set for them
- a targeted approach to assessment is achieved
- when a target is achieved success is felt by student and teacher
- it ties teaching objectives more closely to children's learning targets
- the discussions about achievement of targets have helped to increase the children's vocabulary, so they are more able to talk with each other and the teacher about their learning.

In the target-setting method used by Vanessa the approach acts as a form of achievement reward system. She says 'I find this encourages all children to stretch themselves to a higher level. They are encouraged to want to improve knowledge and understanding, to be more "successful". Achievement of targets raises self-esteem in the children and makes national curriculum assessments easy to record and refer to.'

Although the four teachers quoted are highly committed to using a form of target setting to produce an individualised service for their clients, they also identify areas of weakness in their approaches and these are now their own targets for improvement. These include:

- personal and social targets, included alongside national curriculum targets, not being valued by the children in the same way
- programmes of study and attainment targets not always providing small enough steps for achievement at each level, prior knowledge needed at the lower levels is not stated at times
- children with significant learning difficulties find the self-evaluation aspect of the system very difficult
- practical subjects seem less well incorporated into the approach
- at present there are not enough targets that focus on the acquisition of skills

- there is a possibility that teachers or children may not aim high enough leading to under-achievement: sometimes children may miss out on higher order learning opportunities that could have been of benefit
- knowing when a target has been achieved in terms of learning is not easy, working towards and achieving are two different things: also learning is often highly context bound
- time taken to plan the differentiated learning opportunities across the curriculum can be immense; focusing on the outcomes is as important
- with the range of differentiated targeted activities taking place teaching opportunities for the pushing on of learning at crucial moments can be missed.

As a staff we are conscious that, although we have adapted them, the Statements of Attainment were designed as assessment tools rather than learning targets. Therefore more refining is necessary, particularly as we believe that the national curriculum is far from the whole curriculum, even in the prescribed subjects.

We also realise that children do not always learn in neat stages; the steps are not necessarily sequential. It is therefore important to gain a balance of targets to aim for and to have acknowledgement of learning achievement during and after an activity. This is important because it remains debatable whether it is possible to predict consistently what can be learnt. Is it possible to really know what we are going to learn before we learn it? Doesn't learning often involve moving into the insecurity of the unknown? These are important questions that need addressing within the target-setting framework, in order to achieve an appropriate balance for each learner at each particular occasion in his/her learning.

We are monitoring the approaches taken. We are looking at teachers' planning, children's work, target sheets and hearing directly from children about their views on the approach. This is what some children had to say:

'I think target setting is a really good idea. Now when we work we have targets to achieve and its like we are working towards goals. I really like that.' (Hannah)

'It helps to set personal targets as these could become useful in later life.' (Simon)

'The system we use for targets is really easy to understand. By using an IT database we have easy access to the targets and they can be clearly presented.' (Kimberley)

We are also encouraging teachers to share their experiences and learn from one another. What appears to be emerging is that different individuals, both students and teachers, favour different approaches to target setting and to establishing their own individual learning pathway.

Mereway Middle School Challenge Centre

At our school we have made an active commitment to taking on initiatives on behalf of the customer in our efforts to exceed expectation. We have asked ourselves the question 'How often in the day-to-day course of a child's education does he/she feel positively and fully challenged by the work being undertaken – challenged to achieve at the edge of his/her capabilities. For a multitude of reasons it probably doesn't happen as often as we would like. Last year the staff, governors, parents and children in the school tried to address this by embarking on a major new initiative – the development of Mereway Middle School Challenge Centre. The work of our Challenge Centre greatly contributes to our attempts to customise our service and give opportunities for all to exceed expectation.

The notion of a challenge centre has its roots in a visit to Hamilton in Ontario, Canada in the Easter holiday of 1994. The seed of an idea then germinated when we were able to see a way of bringing together various school objectives. These included:

- an increasing staff commitment to children having the chance to make more choices in their education and have greater control over their own learning
- a desire to facilitate more opportunities for independent learning
- further work on addressing the needs of the most able children in school
- a desire to introduce specific problem-solving challenges that went across age groups and beyond the national curriculum.

These commitments coincided with various significant developments in school:

- the establishment of a DSP (Designated Special Provision) for children with significant learning difficulties
- the appointment of a new special needs co-ordinator (Emma Mead) and the rapid expansion of the curriculum support team
- the announcement of the Dearing Report's 20 per cent flexibility in the curriculum
- re-acquiring the use of a school space previously designated as a kitchen servery area.

After a period of strategic planning and discussion, the kitchen servery area was converted into a learning resource room, now known as 'The Challenge Centre'. The Mereway Middle School Challenge Centre is a multi-purpose facility. It continues to be equipped with up-to-date multimedia technology and communications systems for the children's use. To date these include: computers with CD ROM, laptops, a modem, telephone, fax, Internet connection, cameras, video recorder and video cameras.

The work of the Challenge Centre has three main foci:

- It provides us with an attractive, well-resourced space which can be used by children, and staff supporting children, on special needs programmes; this involves children who require additional special needs help in their education, including children who have been identified as being 'more able'.

- The Challenge Centre provides us with a supplementary facility for advanced IT work with children and IT training for staff.

- It provides a focus for 'Challenges' which are introduced to the children from a variety of sources. These include general competitions and problem-solving puzzles as well as specifically designed challenges proposed by school staff, governors, students, community organisations and local companies. Challenges are often tailor made for the children and relate to real problems or projects. As a consequence of this the children are usually able to see some of their ideas and solutions put into action. Work on the challenges often takes place in the centre, helping to ensure that all children have access to the work of the Challenge Centre.

Challenges are something children choose to do. They are advertised to the whole school or sometimes to target groups. The uptake is usually quite high with 90 per cent of children having taken part in a challenge to date. It has been suggested that achieving customer satisfaction indicates choice for the client, a chance to make decisions. The national curriculum has taken away much of the opportunity for choice for schools, teachers and individual children. However, we only learn what we choose to learn and therefore it is important to acknowledge children's choice and their need to make decisions in their learning.

The centre operates a booking and signing-in system with children making arrangements with the relevant teachers in school. A typical morning might see:

- a small special needs group working with a member of the curriculum support team

- our special needs co-ordinator working on a specific learning programme with a statemented child from our Designated Special Provision

- pairs of children working on their contributions to a challenge

- a child or teacher using the Internet

- pairs of children working on producing articles for our newsletter or computer presentations or databases for use in school

- one or more children, who have displayed particular abilities, working by themselves, or with a mentor, on a specifically designed project.

Our work on extending children has led to an increasingly growing number of children who have shown particular interests and abilities being placed on 'Enhanced Education Plans'.

The Special Needs Programmes, Enhanced Education Plans and the Challenges provide an opportunity for children to work independently or in small groups on projects which fascinate them, encouraging them to take the work beyond the classroom to reach higher levels of achievement. The idea is that children should have access to the very best facilities with opportunities to go to the very finest experts within and beyond the school to assist and inspire them in their learning. This has involved such things as children using the Internet, phoning and faxing and writing to 'experts' and using the video phone. Soon we are hoping to install a computer conferencing facility and we have schools interested in linking up children with similar interests and setting up mentoring partnerships.

Over time, all children and staff have access to the Challenge Centre, its projects and facilities. We are also hoping to gain greater community use, particularly by some of our feeder lower schools. It is of great importance that the Challenge Centre facility is inclusive in its nature rather than exclusive. Indeed, one of its greatest successes to date is the interest and pride that all children have in the centre. The nightmare scenario of a special needs room in which children may feel labelled and de-motivated has not only been avoided but has, in fact, been replaced by the establishment of a high status room where everyone wants to work and achieve.

The future

When Mereway Middle School first opened we said that we were developing an organisation for the twenty-first century; we were not setting up a school for the end of this century and certainly not for the nineteenth century – a century which still has a controlling impact on our schools in this country, particularly in terms of structure and organisation. In our efforts for further improvement, there are a number of areas in which we are planning for the future. We are concentrating our thinking on the areas of:

- organisation for teaching and learning
- the use of IT in school
- staffing issues
- further development as a learning organisation.

We are working hard to release each other from the tendency to try to adapt and develop practice from the existing educational paradigms that tell us this is the way it has to be done, this is the way it has and will always be done. We need to avoid trying to base the future on current paradigms as they can limit our thinking. We need second order change where, instead of change within the system, it is the system itself which is changed. Our future strategic intent often revolves around asking questions to challenge existing paradigms in order to try and rethink education for our rapidly changing world. Below are some of the questions that are presently preoccupying us in our thinking about education.

Organisation for teaching and learning

Should formal teaching and learning be organised on a 8.35 am to 3.05 pm basis? How can we use the school's human and physical resources most usefully and creatively? Should the class in a year group remain the main organisational unit when it comes to setting up educational experiences in school? What are the optimum number of students for certain learning situations? How are the adults in school best deployed to support learning on a minute by minute basis? What are our clients thoughts on each of the above questions?

The use of IT

In what ways can computer-aided learning most benefit young people in school? What has educational research to say about this and what have we found so far within our context? What changes need to be made to ensure that the school can keep pace with technological developments and the demands of young people? How can IT help us to become a data-rich school? Where can IT add to administrative efficiency, rigour and reliability? Where is IT not an effective answer to providing a quality service? What are our clients' thoughts on each of the above questions?

Staffing issues

School structures must not inhibit school development. How can flexible structures be created and how can re-structuring be best managed? In the context of our school what is the most effective balance of different types of staff, i.e. admin. staff, classroom teachers, school managers, members of the curriculum support team, outside 'experts', etc.? Does our present staffing structure best fit the school's needs today and its possible future needs? What should responsibility points be given for? What should be awarded on a short-term, long-term, permanent basis? What appropriate career structures can be created for the twenty-first century?

The school as a learning organisation

What needs to be done in order to enable us all to learn, share that learning and find ways in which that learning may contribute to future practice? What can we find out about the preferred learning styles of all of us as learners in the organisation? How can appraisal be of greatest benefit to staff in the improvement of the school experience for young people? How can educational research, particularly action research, be best used in our organisation to help our development as a research-based profession? Where can research help us to find ways forward to tackling problems, understanding our practice and analysing our successes? What are our clients' thoughts on each of the above questions?

I believe, at Mereway Middle School, that we have a responsibility to set aside out-dated assumptions and practices and to stay true to our mission which includes the statement that:

We will continue to be a forward looking, innovative school, proactive in our pursuit of excellence and continuous improvement.

The movement must always be forward. This is at the heart of the quality movement at Mereway Middle School.

Commentary – quality strategies

BRENT DAVIES AND JOHN WEST-BURNHAM

The three case studies in this section provide detailed accounts of the implementation of specific Total Quality strategies. It will be immediately apparent to the reader that two of the schools, Eumemmerring and Mereway, introduced strategies without consciously adopting a Total Quality philosophy. In both cases they have introduced radical changes on the basis of education strategies to which Total Quality criteria can be applied with the benefit of hindsight. It might also raise the issue of the extent to which the principles of Total Quality are available from other, purely educational sources. This would appear to be a solution to the problem of transferability and to the charge that Total Quality has limited relevance to education because of its commercial i.e. profit-based antecedents. Certainly it is possible to demonstrate that there is a high degree of congruity between the tenets of Total Quality and the components of the school effectiveness and school improvement movements.

In spite of this, as Murphy agrees, schools are not as effective or committed to improvement as they need to be. These case studies provide important insight into significant and valuable innovations which are operating in a culture of focus on the client and continuous improvement. If these prerequisites were met then initiatives would serve to transform schools. Equally all three schools in this section have demonstrated a willingness to change. This is not always the case with schools, nor with many other organisations. Far more businesses fail to implement Total Quality than succeed. This may well be because the totality of Total Quality is too demanding. It may be more appropriate to consider an incremental approach as the schools in this section have done, focusing on specific and particular strategies and then using the conceptual framework of Total Quality to help provide the criteria for success and the agenda for reform.

All three schools demonstrate the impact on a school of challenging existing definitions of commonly used concepts: leadership, teams and child-centred. All three terms are widely used in education without specific frames of reference and without consideration of what the application of the concept in a logically consistent way might mean. The three writers show that the systematic application of a principle has implications across the whole organisation; if a significant change is to be sustained then it cannot be 'bolted-on', it has to become systemic.

In his discussion of leadership, Murphy shows how the new concept has to be derived from values and to permeate language, management structures and processes, perceptions of students and car-parking. In the same way Taylor and McKenzie show how a change in classroom organisation informs almost every other aspect of the school. Trott demonstrates how a relatively simple premise can influence a wide range of practices and supportive principles. The central issue is one of consistency and this is where the overarching principles of Total Quality can help to contextualise a specific initiative.

Of course all three cases cited have problems. The notion of distributed leadership is compromised by external expectations of accountability and the hierarchical career structure of education. The integrity of the team approach will be significantly determined by the extent to which it is exemplified in every aspect of a student's experience. But it is the notion of the child as customer that is potentially the most problematic. It is almost impossible to envisage a school that would deny centrality of the student and yet practice is so very often at odds with the exposed values. The secondary school timetable, prevailing teaching strategies, social facilities for students, the scheduling of the school day, access to resources and meal times are all examples of where it is better to be an adult than a student.

This assumes that the student is in fact the customer. There is a very strong case which argues that, while this may be morally defensible, it is practically naïve. In an era of parental choice, the national curriculum and OFSTED inspections there appear to be a multiplicity of customers most of whom have a direct impact on the school in a way that children cannot. And yet the examples in this section demonstrate that it is possible for schools to make fundamental decisions within externally determined accountabilities.

A further constraint on the notion of students as customers is the extent to which they can be said to be able to differentiate between needs and wants. They need to follow the national curriculum, take SATs and external examinations and develop a wide range of social and intellectual skills. This menu may not always coincide with the wants of the average 5, 10, 13, or 16-year-old. What these case studies demonstrate is the capacity to 'delight the customer'; to develop strategies which focus on the learning of the individual in a way that allows success, supports differentiation and works to recognise and respect individual differences. The control and dependency culture that pervades some schools (and is as detrimental for adults as it is for students) is probably one of the most significant indicators of the lack of a focus on the individual, i.e. a customer focus.

Many education professionals have found a semantic problem with the concept of a customer; they prefer client. This really does not matter, the label applied is less important than the underlying vision and values and how these are exemplified in the daily experience of students. Few teachers would tolerate the quality of service from their garage that they are prepared to administer to their students. Yet this is inevitable if the teachers in turn are not perceived as customers of managers and leaders. Murphy and Trott both provide examples of teachers as customers (in terms of choice, trust and control) which are necessary preconditions to teachers regarding students as customers.

What is significant to all three case studies is the existence in schools of leading professionals who are prepared to innovate, take carefully calculated risks and follow through a strategy to its logical conclusion, in other words learners leading learners.

PART SIX

■ ■ ■

International perspectives on quality

11

■ ■ ■

TQM: Georgia's approach to educational reform and school restructuring

DAVE WELLER

Education is the key to America's future and to its mission of regaining pre-eminence in the global marketplace. The state of affairs existing between the educational product in the United States – graduates of its public schools – and that product's influence on the effectiveness of America's businesses is a given, as is the logic of a working relationship between education and business whose mission is to improve the outcomes of both (Melvin, 1991). Recent reform movements in American education, however, have shown little success in meeting the expectations of its customers (students, parents, and business and community members) or its workforce (teachers, administrators, and other staff members). Both groups have become discouraged with previous unsuccessful school reform efforts to achieve their desired product: students who have the knowledge and skills to be productive, competent, and contributing members of their workplaces and their communities (Weller and Hartley, 1994b).

Murgatroyd and Morgan (1993) and Weller and Hartley (1994a) found that if school restructuring is to succeed, a systematic, structured process is needed which will provide adequate flexibility for teamwork and individual creativity. These researchers note that previous school reform movements comprised fragmented programmes and piecemeal approaches and failed because they lacked a coherent plan and process to implement school reform.

Today, educators have a management improvement process based on Deming (1986) which provides structure, flexible guidelines, evaluative procedures, and a systematic interactive network between principals, teachers, parents, and community members. Deming's fourteen principles of Total Quality Management (TQM) provide a restructuring template for school improvement with a comprehensive delivery system which allows educators to adopt proven research practices and to refine and expand these components to their fullest potential. These include shared decision making, problem-solving teams, training and staff development, and a new approach to leadership.

Many businesses have recognised the potential and reaped the benefits of TQM as a means for product and service improvement. Although TQM is not new to the business world in the United States, the management method is relatively new to education. TQM's emphasis on leadership, teamwork, constancy of purpose, and continuous improvement holds great promise for educators in their efforts to produce a quality product because it combines many of the practices that educational research has shown to be effective. The research on effective schools, for example, with its emphasis on teamwork, shared decision-making, and creating a positive school culture complements the Deming quality philosophy.

Nations throughout the world are pursuing quality in education through the adoption of TQM principles of Deming, Crosby, Juran, and others. TQM has become central to international educational reform efforts in nations such as Australia, Japan, Canada, the United States, and the United Kingdom as they seek higher quality products and services through educational renewal and school restructuring.

In the United States, reform movements have proliferated: the 1960s stressed innovation; the 1970s called for educational accountability; and the 1980s popularised school reform with various federal and state commission reports and their recommendations for excellence which states converted into prescriptive legislation. Often trendy, many reform practices thought to be educational panaceas were short-lived and yielded few positive research-based results.

Murgatroyd and Morgan (1993) and Schenkat (1993) believe that such reform efforts have not succeeded in America because the successful elements of various approaches have not been tied together into a coherent delivery system in order to refine these successful practices or to attack new problems. Moreover, schools for the most part, are focusing on implementing single innovative practices as typified by the 1970s and 1980s approach which called for schools to focus on improving one area at a time. In reality, schools contend with simultaneous interactions and demands and, therefore, require multiple innovations if they are to be successful in their attempts at reform. For this reason, TQM's systematic, structured delivery system holds great promise for educational renewal (Fullan and Stiegelbauer, 1991).

School restructuring, the educational reform movement of the 1990s, is more intensive and diverse than previous reform movements. It emphasises local rather than state reform initiatives and focuses on bottom-up policy-making and fiscal control (Weller and Hartley, 1994b). This concept centres on redesigning the school's instructional delivery system and its governance policies by allowing the schools themselves to create their own policies and to be held accountable for their own successes and failures. This thrust toward internal school reform runs counter to past reform movements which were externally mandated, hastily conceived, functionally narrow in scope, and lacking in research-based data to support their reform paradigms (Weller, 1996a). According to English (1994), these variables were major reasons for their failure as well as the reason many educators were left sceptical of the promises of reform movements in general and with many educators being reluctant to be optimistic about any programme being capable of reforming public education (English, 1994).

Background to the TQM initiative in Georgia

Georgia was the first state to legislate sweeping school reform measures in the call for educational excellence following the publication of *A Nation at Risk* (National Commission on Education, 1993). In its initial efforts in 1985, Georgia adopted the Quality Basic Education (QBE) Act. QBE was designed to promote school excellence, and it was Georgia's hasty response to the national call for excellence. The primary impetus for excellence came from external sources, business leaders and state government officials. State legislators, with minimal input from professional educators, passed the QBE Act which was highly regulatory in nature and, using the typical top-down strategy, mandated uniformity in public education through an abundance of prescriptive rules and regulations which were often contradictory in nature (Weller and Hartley, 1994b).

Outcomes from QBE proved less than satisfactory since school efficiency, through school conformity to policy, was emphasised over school excellence. Conflicting policy statements led to confusion and frustration on the part of educators trying to follow QBE mandates which often ran counter to sound educational practice. Teachers and administrators at the local level, having no say in these improvement policies, lacked a sense of commitment to and ownership of QBE. Moreover, these mandates were in opposition to the existing research on the effective schools movement which had found benefits in local control, shared decision making, and goal setting among school personnel. Good and Brophy (1984) reached similar conclusions about improving schools when they found effective schools to be virtually synonymous with a minimum of regulations prescribing teacher classroom behaviour. Excellence in teaching, they maintain, is a very personal and complex task which cannot be achieved by mandated uniform measures.

Finally, as with most top-down, externally mandated measures QBE focused on the symptoms rather than the causes of Georgia's educational distress.

Taking the recommendations from *A Nation at Risk*, QBE emphasised curriculum reform, the allocation of more state Monies, increased graduation requirements, more rigorous grading practices, and alternative student scheduling options. No thought was given to the effective schools research which found that people from *within* the organisation make change; external mandates and redesigned traditional delivery systems do not.

TQM initiative: grassroots interest and pressure

The interest in TQM for local school reform in Georgia came from a variety of sources. Educators as well as non-educators shared basic frustration over QBE and past reform efforts. Primarily, student test scores on standardised achievement tests were not showing significant increases, there was external criticism from business leaders and government officials about the quality of high school graduates, student dropout rates and high absenteeism showed insignificant decline, and there was general teacher and parent dissatisfaction with the educational programmes offered by the schools. In short, both groups recognised that traditional top-down reform measures were not yielding the intended educational results and that 'something' had to be done quickly to improve education. Businesses were beginning to see success with TQM, and industry leaders were offering the opinion that TQM was applicable to education as well. Many educators were sceptical about becoming involved in TQM fearing yet another bandwagon routine which would lead to more frustration. Others were wary of a business-oriented approach to improve education. After all, what can business contribute to education when we do not even talk the same language, let alone produce the same product? But the need to improve education was real and in the end, the need to try something different, something that had already proved successful in producing quality results, was too tempting to resist.

Georgia's TQM reform movement

In 1991, a small group of leaders in business, government, and education took an active interest in reforming the state's public schools through TQM by forming the Next Generation School Project (NGSP). The idea behind the NGSP was to promote school excellence through a school–community collaboration to achieve quality education at the local level with state-level support. The NGSP had a three-pronged mission:

- to infuse the quality principles into the educational delivery system at the local school level

- to prepare students to meet the needs of Georgia's twentieth-century workforce
- to develop a community collaborative network to assist schools in their quality efforts.

By 1992, over 300 Georgians representing education, business, and government were NGSP members with the business community having the most significant impact on the adoption of the TQM principles as the primary vehicle for school restructuring. Business leaders who evidenced success with the Deming quality model drew direct parallels between business and education, and educators were quick to realise the value of a grass roots, bottom-up model to reform education. Many educators saw in TQM many of the fundamental practices of the effective school movement which yielded success but at varying rates and outcomes. Most appealing to Georgia educators was the systematic, structured delivery system that TQM offered to implement shared school governance through team decision-making, problem-solving, and continuous improvement. By 1993, the Quality Design Committee (QDC) was formed and it developed a nine-point template modelled after Deming's fourteen points, for Georgia's communities to use in designing their next generation schools. This nine-point template is an umbrella concept which allows the schools and their communities to develop their own quality paradigms, based on their own educational priorities and available resources, to promote and sustain their own quality improvement goals. Central to the template are the quality principles of participatory leadership, teamwork and shared school governance, customer satisfaction, joint vision building, and continuous improvement. This approach to school restructuring creates a *seamless* educational community in which educators, community and business leaders, parents, and students work together to develop their own quality educational programmes and set their own quality goals. This unified commitment to quality education promotes shared ownership, vested interest, and pride in achieving educational outcomes.

With moneys appropriated from the Georgia General Assembly and through private sector donations, $4 million were available for 1993–94 and 1994–95 for NGSP competitive, quality-improvement grants. Thirty grants were awarded over the two funding years and required matching funds on a 1:2 ratio of local funds to grant funds. Grant moneys were awarded on a competitive basis with Requests for Proposals (RFPs) going to all 183 school system superintendents in Georgia. Each grantee had to designate at least three of the following nine NGSP criteria to implement:

- establish a community collaborative
- emphasise world class performance
- implement improvement
- emphasise vocational skills
- reorganise the learning environment

- use instructional technology
- attend to at-risk students
- adopt the quality philosophy
- provide continuous staff development.

Successful funding for the first year did not mean school systems automatically received second year funding. Only six of the fifteen first-year sites received continuation grants which were primarily based on evaluation results of their project accomplishments.

Georgia's NGSP results (1993–95)

Georgia's Next Generation Schools, having the option of choosing at least three of the nine quality criteria to implement, evidenced similar results to those reported nationally, a summary of which can be found in Weller (1996). Of the thirty funded sites, fifteen per year, some had begun to implement TQM prior to NGSP funding because of their belief in TQM as a promising school reform method, while others waited for NGSP grant moneys to begin their quality venture. Each of the project sites chose as one of their nine quality criteria to 'Adopt the Quality Philosophy' which covered Deming's fourteen points of quality management. Most of these schools only began to gather base-line data on student achievement scores as part of their NGSP funding, which accounts for the lack of longitudinal data. Schools receiving NGSP grants represented rural, suburban and urban school systems and grades kindergarten to 12. Grant sites could be individual schools, two or more schools, or an entire school system. The decision on how the quality principles should be implemented and at what level of implementation, was left up to the community collaborative writing the grant.

NGSP 1993–94 sites

In one rural Georgia school system, which emphasised teamwork, personalised instruction and continuous improvement, middle school students with a 60 per cent plus at-risk student population, demonstrated an 80 per cent increase in average student scores in Grades 6–8 by one grade level in reading and maths, and high school students in Grades 9–12 increased their achievement scores by an average of 0.3 grade levels in reading and maths. Student absentee rate in the middle schools decreased by 90 per cent while the dropout rate decreased by 21 per cent. High school dropout rates decreased from 38 to 26 per cent with average student attendance increasing to 72 per cent.

Two other rural Georgia school systems, emphasising personalised instruction and continuous improvement, reported decreases in student grade-level retention by over 60 per cent for Grades 9–12 with student dropout rates declining by an average of 35 per cent. In these school systems, cases of vandalism decreased an average of 40 per cent. In three suburban school systems, teacher morale and student self-esteem increased and student absenteeism decreased an average of 30 per cent. Personalising student instruction through the use of computer programs, small group instruction, after-school tutorial programmes, and the use of community volunteers as classroom aides has a positive impact on student learning by raising student achievement scores by almost 7 per cent. Increasing parent involvement in school activities and forming home–school parent support groups reinforced the importance of the school's goals at home, impacted positively on student increased attendance, and produced decreases in student dropout rates and cases of school vandalism. Emphasis in these school systems was placed on the Deming principles of constancy of purpose, continuous improvement, and involving everyone in the quality transformation.

In another suburban school system, with a 40 per cent plus at-risk student population, gains in maths and reading increased by 0.7 and 0.5 grade levels respectively for middle school students (Grades 6–8) while gains in maths and reading at one elementary school increased an average of 1.2 years in maths and 1.3 years in reading in Grades 3 and 5. In another elementary school, Normal Curve Equivalent (NCE) scores on the Iowa Test of Basic Skills (ITBS) for test data from 1992–94 show gains for students in Grades 3 to 5 for maths and reading with gains of greater than one-third of a standard deviation at Grades 4 and 5 for maths. Gains of one-third of a standard deviation are considered statistically significant <0.05. With the rise in student achievement scores, teacher morale at these schools also increased by 67 per cent and is attributed to the use of quality improvement teams and classroom team teaching practices, and the success of their students as a result of their quality improvement efforts. In this elementary school, parent participation increased by 41 per cent and student attendance increased by over 60 per cent and was attributed to teacher efforts to get parents involved in adopting the quality philosophy in their homes.

In another rural elementary school, discipline problems decreased by 81 per cent and student absenteeism decreased by almost 40 per cent. Personalising student instruction through computer assisted learning, using peer and parent tutors in classrooms, and applying the team-teaching concept contributed to student achievement. Increases in teacher morale are attributed to team-teaching, evidence of student achievement through the application of the quality principles, and active parent support for the school's goals. Here, efforts were made to actively involve parents in quality improvement teams which examined the school's disciplinary codes and classroom teaching methods. Parents were also used as classroom tutors and instructional aides and served as regular members of each grade level's quality improvement team.

Two of Georgia's large urban school systems, both with over 60 per cent at-risk and low socio-economic status (SES) student populations, reported increased attendance by parents at PTA meetings by over 50 per cent, parent volunteers were up by 47 per cent, the rate of student absentees decreased by 60 per cent, and the dropout rate decreased more than 25 per cent. Vandalism cases were down by more than 40 per cent. In both of these school systems, parents were members of school governance committees which revised school disciplinary codes and restructured the school's curriculum. Parents as Teaching Partners programmes were formed which provided instruction to parents on how to be effective tutors and learning partners with their students while completing school work at home. Parents in these programmes also assisted teachers in reinforcing the importance of being good citizens, taking pride in completing their school work, and having respect for the rights and property of others.

Student gains in these two urban school systems increased an average of two to ten percentile points on the ITBS for at-risk students in Grades 2 to 8 in both maths and reading from 1992–94. Greatest percentile gains were evidenced in Grade 3 (up three percentile points in reading and four points in maths) and Grade 7 (up three percentile points in reading and six points in maths). Here, the use of computer assisted instruction, small group instruction, the use of teacher team planning, and the use of community volunteers as classroom tutors impacted positively on student achievement.

NGSP 1994–95 sites

Of the fifteen NGSP funded sites, nine received first-year funding. These nine school systems concentrated on implementing the quality philosophy through year-long in-service and workshop programmes, establishing community collaborative programmes and partnership with local businesses and government agencies, redesigning their vocational education curriculum through emphasis on interdisciplinary instruction, and training teachers and support staff in the use of telecommunication and computer technology to improve classroom instruction.

Six NGSP sites received second-year funding to either work towards new project goals or complete their 1993–94 goals. In one Georgia rural school system using 1993–94 base-line data, student average test scores on the ITBS for Grade 8 increased in reading by 1.4 grade level and in maths by 2.9 grade level. Student gains in two predominantly low SES rural kindergarten classes evidenced student gains in reading on the Developing Skills Checklist by an average of 70 points with teacher morale increasing by 62 per cent. In both these school systems, the use of computer assisted learning programmes, team teaching, and small group instruction contributed to the positive gains in student achievement. Teacher morale increase was attributed to student progress and the professional interaction and professional growth which comes from team teaching.

Another rural school system with over 60 per cent SES showed increases in average grade equivalent scores on the ITBS in four schools at the third grade level of 0.9 in reading and 0.8 in maths. Grade equivalent scores for students at Grade 5 went up 0.6 in reading and 0.4 in maths, and eighth grade student achievement scores increased by 0.5 in reading and 0.4 in maths. In two of these four schools, students in Grades 3 to 5 were at an average of 0.5 grade level below in reading and in two other schools students were below an average of 0.7 grade level in maths. Here, student success was attributed largely to parent and community volunteers who served as classroom tutors, small group instruction, and computer assisted learning programmes. However, parent–student assistance programmes, teacher team planning and team teaching, and the commitment to continuous improvement were central to each of these four schools' instructional programmes.

In one urban school system with a high percentage of at-risk and SES students, overall students achievement scores increased. Average scores on Georgia's Tests of Achievement and Proficiency (TAP) for eleventh graders increased from 1993 to 1995 with greatest gains in maths and social studies (six percentile points each) and in written expression (four percentile points). At the elementary level, students in Grades 2 and 4 averaged a 7.8 percentile gain in reading and a 7 percentile gain in maths on the ITBS. At Grade 5, a 2.5 average percentile gain occurred in reading with a 3.1 percentile gain occurring in maths. At the middle school level, students in Grades 6, 7 and 8, student achievement scores in reading and maths increased an average of 2.6 percentile points for reading and almost one percentile point in maths. In this school system, team teaching, team planning, and computer and personalised instruction were emphasised and attributed to the improvement in student learning in reading and maths. However, at the high school level, increases in written expression scores were also attributed to more assignments requiring writing by students and increases in social studies scores were attributed to the teaching of more social studies topics such as geopolitics and economics, and teaching map reading and chart and graph skills. These topics and skill areas, while tested on the Georgia TAP, were not emphasised as being important to the social studies curriculum in previous years.

In another urban school system, a comparison study of low SES seventh grade students (N = 78) and a cohort group of eighth grade students (N = 75) having matching variables was conducted with results as presented in Table 2.

Table 2: Comparison study of low SES students

	Quality principles 7th grade (N = 78)	Standard instruction 8th grade (N = 75)
Number passing all subjects	67 (86%)	30 (40%)
Number failing only one subject	3 (4%)	17 (23%)
Number failing more than one subject	8 (10%)	28 (37%)
Promoted to Grade 9	67 (86%)	45 (60%)
Promoted to Grade 8	5 (6%)	
Not promoted	6 (8%)	30 (40%)
Days absent	981 (7%)	2,837 (21%)
Attendance rate	93%	79%
Discipline incidents	64	111
Students sent to Alternative School	3 (4%)	10 (13%)

Note: Data were presented and provided by the descriptive statistics of frequency count and per cent. No inferential statistics were applied to further analyse these data.

In this NGSP school, seventh-grade teachers emphasised personalised and small group instruction and continuous improvement for their students. Students were told that they could and would succeed in their classwork, teachers had high expectations of success for each of their students, and teacher expectations for student success were communicated to students regularly. Emphasising these factors through the year, seventh-grade student achievement rates more than doubled, there were fewer students failing one or more subjects, more students in Grade 7 were promoted than in Grade 8, and absenteeism and discipline problems were fewer in Grade 7.

Students who were promoted from Grade 7 to Grade 9 (67 or 86 per cent), as presented in Table 2, were students who had passed a certain number of eighth grade course requirements but lacked the minimum credit hours to be fully promoted to Grade 8. With an extended day schedule, seventh grade students were provided with individual tutoring by teachers and student volunteers from a local university. During the extra hour of instruction each day, these seventh grade students were taught the required course content to be promoted to Grade 9 with computer assisted instruction and other instructional materials which met their individual interest and needs. This highly personalised instructional programme promoted their self-esteem and fostered learning through instructional materials which matched their individual interests.

This same school system also demonstrated gains in student test scores in Grades 2 to 4. Over two years, Normal Curve Equivalent scores on the ITBS for third grades increased in reading an average 2.75 points and in maths an average of 3.9 points. Students in Grades 2 and 4 increased their writing scores by over 70 per cent on teacher-made tests. Teachers increased the use of co-operative learning activities and personalised instruction in their classrooms.

Again, the use of computer programs and team teaching were also credited for gains in student achievement. Increased teacher morale was attributed to increased student learning and a decline in classroom discipline problems.

A suburban school system concentrated its instructional improvement efforts on student language proficiency in Spanish in the fifth grade and ninth grade algebra through Learning Logic algebra computer labs. Over two years, Spanish proficiency increased from 30 to 95 per cent in the novice range for speaking and writing while ninth grade Learning Logic algebra pass rates increased from 60 to 87 per cent with 76 per cent of the remaining students passing in summer school. Here, the use of technology, teacher team planning, and personalised instruction played a major role in student achievement.

Test scores on the ITBS for another Georgia suburban school system, with over 60 per cent SES students, showed average gains in percentiles for 1993–95. Grade 1 increased 3 points in maths, Grade 2 increased 3 points in reading, and Grade 3 increased 0.6 points in both maths and reading. Grade 4 students increased 4 percentile points in reading and Grade 5 students increased 6 points in maths. Students in Grade 6 increased in maths by 5 points, seventh grade students increased maths scores by 9 points, and eighth grade students increased 4 percentile points in maths. Eleventh grade students gained 15 percentile points in maths, 6 points in science, and 10 points in expressive writing. This school system's major goal was increasing student achievement with the use of computer assisted instruction and a strong home–school collaborative programme. Parents were provided with instruction on how to reinforce the school's goals in the home by helping students with their school assignments, emphasising the importance of school work and doing one's best, and more frequent parent-teacher conferences about students' progress.

In Georgia, the results of implementing TQM for school improvement closely parallel the findings reported nationally (Schmoker and Wilson, 1993; Weller and Hartley, 1994b). Results of the NGSP are highly promising, but should be viewed with an air of cautious optimism since the research efforts are ongoing and data are being collected to make longitudinal comparisons. What is evident from the current findings, however, is the need for strong and enthusiastic support from superintendents if TQM is to be a viable vehicle for school reform. Top-down initiation of the quality movement in American public schools is essential if TQM is to have the all-important foundation needed for success. This support, coupled with intensive training in the TQM principles for school personnel promotes a greater commitment to the quality philosophy and the goals of continuous improvement and constancy of purpose. Teamwork, team planning, computer-assisted instruction, parent involvement programmes, and personalised instruction are central to promoting instructional improvement and student achievement. Teacher morale is increased through the TQM philosophy of shared governance, team teaching and team planning, and improved student achievement. Parental and community support for the quality goals, parental involvement in classrooms and on instructional planning teams, and the assistance of parents in helping their children to achieve academically and socially are major factors contributing to the success of the Next Generation School Project. Consequently, the application of the TQM principles is showing positive results as Georgia schools are adopting TQM as a school reform and restructuring process.

References

English, F. W. (1994), *Theory in Educational Administration*, New York, HarperCollins.

Fullan, M. G. and Stiegelbauer, S. (1991), *The New Meaning of Educational Change*, New York, Teachers College Press.

Good, T. L. and Brophy, J. E. (1984), *Looking Into Classrooms* (3rd edn), New York, Harper & Row.

Melvin, C. (1991), 'Restructuring schools by applying Deming's management theories', *Journal of Staff Development*, 12(3), 16–20.

Murgatroyd, S. and Morgan, C. (1993), *Total Quality Management and the School*, Bristol, PA, Open University Press.

Schenkat, R. (1993), *Quality Connections: Transforming Schools through Total Quality Management*, Alexandria, VA, Association for Supervision and Curriculum Development.

Schmoker, M. J. and Wilson, R. B. (1993), *Total Quality Education: Profiles of Schools that Demonstrate the Power of Deming's Management Principles*, Bloomington, IN, Phi Delta Kappa.

Weller, L. D. (1996), 'Total Quality Management and Georgia's School Reform Effort' *Quality Progress*.

Weller, L. D. and Hartley, S. H. (1994a), 'Why are educators stonewalling TQM?' *The TQM Magazine*, 6(3), 23–28.

Weller, L. D. and Hartley, S. H. (1994b), 'Total Quality management and school restructuring: Georgia's approach to educational reform', *Quality Assurance in Education*, 2(2), 18–25.

12

■ ■ ■

An analysis of the application of Total Quality in US and UK education

JOHN MARSH

Introduction

If changing is really learning, if effective organisations need more and more intelligent people, if careers are shorter and more changeable, above all, if more people need to be self-sufficient for more of their lives, then education has to become the single most important investment that any person can make in their own destiny . . . Education needs to be re-invented. (Handy, 1990, p. 211)

If the USA and the UK are to avoid becoming solely low labour cost economies then both countries need to be obsessed with investing in education and learning. Thankfully a transformation is under way in both countries. Total Quality philosophy and tools are being adopted throughout the education systems in the USA and the UK. As with any innovation, success is variable and applications reflect the different political and social environments. This chapter presents the principles, analyses successful applications, investigates the differences and similarities between the two nations' approaches and identifies challenges for the future.

What is Total Quality in Education?

The industrial model does not have all the answers. Successful practitioners are taking the best from industrial experiences and combining it, in an holistic framework, with the best learning theories and methods. The result is a fascinating hybrid which naturally varies from school to school. There do appear to be at least three levels of application.

The first, and possibly lowest level of application, is to the management processes of a school, or other educational establishment. Schools do have many processes in common with other organisations. They produce strategic plans, recruit and develop staff, deploy resources and require principle-centred leadership. While the application of Total Quality at this level can produce improvements in efficiency it is unlikely to inspire students and teachers, or deal with the real root issues which lie within the learning processes.

The next level up is the teaching of Total Quality to students. The philosophy, in its totality, needs to be covered along with methods and tools. This becomes more exciting because it enables the school to move to the highest level.

The highest level is Total Quality in Learning. This is where application impacts the classroom. Todd Bergman, Quality Co-ordinator, Mt Edgecumbe High School, Alaska, and myself define Total Quality in Learning as a philosophy, supported by a comprehensive Toolkit (Marsh, 1993), driven by students and staff, in order to identify, analyse and remove the barriers to learning. One view of the teacher's rôle is to motivate students to learn. Another is for the teacher to work with the students to remove the barriers to motivation. All of us are born with an inherent love of learning and the 'forces of destruction' (Deming, 1993) which are built into our systems, work to drive this out of us. Some of us are lucky enough to survive the system.

An important myth in education needs to be destroyed. There is no such thing as 'value-free' education. Any human activity, or process, is going to be influenced by principles or values. These need to be managed to avoid the systemisation of unhealthy or negative values. Results cannot be achieved without applying methods, and methods will embrace certain values and principles. One way of viewing the relationship between results, methods and principles is as a pyramid (*see* Figure 8). They need to be founded on a solid understanding of practical psychology, theories of learning, systems and variation. This was referred to as Profound Knowledge by Deming.

The desired results vary according to the stakeholders being questioned. Students want schools to equip them to deal with very uncertain futures. Rather than being 'stuffed full' of information they need to leave their formal education with a love of learning and an understanding of how they learn best. Parents want greater choice and involvement in their children's education. They expect higher academic standards to be achieved but want their children to be balanced, mature citizens. Employers require greater learning skills,

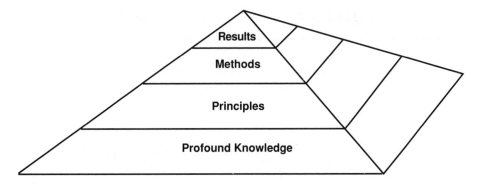

Figure 8: The transformation pyramid

teamwork and self-motivation based on a good grasp of the basics. Governments, however, while in theory representing the electorate, require much more from less. Western economies, particularly the USA and the UK, have been in a gradual process of decline since the Second World War. As the profitability of industry has declined the available resources to invest in education have also declined. Governments are under intense pressure to reduce public spending. In these circumstances quality is the answer not the problem. It is the only way to increase outputs and reduce costs, as the leading industrial practitioners discovered in the 1980s.

In order to achieve the desired results for all of the stakeholders, schools and other educational establishments are having to question their core processes and methods. New ideas are emerging but these need to be based on sound educational and management principles. The most holistic set of principles for quality is Dr Deming's fourteen points (Deming, 1986). When combined with his system of *Profound Knowledge* and the *Deadly Diseases* one has a solid foundation on which to develop methods. If methods contravene these principles then they should be ignored. If they align well, then they should be considered for development. The students and staff at Mt Edgecumbe have interpreted the fourteen points for an educational environment. Some of their conclusions will challenge the core beliefs of our current approach to education.

In terms of methods both the Baldrige Award and European Quality Award Frameworks can be usefully applied to education if they are interpreted sensitively. Figure 9 shows a translation of the European Quality Award framework for a school. This gives an overall framework into which to fit more detailed methods such as self-assessment, portfolios, cross-curricular, project based learning, student improvement teams.

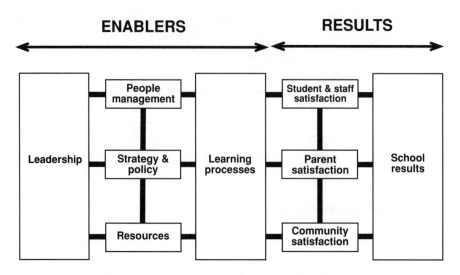

ENABLERS

RESULTS

Figure 9: The European Quality Award framework adapted for a school

Any application of Total Quality in an educational establishment needs to be founded on sound principles. Frameworks such as the Baldrige Award can be useful but they must allow for flexibility and diversity. The school must fit the approach to itself, not the other way round. The best must be taken from the industrial model and combined with the best from the world of education.

Progress in the UK

If you don't shape the future someone else will. (Barker, 1992)

The Conservative Government in the UK had long seen education as a bastion of 'trendy' progressive, left-wing thinking, focused on ideology rather than service. This perception is far from true, with some of the more progressive schools being closely aligned to Quality principles. However, by careful use of the media, teachers were portrayed as in need of a radical 'shake up'. Change was definitely required but the Government went about this in a very confront-ational style. A series of Central Government changes were implemented in record time. The speed and magnitude was unprecedented and some would argue poorly managed.

The first major change was the introduction of a national curriculum. This was implemented rapidly with little stakeholder involvement. Those in tune with Government philosophy designed and implemented a very well defined cur-riculum based on key stages with standardised tests to evaluate performance. The English National Curriculum is very prescriptive and bureaucratic. Inevitably there was a backlash from the teachers who refused to co-operate with the testing regime. After many months of conflict the Government listened and the curriculum was redesigned to allow schools 20 per cent of teaching time to use as they wish.

A cornerstone of John Major's Government has been the Citizens' Charter. This aims to ensure that all citizens receive high-quality services, responsive to their needs, provided efficiently at a reasonable cost. For schools, the parent is identified as the main customer. The Parents' Charter defines standards and encourages openness of information. League tables have been introduced and choice has led to greater competition. Many teachers have responded negatively to the Charter but initial simplistic measures are being improved.

The Government also introduced major changes to the way schools are inspected. The Office of Standards in Education (OFSTED) was established and inspection was opened up to market forces, including lay people on inspection teams. Schools have to 'buy in' a full inspection every four years. This is a very expensive approach and the quality of inspection varies considerably. Deming's third point, cease dependence on inspection to achieve quality, seems to have been ignored by the Government, which appears to be doing the opposite.

Very little in British education has remained constant over the last ten years. Funding mechanisms have also been completely revised. One very successful change has been the introduction of Local Management of Schools (LMS). This has empowered schools considerably and has led to more innovation. Also the Government has offered schools large financial incentives to leave local authority control and to receive their funds direct through a central funding agency. Schools can thus 'opt out' and become grant maintained (GMS). Many argue that GMS is creating a two-tier state education system. The take-up varies considerably across the country. Some might conclude that this is another attempt by a Conservative Government to undermine traditionally left-wing local authorities.

Finally, two voluntary standards are being implemented in education. The first is Investors in People. This is a national initiative designed to help organisations to improve performance through a planned approach to setting and com-municating goals and developing people to meet these goals. Designed by Britain's best companies, IIP is proving popular and effective in schools. It is starting to address years of under-investment in teachers. We will not have competent, confident students unless we have competent, confident teachers.

A less welcome development has been the application of ISO9000 to certain educational establishments. ISO9000 is an international standard which aims to introduce disciplines, procedures and systems to assure that the production of goods and services meets the customers' requirements. It has its origins in the defence industry and is completely manufacturing focused. This causes a lot of resistance in education. More importantly ISO9000 ensures consistency. A registered company 'does what it says it does' even if this is not the best approach. Our schools need to re-invent themselves not proceduralise ineffective and inefficient ways of working.

The British education system has gone through a period of unprecedented change. Much has been imposed on the system by Central Government. Some of the initiatives align well with the principles of Total Quality. Others have conflicted with basic principles and created a real tension for schools trying to apply continual improvement.

Many applications of Total Quality are being reported across the UK. These are spread across the spectrum of educational establishments. Often these initiatives come with different labels, such as School Improvement or Effectiveness, but they embrace many of the underlying principles of Total Quality. Hamblett School in St Helens was one of the first special schools to officially introduce TQM (Brownlow, 1994) but many others have been close to the spirit of the philosophy for a long time. The idea of focusing on the individual's wants and needs is more second nature in this environment. Also special schools are less constrained by the national curriculum and are often allowed to be more innovative. The level of commitment from teachers is usually very high. Similarly the concepts of Total Quality, particularly based on the teachings of Deming, are generally well received in primary schools. The more progressive primary schools have been developing collaborative, project-based learning approaches for many years. Some have even questioned reward and punishment concepts and moved away from grading and ranking to concentrate on intrinsic motivation. Ironically Government initiatives designed to improve quality, by concentrating on standards and testing, have forced many of these pioneers to abandon their work and return to 'chalk and talk' and 'teaching to the test'. Many primary teachers have a fundamental belief in the same principles articulated by Deming but they are frustrated by a national system that seems to be driving them backwards.

Many secondary schools around the country have been making gains. Somervale Comprehensive School, Midsomer Norton, has been implementing Total Quality for three years. They were supported by Avon Training and Enterprise Council, a Government-funded organisation aimed at improving prosperity by increasing investment in education and training throughout the community. Somervale, which is now exchanging students with Mt Edgecumbe High School, started with a strategic review involving all stakeholders, including students. This identified the critical processes for improvement. Improvement teams involving parents, teachers, support staff and students were established and facilitated through a cycle of Process Improvement (Marsh, 1993). A steering group was established and still meets every month. A major breakthrough occurred when some teachers, support staff, students and a parent went through a training process spread over six months to become facilitators. These people then went on to lead improvement initiatives in many areas. One of the most successful was the complete redesign of the process for reporting with parents and students. Another facilitator course is about to start with a similar mix of people. This will concentrate more on the learning processes themselves. Somervale now intends that all students will experience Total Quality. This is in order to use the philosophy and tools at the centre of the curriculum.

There are many other examples of secondary schools implementing Total Quality across the country. Another innovator is Westwood St Thomas School, Salisbury. They have used Total Quality to engage 150 stakeholders in Strategic Planning. They too are using the tools in the classroom. Most of these schools realise that they are at the start of a long process and that there are no quick fixes.

Sometimes the impetus for Total Quality comes from outside of the educational establishment. Leading Total Quality employers such as Rank Xerox, ICL and the Royal Mail have been assisting local schools to start implementation. It is clearly to their advantage if the quality of students can be improved. The Royal Mail has in fact sponsored the Centre for Total Quality in Education and Community which exists to promote TQ nationwide. Other bodies such as Local Education Authorities and Training and Enterprise Councils have been acting as catalysts. The British Deming Association has taken a lead, mentoring many schools throughout Leicestershire.

Progress in the USA

The pioneers of Total Quality in Education are generally American but the ideas have spread rapidly around the world, particularly to the UK, Canada, Australia and New Zealand. The USA can boast of schools which have been implementing for the longest period of time and as a consequence have learnt a great deal. Their willingness to share has helped many others. Every year 'Quality Progress' publishes the results of its survey into Quality in Education. The list is growing dramatically each year but only a handful of schools have been going for more than five years. These leaders include Mt Edgecumbe High School, possibly the most famous, Fox Valley Technical College, George Westinghouse High School and Millcreek School District.

Mt Edgecumbe's quality journey started in 1988. At the heart of a quality school must be a quality curriculum. Quality philosophy, tools and techniques, learning theories and practical psychology, including Covey's Seven Habits, are taught to all students entering the school. They then have opportunities to apply this core knowledge in all subject areas. Some quality experts used to think that adults define the curriculum and then the students work with the teachers on improving the process of delivery. Mt Edgecumbe has gone further than this. Because the students are engaged in understanding why they are learning something, and in regular reviews of the curriculum, they are now directly influencing future curriculum as well as delivery. This is achieved through the use of competence based learning and Bloom's taxonomy. The original curriculum was influenced by state guidelines and other reports about the type of skills that will be needed in the future.

Delivery of curriculum does not just happen in the classroom. It happens throughout the student's time at a school. Marty Johnson, science teacher at Mt Edgecumbe refers to the kiss principle. Most people remember their first kiss. They do not remember when they first heard about kissing and were told how it is done! Learning must relate to application and so great effort is placed on cross-curricular projects.

Finally, the most controversial subject of all, assessment. Dr Deming taught about the harmful effects of grading and ranking, as well as depending on mass inspection. Applying his teachings to education, as Mt Edgecumbe have done, means monitoring learning, not controlling the students. The school uses the learning matrices and Bloom's taxonomy in order for students to assess their own learning. This is not done lightly. Students are taught learning theories and assessment techniques. They have to document, demonstrate and defend their learning. The documentation ends up in extensive portfolios, soon to be put on CD ROMs.

Some of the results achieved by Mt Edgecumbe are listed below:

- 68 per cent of graduates continue onto college or university. Another 28 per cent go to technical/trade school or into military service. The average progression rate to college for rural high schools is below 5 per cent.
- The drop out rate varies between zero and 0.5 per cent.
- 97 per cent of students believe that the quality of education received was better than available in their home communities.
- 92 per cent of the 1992 graduates would like their children to attend. The academic challenge was cited as the main reason.
- 75 per cent of graduates felt that the school did a good job preparing them for continuing education.
- Drug and alcohol abuse has fallen dramatically.
- Parent satisfaction has risen.

Fox Valley Technical College, Wisconsin, has achieved similar results but on a larger scale (Osborne and Gaebler, 1993). It started implementing Total Quality in 1985 by understanding the students and the business community's wants and needs and has also directly engaged the wider community in the process.

As a result of listening to customers Fox Valley created customer driven measures and indicators. Because achievement of jobs is so important to students they developed a job placement tracking system. This emphasis encouraged lecturers to focus on the relevance of their courses in preparing students for the world of work. Guarantees are offered to students and businesses to compensate in cases of dissatisfaction. Fox Valley has been prepared to challenge paradigms like the traditional academic calendar. They recognise that all students are different with different wants and needs and different learning styles. However, it must be remembered that the student is not only the customer but the supplier and is responsible for their own learning processes. They are co-workers in improving the learning process, but ultimately they remain the primary customers.

The National Alliance of Business Report, *The Cutting Edge of Common Sense*, (Siegel and Byrne, 1993) investigated seven leading examples of TQM in Education. In the report they used the Baldrige Award framework to compare the different approaches. The schools are all 'courageous pathfinders and worthy role models'. They are showing, without doubt, that Total Quality in Education does work and is essential in transforming the system. What is apparent is the sheer diversity of application based on some common principles.

The Federal Government has identified the need for change but the failing America 2000 schools initiative is another example of using the old paradigm to assess the new. The highly innovative New American Schools initiative is falling victim to short-term and narrow measures of performance. Total Quality is not a quick fix and does not sit comfortably with the rampant short-termism of many Western governments. There are few world leaders who appear to understand the quality paradigm.

US educators are fortunate in having at least two excellent sources of information on Total Quality applied to education. The American Association of School Administrators has been running a Total Quality Network for many years and the American Society for Quality Control has established an Education Division.

Every year there seem to be more and more schools starting on the Total Quality journey in the USA. The innovators are highlighting a clear path and developing new and creative solutions to some of society's most systemic problems. While a handful of American schools have been in the vanguard, the majority will benefit from looking at best practice across the world as others rapidly adopt Total Quality principles and tools.

Differences and similarities

The main differences in the approaches adopted to Total Quality in the USA and the UK are rooted in the past. The social and political systems are very different. The USA was started as one great experiment to break away from the traditional. In the UK there is a long history of strong Central Government. Over the last fifteen years more and more power has gone to the centre and Local Government has become very weak. The schools are caught up in this process with some interesting irony. Just as the most critical process, curriculum design, has gone to the centre, schools have been given much greater responsibility for their own management. This creates an enormous tension because many of the root cause problems lie outside of the influence of the teachers. The only way to resolve this is to work, in partnership with other stakeholders, on the system itself. With many Government initiatives contradicting Total Quality philosophy this is getting increasingly difficult and frustrating.

In the USA there has always been a mistrust of strong Central Government. Communities were founded on the principles of empowerment. The raising and spending of taxes is more transparent. Strong communities and local freedom were key components of the American Way. These social and political differences encourage a great desire for innovation in the USA and it is innovation which is the key differentiator.

Because of greater freedom and a strong desire to innovate it is not surprising that the first schools to implement Total Quality were American. However, a natural consequence of innovation is failure. Another is a wide variation from the very good to the truly dreadful. This range is apparent in educational innovation. Some approaches being tested in the USA are so far from the principles of Total Quality that they should probably be left well alone. However, paradigms will never be challenged without the pioneers and change is a messy process.

In the UK the approach to Total Quality has centred on more traditional aims like improving academic standards. Government defines what will be learnt and then uses an array of methods to inspect and monitor. Many of the approaches adopted by the more progressive US practitioners would be illegal in the UK. However, there is a limit to how much you can improve a fundamentally flawed system and if the UK is to survive economically a radical rethink of the purpose of education is required. Going 'back to basics' is not going to equip future generations with the necessary skills to survive in a very uncertain world.

One interesting area of common ground is how well Total Quality philosophy is accepted in schools if it is presented sensitively. Deming's teachings are well received because he made a mockery of blaming individuals and stressed working on the whole system. His teachings are founded on Profound Knowledge which includes the 'softer' subjects of psychology and theory of learning as well as the 'harder' areas such as systems and variation. This is a good balance which allows for the integration of best practice from the world of education.

Challenges ahead

To face up to the future both US and UK educators need to be prepared to challenge many of the paradigms which exist today. Why do we grade and rank people? Why do we put such emphasis on testing and inspection? Why in complex, interdependent systems do we link peoples' pay to performance? Nothing should remain unchallenged and teachers need to work with the whole community to develop new solutions.

The political systems are not going to be immune from this challenge. How can constancy of purpose be achieved in a system which encourages such short-termism? The media too, will have to learn the difference between special and common causes of problems and accept greater responsibility. The transform-ation of education cannot be considered outside of community-wide systems and everyone will have to play their part.

Perhaps the greatest challenge will be one that has perplexed industry for many years. The days of 'any colour as long as it's black' are over. People want diversity and choice but this often has to be done in a mass production system to be economic. In the same way educators are going to have to develop learning processes that can meet all of the individual wants and needs in a large scale system.

Both the USA and the UK are facing unprecedented change. Both have had to face unpleasant questions about their rôles in the world. But one thing is certain, the future belongs to those nations which can release the infinite potential locked up in their people.

Note

An edited version of this chapter appeared in the September 1995 edition of *UK Quality* as 'Education's Toughest Exam'.

References

Barker, J. (1992), *Future Edge*, New York, Morrow.

Brownlow, R. (1994), 'TQM at Hamblett', *Quality and Learning*, Journal of Centre for Total Quality in Education and Community, Vol. 1 No. 1.

Deming, W. E. (1986), *Out of the Crisis*, Cambridge University Press.

Deming, W. E. (1993), *The New Economics for Industry*, Government and Education, MIT, CAES.

Handy, C. B. (1990), *The Age of Unreason*, Boston, Harvard Business School Press.

Marsh, J. (1993), *The Quality Toolkit – An A to Z of Tools and Techniques*, IFS International Ltd.

Osborne, D. and Gaebler, T. (1993), *Reinventing Government*, New York, Plume.

Siegel, P. and Byrne, S. (1993), *The Cutting Edge of Common Sense*, National Alliance of Business.

Commentary – international perspectives on quality

BRENT DAVIES AND JOHN WEST-BURNHAM

The two chapters in this section provide a comparative overview of the application of Total Quality principles in the UK and the USA. We are aware of Total Quality initiatives in many other countries, notably Australia, Denmark, Germany, Kazakhstan, Malaysia, The Netherlands, New Zealand and South Africa. At present there is relatively little public data available as to the success or failure of these initiatives. This is why the detailed evaluation of the project in Georgia by Weller is so welcome. A major issue for all innovative projects in education is the development of meaningful evaluation models that actually inform policy making *and* that reinforce, motivate and celebrate.

It is possible to extrapolate a number of broad conclusions from the reviews by Weller and Marsh. First, it appears that the use of Total Quality strategies does make a practical and immediate difference to the performance of schools, most importantly in terms of student experience. This is not to argue for a monopolistic or exclusive view of Total Quality as a panacea; other strategies have produced equally dramatic results without the use of Total Quality approaches. What is clear is the need for an *integrated* approach that is used consistently and demonstrates coherence in all aspects of a change in policy. Total Quality can serve as a unifying process creating a common vocabulary and shared frames of reference.

The second conclusion relates to the emphasis on the involvement of all practitioners. Policy-making by central, regional or local government may not be posited on involvement and recognition of the need to respect existing skills and knowledge. Indeed the more generic the policy the more likely it is to be founded on a control culture with models of accountability which are actually hostile to improvement at the classroom level. Both studies in this section endorse the view of the need for 'top-down' leadership to be balanced by 'bottom-up' interpretation and application. National policy-making seems to be increasingly focused on 'how?' as well as 'what?' thus effectively disempowering local initiatives. And yet, as has been demonstrated throughout this book, it is at the institutional level that the most significant and profound changes are taking place, often in spite of national initiatives.

Third, the improvements that have been described in these two chapters have been the result of community action. It is highly significant that the greatest successes have been the result of partnerships between schools, local government, parents, employers, public bodies, voluntary agencies and higher education. There is no doubt that political will can make a significant difference but it may well be that the philosophy of Total Quality sits uncomfortably with the prevailing culture of governments. Just as Total Quality has changed the culture of many large companies so it will inevitably have an impact on the way in which communities perceive themselves and, more importantly, the way in which they learn to work together. What is increasingly clear is that educational improvement cannot be carried out in isolation from other social forces. Schools are highly significant factors in student success but they are only one of the variables that have to be managed. The greater the amount of horizontal integration within communities the more likely it is that educational reforms will become pervasive and sustainable. Mt Edgecumbe school as described by Marsh in Chapter Twelve is responsive to its local and wider community as an essential component of its *total* strategy.

The fourth element, highlighted by Weller, is the issue of funding. This is not to argue that the implementation of a Total Quality strategy requires special or additional funding but rather that the initiative has to be resourced in a variety of ways, for example through the use of advice and support from commercial organisations. It is also worth suggesting that Total Quality is a better way of doing what has to be done and this could actually result in savings. What is clear is that the implementation of any radical reform programme requires commitment of physical as well as emotional and intellectual resources.

The final point that comes through from these two chapters is the awareness of the need to change – at national, local, institutional and individual levels. For many commercial organisations the primary motivation to adopt a Total Quality approach has been economic survival. This imperative has been fully endorsed at national level by the governments of the UK and the USA but there the similarity ends. Instead of creating a system based on trust and subsidiarity, the British government and some states in the USA have introduced a draconian control culture based on formal accountability and the belief that performance can be improved through sanctions. Fortunately many systems still have the flexibility to allow for local initiatives and that is what the case studies in this book have described.

PART SEVEN

Mapping the future

Mapping the future

BRENT DAVIES AND JOHN WEST-BURNHAM

Introduction

In this part we explore the generic implications of the changes in the leadership and management of schools described in the case studies. It is possible to extrapolate a number of key themes which will inform effective leadership in the twenty-first century and which will extend the reengineering and total quality principles outlined in this book. Before any change can take place, however, some fundamental barriers have to be challenged.

As every school pupil will be aware, the battles of Crécy and Agincourt loom large in any study of English history. In a management interpretation of these events, Richard Luecke (1994) in his book *Scuttle Your Ships Before Advancing* recounts these two episodes from history. Our colleague Brian Caldwell (1997, p. 267) gives his interpretation of Luecke's work:

> ... in August 1346 as England's King Edward III faced the superior forces of the French at Crécy. His front line consisted of yeoman archers who could deliver up to fifteen arrows per minute, hitting human targets at one hundred metres or formation targets at three hundred metres. On the other side, French knights on horse back were supported by Genoese mercenary crossbowmen who could fire two bolts per minute, each able to pierce heavy armour at great distance. The English were drawn in a circle around their supply carts; the French relied on the shock power of war horses at high speed.

> The outcome was the loss of just 300 English. Up to 16,000 French perished under the barrage of English arrows 'that must have appeared like a dark swarm of hornets lofting into the sky, hanging there briefly before raining down with a thousand hissing voices'.

> Sixty-nine years later, in October 1415 at Agincourt, the same result was achieved by England's Henry V: some 6,000 French lives were lost to Henry's 150.

In continuing the string of French disasters, Agincourt demonstrated the tenacity with which the nobility clung to the technologies and tactics that had accounted for past glories, even in the face of overwhelming evidence that their usefulness had long faded.

What this demonstrates was that the French army was not a learning organisation adapting to fundamental change but, rather, was repeating the mistakes of the past. School leaders need to realise that we are in a period of fundamental change where the following trends can be observed:

- profound social, economic and cultural change is taking place
- organisations are changing from a nineteenth-century factory model to a twenty-first-century learning model
- the purpose of schooling is changing because of changes in the global economy, technological change and social change.

This creates the need to shift the emphasis of schooling away from the replication of knowledge to the capacity to 'learn how to learn'. Schools must, therefore:

- increase confidence that every individual is learning to optimum effect
- make information technology implicit to learning and school management
- see leadership and management as learning processes in their own right
- create cultures based on review and responsiveness
- challenge existing models of resource management and concepts of cost-effectiveness.

We believe that proactive leaders in schools must consider each of ten key elements for effective school leadership in the next millennium. We explore these in the sections below.

1. A focus on learning.
2. Moral purpose as the purpose.
3. The need for human scale organisations.
4. The centrality of leadership.
5. Developing and sustaining a learning organisation.
6. The redefinition of the resource base.
7. The need for responsive cultures.
8. Performance management as the critical factor.
9. The need for global awareness and community interdependence.
10. Personal effectiveness as the synthesising agent.

1. A focus on learning

One of the great fallacies of late twentieth-century educational policy-making, at macro and micro levels, is that there is a necessary and contingent relationship between teaching and learning. Teaching can take place without any learning resulting from it and a great deal of learning is achieved without the benefit of teaching. A major reason for this situation is that there is an emphasis on teaching as an activity rather than learning as a process. This is easy to explain as it is much easier to define, control and evaluate a physical activity than a subjective process.

If education systems are to help people of all ages to come to terms with a rapidly changing world then it would seem appropriate to argue that those people should become learners. Yet the structure and organisation of the curriculum, its delivery and assessment is posited on the notion of something that is delivered. Thus the criteria for success such as GCSE and 'A' level results are seen as indicators of successful teaching, that is the reception and replication of knowledge.

What is lacking is a definition of learning which is as coherent, accessible and transferable into actions as definitions of the relationship between teaching and knowledge. The national curriculum, GCSE and 'A' level syllabuses and many post-compulsory and higher education courses have their a priori knowledge as content rather than learning as an individual, subjective and highly variable process.

This explains the organisation of most schools – compartmentalised activity following a generic chronology based on the premise of essentially homogeneous groupings. It is difficult to find any other examples of this degree of regimentation and standardisation outside the education system. Even mass production factories are now designed on the premise of delegating high degrees of control to the appropriate level. If young people are being 'prepared for the world of work' then it is for an essentially nineteenth-century view of the workplace.

It is possible to envisage considerable changes taking place in the way in which schools address the significance of individual learning and the rôle of the teacher. Most of the chapters in this book provide examples of innovative approaches which are derived from the premise of effective learning. What is significant is that they demonstrate that it is possible to shift the focus from teaching to learning and to enhance academic performance as judged by current criteria. The challenge remains, however, to create autonomous learners in a management culture which is based on dependency and formal models of accountability. It may well be that the culture of many educational organisations is profoundly hostile to learning qua learning and there will need to be fundamental and profound changes to every component of the school as an organisation.

By any criteria learning is a highly complex process. The management structures and processes in schools do not reflect this. There is a natural organisational imperative to seek to codify and simplify. If this is done at the expense of the integrity of the effective learning of any individual, then the validity of those structures and processes has to be questioned. It is difficult to find a justification for the design of schools as places for learning in the current literature. The complexity of learning may be directly proportional to the amount of time that is devoted to understanding how individuals learn and what the appropriate supportive infrastructure might be. Schools need to put learning on the agenda of every meeting in order to demonstrate that the focus on learning is tangible and significant.

2. Moral purpose as the purpose

Schools are moral communities. Every day in every school hundreds if not thousands of decisions are taken which have implications for the lives of the people within the community; they are therefore moral decisions. Some will be relatively insignificant while others will have a profound bearing upon the nature of the school as an organisation and its impact on the lives of those within it. If this basic premise is accepted then a starting point for any re-evaluation of the nature and purpose of schooling is the development of moral competence which in turn will lead to moral confidence. Murphy provides an excellent example of this process in Chapter Eight.

Moral competence is found when there is knowledge of the options and implications surrounding any decision and the skills necessary to make and implement decisions which are logically consistent with the particular ethical framework pertaining at a given time and place.

We are not arguing for an artificial hegemony based on a lowest-common denominator view of social responsibility. One of the implications of leading and managing schools in a society that has aspirations to be democratic and pluralist is the need to respect difference. A wide range of variables will inform and influence the precise nature of a school as a moral community. Issues such as race, culture, social and economic focus will all serve to produce varying sets of priorities and criteria.

The issues are those of explicit articulations of the values and their consistent application. This is to argue for a moral relativism that is bounded by a common ethical framework, that is a tolerant, democratic society based on respect for the individual and creation of opportunity for improvement. The problem for schoolteachers is that the approach in education has often been reductionist and/or academic; this is best exemplified in the difference between imposed school rules and a consensual code of conduct. The demands on pupils are not always reflected in an explicit and consistent reciprocal set of demands upon the school.

If schools are preparing young people for adult life then they are essentially preparing them to make decisions of varying significance. The more the ethical basis of those decisions is understood the more likely it is that they will be translated into moral behaviour. This implies that schools become increasingly more sophisticated in terms of moral competence so as to create moral confidence. In a period of moral ambiguity the impositions of a moral code will only serve to reinforce that uncertainty; a more appropriate response might be to work for moral competence in every aspect of the school's life.

3. The need for human scale organisations

As Naisbitt and Aburdene have expressed it:

> *The dominant principle of organisation has shifted, from management in order to control an enterprise to leadership in order to bring out the best in people and to respond quickly to change. This is not the 'leadership' individuals and groups so often call for when they want a father figure to take care of all their problems. It is a democratic yet demanding leadership that respects people and encourages self-management, autonomous teams, and entrepreneurial units.* (Naisbitt and Aburdene, 1990, p. 218)

The notion of the self-managing team is in danger of becoming one of the great clichés of management writing in the late twentieth century. And yet the evidence seems consistent and overwhelming – teams are better units to work in than any of the alternatives. Social psychology theory and sociometric studies point to the fact that people do not relate to the totality of any organisation but rather achieve meaning through a highly specific and limited context. There seems to be a consensus that six to eight people constitute a manageable social network and, according to Taylor and McKenzie in Chapter Nine, groups for effective learning are even smaller. A consistent feature of the accounts of change in this book is the use of teams.

In spite of this evidence, the education system remains stubbornly resistant to creating schools as organisations fit for learning rather than using administratively convenient structures. In terms of an organisational type most schools are, in essence, hierarchical and bureaucratic. Hierarchy appears to be endemic to public sector organisations. What is bizarre is the number of schools that have a formal hierarchy but then argue that the school doesn't actually work like that. No organisation does, but many in the commercial sector have recognised this and recast themselves into appropriately functional units not just in terms of an organisational structure but also in terms of appropriate levels of authority commensurate with the amount of responsibility that has been delegated.

225

A further bizarre feature of school organisation is the fact that teachers form one of the most highly qualified and skilled workforces in the country and yet operate in highly dependent cultures with extremely limited levels of autonomy. This costs money, wastes time, diminishes those who are not trusted and places greater burdens on those who have to manage.

Rather than try to manage a hierarchy it may be more appropriate to talk of leading teams and to conceptualise the school as a network of interdependent teams, some long-term and structural, some short-term and protean. If this is done within the context of a theoretical framework of subsidiarity rather than delegation then each team will have genuine control over its own working.

Working in such groupings is socially more appropriate, managerially more cost effective and, most importantly, is more likely to create a moral community. A team-based structure is also a more appropriate preparation for higher education and employment. There is no doubt that many of these features are found in schools and that there is exemplary practice. The issues are the extent to which such practice is found across the whole school and the extent to which formal structure recognises and facilitates the social relationships which are the actual basis on which any organisation functions.

The shift from formal bureaucratic hierarchy to social interdependence and focused teams is a complex one. It may well require significant reengineering in order to reconceptualise leadership and management rôles and to take away historic patterns of dependency and permission seeking. Perhaps the greatest challenge for schools is to translate their vision of themselves as caring communities into the actual experience of every individual through the development of valid and appropriate structures.

4. The centrality of leadership

Leadership is the current talisman of school effectiveness and improvement. There is a high level of confidence from a range of sources that leadership is the panacea, the 'magic wand' that transforms schools. This would appear to be reinforced by a wide range of anecdotal evidence which seems to point to school success or transformation being causally linked to the behaviour of the headteacher. Although a wide range of variables will determine a school's success (including the definition of success) there appears to be an overwhelming consensus that leadership is the key determinant. A number of concerns emerge from this view.

First, there is the focus on the individual as prime mediator which places an unreal burden on any individual and, according to Gronn (1995, p. 23)

... the terminology about elevating people to previously unheard of levels of potential, altered levels of awareness, autonomy, mission and vision, and even the very idea of transformed individuals and organisations carries with it all the hallmarks of a religious crusade.

The problem with any crusading approach is that the ratio of cost to success is usually highly disproportionate. The emphasis on the solitary leader has problems for the leader and for those who are led. Any hierarchy disempowers; empowerment (a much vaunted strategy) has connotations of subordinates being given permission to be themselves.

Second, there is the issue of how such leaders are to be identified and selected. The education system continues to place high reliance on the interview as a means of discrimination yet its reliability as a discriminatory tool is highly suspect. Most selection procedures are historic and this is compounded by the lack of appropriate criteria, especially with regard to the transformational component of the task.

Closely allied to these concerns is the whole issue of how such individuals are to be trained and developed. There appears to be no consensus as to the most appropriate techniques which will enhance and sustain the qualities of the transformational leader. There is a danger of a reductionist approach which stresses the significance of that which can be defined and relies on hope and fortuity for the rest.

What has not been fully explored is that the rôle of headteachers in effective or improving schools is largely expressed through the leadership *and* membership of a team. Given the complexity of the modern school it seems highly improbable that any one individual could (or should) combine all aspects of leadership.

Equally, the successful school is made up of many elements which it is practically impossible for the headteacher to be involved in. Leadership in the department, pastoral group and, crucially in the classroom is what makes the actual difference in terms of performance. The successful school is an amalgam of successes, not all of which can be directly attributed to one individual, who, on the limited evidence available does not have the time or expertise to be directly interventionist. This applies equally to primary and secondary schools, though for different reasons.

If schools are to develop to meet changing needs then the emphasis will have to be on leadership as a shared function rather than a status-orientated rôle. The British obsession with personal accountability has led to an unhealthy (literally for some) obsession with the 'hero-leader' rather than the enabler, facilitator and creator of effective processes.

5. Developing and sustaining a learning organisation

To argue that schools should become learning organisations might seem tautological. Yet, in response to national policy initiatives, schools have a very high product orientation which has led to a focus on 'What?' at the expense of 'Why?' and 'How?'. One of the most significant indicators of this is the extent to which schools perceive review and evaluation as axiomatic to management processes. The emphasis on planning of the past few years has not been mirrored by an equal emphasis on monitoring. Equally, the leadership and management style of many educationalists is often, for very good practical reasons, constrained when it comes to personal reflective learning.

Learning organisation is, of course, a misnomer. It is the individuals in the organisation who learn and through the application of their learning enable the organisation to change and develop. The change comes when individual and team learning is integrated into organisational processes which are in turn seen as heuristic. In order to achieve this symbiotic relationship, a number of criteria have to be met:

- a clear statement of the purpose, vision and mission of the organisation
- an explicit policy defining the characteristics of the learning process
- re-definition of core management processes (e.g. planning, implementation and evaluation) in terms of their cyclical and interrelated nature
- realignment of rôles to include reflexive learning as a component of any task
- use of systems thinking to help analyse the relationship between functioning variables
- enhancing the capacity of individuals to learn
- planning for learning as much as for any other organisational function.

In one sense the school becomes a learning organisation if the very best practice to be found in the classroom, lab, workshop or gym is seen as a microcosm for the whole school processes. In this way there is no artificial dichotomy between students and adults as learners – the same techniques are practised throughout the school. This increases the likelihood of effective learning strategies becoming pervasive throughout the school and can help to ensure that form follows function in such a way that leadership and management behaviour models effective learning strategies.

6. The redefinition of the resource base

Traditional views of schools are associated with the practice of teaching. If you ask the question 'what is a school?', the responses elicited are likely to emphasise the building, classrooms with thirty pupils in them and teachers at the front of the class addressing the whole group. At the secondary stage, additional divisions of the physical side of a school such as sports fields, technology and music rooms are likely to be added to the list. Similarly, focusing on the staff of the school is almost always likely to draw responses that talk about teachers and, even when it does not, it clearly draws the distinction between teaching and 'non-teaching staff'.

Futures thinking often draws what are likely to be considered as 'way out' or 'unrealistic' pictures of learning in the future. Below is one provided by Graham Hewitt of Abbey Grange High School.

It was Friday morning 10.00 am and Millennium lay in bed putting the finishing touches to her history project. As usual she had left it until the last minute but she had experienced one or two problems with the voice recognition system on her Personal Active Learning Link (PALL). A bout of flu and a sore throat had slowed down the entry of data for a few days. This history project had involved many hours in bed surfing through archives, newspapers, books, TV programmes, CDs and talking with other pupils across the country.

With the project completed, Millennium got out of bed and instructed her PALL to download the work to school. It would be marked electronically and a report would be returned to her before she would be out of the shower. The hard copy would form part of her Personal Record of Progress (PROP) and would aid her in planning her future learning and target setting in consultation with her personal tutor.

Friday is Millennium's favourite day. It is the only day each week when she is timetabled to attend school. She had an appointment with her personal tutor at 12.00 noon to discuss her individual budget. There are only ten supervisors in school now to advise 1,000 students. Most interviews revolve around personal budgets, study plans and target setting. She would like to book time on the satellite link for her geography and psychology work and update her PALL to include the 'music tutor' for her cello. The update would be expensive but it will allow Millennium to be 'tutored' at home with instant feedback and the option to play as part of a small group or even a whole orchestra while sitting in her own bedroom.

From 1.00 pm to 6.00 pm there will be 100 students in school, along with the ten supervisors. The five hours are structured for drama/dance, practical science and technology, PSE group discussion work, orchestra practice, sport, community work and socialising.

The school is now very much part of the community with its own pre-school nursery, drop-in centre for the unemployed, sports centre, special learning centre, library, cafeteria, adult learning centre, private study rooms, conference facilities, and a number of rooms which are let as private offices.

The history project has been an eye-opener for Millennium. Schools in the last century had over 1,000 students in every day and lunches were served to most of them. Chalk, keyboard, exercise books, and uniform were to be found in most schools, and some students even skipped school because they didn't like it!!

The value of engaging in this futurist type of thinking is that it completely shifts the consideration of resources for teaching to resources for learning. Previously, they were often seen, erroneously, as the same thing but now the difference is being brought into sharp relief. The use of technology discussed by Dettman and Southorn is just one small example of the impact that technology is having on the learning process. Indeed we may be undergoing a very fundamental change which Peter Drucker (1993, p. 1) describes as:

> *Every few hundred years in Western history there occurs a sharp transformation . . . Within a few short decades, society rearranges itself . . . its world view; its basic values; its social and political structures . . . We are currently living through such a transformation.*

Drucker goes on to state that 'knowledge is fast becoming the sole factor of production, sidelining both capital and labor' (Ibid., p. 33). For those of us employed in the education service the implications are profound. We are increasingly going to have to focus on resourcing learning rather than resourcing teaching. This presents several problems. One is the traditional view of parents who see one teacher with a small class as the ideal. It is often not perceived as advantageous to have larger classes with combinations of a qualified teacher, other adult helpers and high technology provision. Changing the 'mind set' of parents from the teaching to the learning environment is a major leadership challenge. The second problem arises from the way that teachers themselves see their rôle in the future and how they adapt to being 'lead learners' co-ordinating learning rather than being the only 'deliverers' of knowledge.

Fundamentally, of course the amount of resources *per se* that is put into education is a critical factor. There is a danger of the gap in funding and its relationship to achievement widening as schools with greater resources further enhance their technological and other provision. The other element in this debate is the mix between public and private funding in education. During the 1990s there has been a considerable shift from state-only funding to increasing the proportion of private funding, including increasingly large parental contributions as grants only cover part costs. With increasing pressures on the public sector this trend is likely to continue. The shift to a learning-based resourcing and the incremental erosion of 'free education' calls for a radical assessment of alternative funding mechanisms.

7. The need for responsive cultures

The global economic market changed fundamentally during the 1980s and 1990s. Increased global competition and customer power have radically altered the balance between suppliers and customers. This has been accompanied by the restructuring of global political systems. The collapse of communism and the triumph of market economies can be seen as a global phenomenon. In the UK the privatisation of virtually all state enterprise and the introduction of market forces into government services such as health and education can be seen as a very radical shift of policy. Central to this change nationally has been the enhancement of customer power. This can be seen in attempts to encourage parental choice of schools and in the introduction of vouchers for nursery education.

These changes have run alongside management developments such as Total Quality which sees accountability less in terms of formal reporting and more in terms of customer satisfaction. The concept of defining customers' wants and needs and responding to them has moved significantly into the public sector over the last decade. Most significantly is the attitude shift from the defining of outcomes by the suppliers of education (teachers) to seeing things from the point of view of the consumers of learning. The fundamental challenge that we face is deciding how to involve those customers in designing and operating the process instead of just being the passive recipients.

Thus, the challenge is to move schools to develop responsive cultures for the moral purpose of more effectively working with students and parents to enhance the level of student learning. Schools have moved a long way from the culture which can be expressed by teachers' comments such as 'schools are great places when students aren't there' to the development of learning communities of partnerships between students and teachers. Two principles from the Total Quality movement can be used to focus management thinking.

The first is 'fitness for purpose' and the second is 'monitoring and evaluating'. Fitness for purpose exists in a responsive culture where the school is constantly defining and redefining the needs of the students and providing the appropriate learning strategies and support for them. It is not about some predetermined 'gold standard' that is imposed on the students' education but defining for *this* cohort of students the appropriate structures, strategies and content of learning that best meets their needs. This involves listening to the customer (student) and assessing the appropriate information from the environment to define the most appropriate education. This means the school has to develop proactive approaches to meet the changing needs of its client group. The client group, is of course, itself changing as different cohorts of students have differing needs.

Monitoring and evaluating is a key feature of the responsive school. In this context we are not advocating an OFSTED type four-year health check but more of the detailed feedback as described by Davies and Ellison (1997). In their work they report on client attitude surveys carried out on an annual basis that provide student, parent and teacher perceptions of the quality of the schooling process. This provides regular management information so that the school can evaluate its performance and can involve itself in a continuous improvement process. This continuous improvement is a key feature of a responsive culture.

We talk in this chapter of a number of key factors; the responsive culture is one that binds those factors into a constantly improving organisation that is adapting to change and growing as a learning organisation.

8. Performance management as the critical factor

Organisations exist to perform, to deliver outcomes and to demonstrate that they have added value to the inputs. This language is at odds with many perceptions of the nature of education and, it has to be stressed, with notions of what many businesses are about. The emphasis on imposed results has led to a number of inappropriate managerial strategies such as performance related pay, appraisal as assessment of performance, league tables of results and externally imposed inspection. For students, the equivalent manifestations include summative assessment, reward and sanctions systems and 'death or glory' examinations.

What is significant about all these strategies is that they are ultimately concerned with manifestations of power; they reinforce dependency and at a philosophical level they assume that there are right answers. Very few experienced and reflective leaders, managers and teachers would claim with total confidence that there is a direct correlation between any of these strategies and improved and sustained performance.

In any increasingly questioning society, schools of the future will have to look to improve performance on the basis of:

- acceptance of the core purpose
- shared and agreed definitions of performance
- reinforcement through praise and recognition
- acceptance of intrinsic motivation as the key determinant
- stipulation of ends, not means
- recognition of the possibility of multiple outcomes.

The practical implication of this approach is to move towards a strategy of target setting for both students and adults. Targets help to define destinations (helpful in any journey), to prioritise, to set success criteria and to translate generic requirements into personalised action. It is difficult to envisage how personal autonomy can be sustained without the regular negotiation of time-constrained targets which then become the responsibility of the individual, with appropriate support. The skill for leaders in schools or classrooms is to negotiate in a genuine way so that the targets themselves are the motivating force and individuals become responsible for their own performance management. The imposition of arbitrary goals may be good for the ego needs of the imposer but may do very little to help the individual take full personal responsibility for her or his own work. The first response to failure to achieve the target is that either the target was wrong or that there was insufficient support to achieve it. Thus we can forget about timetables, job descriptions and so on and replace them with targets which facilitate planning, implementation and evaluation at the personal level and so act as a microcosm for the leadership and management strategies of the school as a whole.

9. The need for global awareness and community interdependence

The introductory chapter looked at the three factors driving the reengineering revolution, those of customers, competition and change. The significance of these is that they are global factors. Large corporations move their production facilities, and hence employment, around the globe in order to gain the benefits of competitive wage range and government incentives. Technology enables those with access to it (a significant factor) to have an ever-expanding exposure to education and ideas.

> *Knowledge as the key resource is fundamentally different from any of the traditional key resources, that is, from land and labour, and even from capital. It is not tied to any country. It is transnational. It is portable. It can be created anywhere, fast and cheaply.* (Drucker, 1995, p. 227)

Ohmae (1995) provides an illustration of 'the new melting pot' in education, choosing Keio University's experimental Fujisawa campus in Japan:

> *Because [all students] are on-line, they can offer real-time reactions and contributions to the curriculum, to the structure of their own programs of study, to the content of their courses, and to the quality of their instructors. If they need information to supplement a text they are reading or a report they are writing, they can track it down through the Internet. If they want to consult an expert anywhere in the world, they can reach him or her the same way ... They have stopped being passive consumers of an educational experience defined, shaped, and evaluated by the Ministry of Education. The technology has allowed them, in a most non-Japanese fashion, to become definers and shapers and evaluators – and questioners – themselves.* (Ohmae, 1995, p. 36)

What does this mean for schools? The significant information and ideas in education and commerce will transcend national boundaries. Schools can harvest the best lesson preparations on the Internet or the experience of self-managing schools from Victoria in Australia or Edmonton in Canada. Access to knowledge is focusing on the quality of the idea and not the location of its origin. As a result, schools need to become outward-facing and proactive organisations instead of being inward-looking reactive organisations.

As well as being part of the new global community and building cross-national interdependence, schools also need to look to new organisational relationships with the local, regional and national community. One of the problems of working with an essentially nineteenth-century construct of the 'school' is that it is an isolated and monotechnic institution. For a school to achieve its core purpose it has to recognise the need to move away from reaction to social pressure into proactivity. Issues related to health, drug abuse, crime, poverty and social distress are often dealt with by a multiplicity of agencies which inevitably leads to fragmentation. It is not enough for a school to make its sports facilities available, rent its hall to local groups and invite the police, health education workers and so on to speak at assemblies. Equally, links with other schools, further and higher education and employers have to move beyond the symbolic and ritual.

The sophisticated networks that have been made possible by information technology have to be replicated at local level. This would seem to point to community initiatives with a shared strategy, multi-disciplinary teams and a movement away from consultation and co-ordination to integration and intervention.

10. Personal effectiveness as the synthesising agent

One of our key concepts in reengineering is that it is first necessary to reengineer 'mind sets' before it is possible to reengineer processes. The crucial factors in bringing together the diverse elements in the leadership and management process are the way that we think and interact and how effective we are. A common definition of management used over the last forty years has been that management 'is getting things done through people'. We believe that effective leadership and management in the new millennium involves knowing yourself, knowing others and integrating that knowledge with communicative and business skills to achieve new and powerful outcomes.

We discussed earlier in this chapter 'performance management as the critical factor'. We believe that to create an effective performance culture several personal skills are necessary:

- To become outcome-orientated. This is what Covey (1989) calls 'begin with the end in mind', and involves a sharp focus on the core result/activity that is being sought with continual redirection of personal goals to achieve that. Schools exist to provide children with an effective learning environment to enhance their education, not to provide teachers with jobs!

- To take charge of the agenda by becoming proactive. Individuals do make a difference and can interpret the organisational situation and reorganise it best to suit the educative process. This contrasts with the reactive stance where teachers always see themselves at the receiving end of externally imposed methods of working.

- To challenge incremental ways of thinking and think in diverse and different patterns. The rate of change does not allow us the luxury of minor adjustments; we need radically different solutions to many of the challenges we face. Taking this approach and using more right brain creative thinking is the key to meeting the challenge of organising the next generation of learning.

A great deal of effort has been devoted within the competency movement to the defining of effective personal competencies. We believe that effectiveness in the personal skills listed above depends on three further factors:

- *Self-knowledge* of our own skills, abilities and leadership and management traits is a precondition of effectively managing others. It is important to avoid the biblical problem of identifying the speck in someone else's eye while ignoring the plank in your own. First we have to know and manage ourselves. The McBer group of generic management competencies is a good framework to start this process.

- The next factor is *knowing others* and becoming attuned to their needs and perspectives. Covey (1989) calls this 'listen first before you can be understood'. This is aligned to becoming sensitive and tolerant of others to enable you to maximise their contribution by fully understanding 'where they are coming from'.

- Finally, *effective communication skills*, including the effective use of information technology, can significantly aid leadership and management effectiveness.

The problem with any menu, like this one, is that the components can each achieve significance in their own right and that we naturally tend to focus on those which our own history or personality makes more available to us. There needs to be a unifying agent which helps to create a balance and which stresses the significance of each in an interdependent way.

For want of a better term this might be described as spirituality, not necessarily in a metaphysical sense but, rather, something that integrates, gives meaning and encourages questioning to create understanding. For some this could well be a religious faith, for others a humanistic approach, for yet others it might be encompassed in the notion of being a professional. The precise nature of the focus is less significant than the existence of a framework which supports reflection, helps to practise and contextualise and stresses overarching purpose when the rigours of the daily routine become dominant. It is difficult to see how individuals will work effectively in an increasingly ambiguous environment unless there is some notion of a transcendent purpose.

Just in the way that this is necessary to be able to work effectively, so there is a need to achieve a harmonisation of the self at work, the self as an autonomous being. The creation of an holistic and balanced approach means that each element is able to support and enhance the other. This approach has probably been one of the major casualties of the education reforms of recent years; the emphasis on the singular nature of leadership has compromised balance and led to neglect of others and self.

It is worth advancing the speculation that the effective and improving school has a direct correlation with effective and improving individuals.

References

Caldwell, B. J. (1997), 'Thinking in time: a gestalt for the new millennium', in B. Davies and L. Ellison, *School Leadership for the 21st Century*, London, Routledge.

Covey, S. R. (1989), *The Seven Habits of Highly Successful People: restoring the character ethic*, London, Simon & Schuster.

Davies, B. and Ellison, L. (1997), *Strategic Marketing for Schools*, London, Pitman.

Drucker, P. F. (1993), *Post-Capitalist Society*, New York, Harper Business.

Drucker, P. F. (1995), *Managing in a Time of Great Change*, Oxford, Butterworth-Heinemann.

Gronn, P. (1995), 'Greatness revisited: the current obsession with transformational leadership' *Leading and Managing*, Vol. 24, No. 1, pp. 7–30.

Luecke, R. A. (1994), *Scuttle Your Ships Before Advancing: And Other Lessons from History on Leadership and Change for Today's Managers*, New York, Oxford University Press.

Naisbitt, J. and Aburdene, P. (1990), *Megatrends 2000*, London, Pan Books.

Ohmae, K. (1995), *The End of the Nation State: The Rise of Regional Economies*, London, HarperCollins.

Index

■   ■   ■